A NEW LIFE IN THE ALGARVE, PORTUGAL

An anthology of life stories

ALYSON SHELDRAKE

Copyright © 2021 Alyson Sheldrake

Cover Design and Images Copyright © 2021 Alyson Sheldrake

All Photographs Copyright © 2021 Dave Sheldrake Photography

Except chapters 6, 11, 13, 19 - Images provided by the subject and edited by Dave Sheldrake Photography

Published by Tadornini Publishing, 2021

Formatted by AntPress.org

First Edition

Paperback ISBN: 9798735484431

Large Print Paperback ISBN: 9798735488385

Hardback ISBN: 9798736452309

The author asserts the moral right under the Copyright, Designs and Patents Act 1988 to be identified as the author of this work. All rights reserved.

No part of this publication may be reproduced in any form or by any electronic or mechanical means, including information storage and retrieval systems, without the prior written consent of the author, except for the use of brief quotations in a book review. This is a work of creative nonfiction. All the contributors to this book have tried to recreate events, places, and conversations from their memories as truthfully as their recollection permits. As the curator, I tried to ensure that the information in this book was correct at the time of going to press. I make no representation, express or implied, about the completeness, accuracy, reliability, suitability, or availability regarding the information, products, services, or locations described in this book for any purpose. Any use of this information is at your own risk.

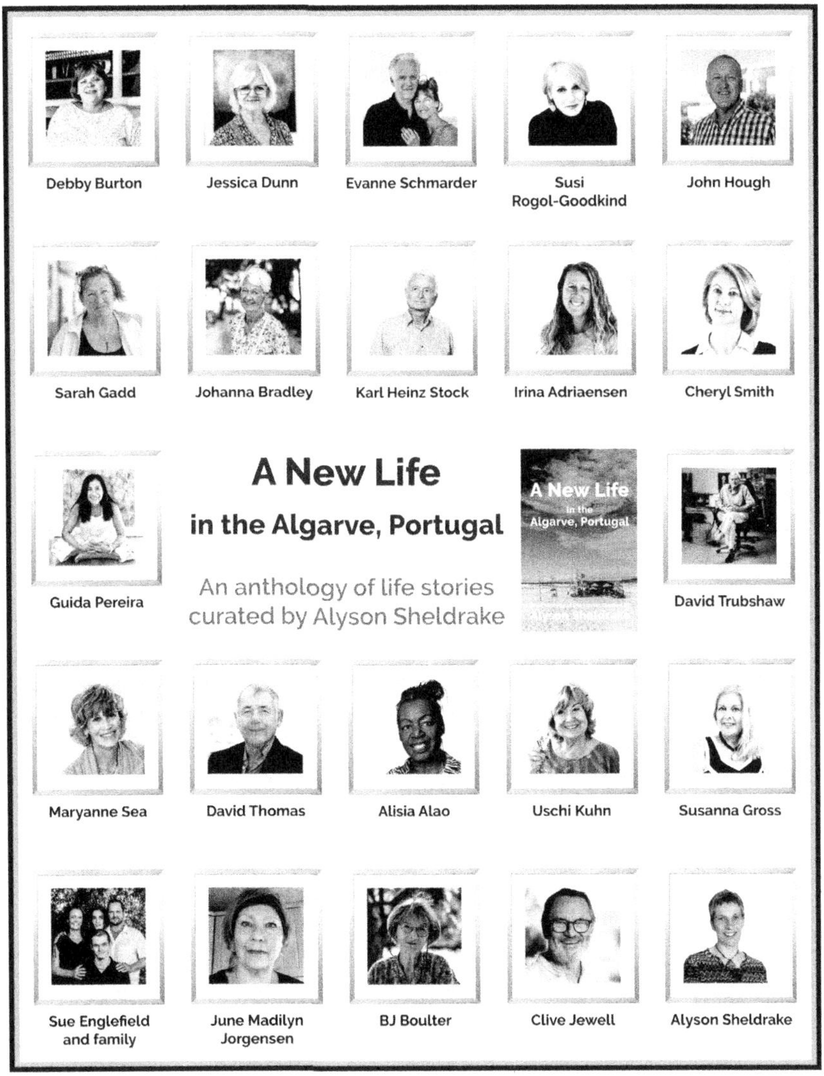

Debby Burton	Jessica Dunn	Evanne Schmarder	Susi Rogol-Goodkind	John Hough
Sarah Gadd	Johanna Bradley	Karl Heinz Stock	Irina Adriaensen	Cheryl Smith

A New Life
in the Algarve, Portugal

An anthology of life stories curated by Alyson Sheldrake

Guida Pereira				David Trubshaw
Maryanne Sea	David Thomas	Alisia Alao	Uschi Kuhn	Susanna Gross
Sue Englefield and family	June Madilyn Jorgensen	BJ Boulter	Clive Jewell	Alyson Sheldrake

Contents

Foreword *Chris Sainty, Her Majesty's Ambassador to Portugal*	7
Introduction *Alyson Sheldrake*	9
1. Alerta – Supporting the Bombeiros *Debby Burton, BEM*	13
2. An Artist's Eye View *Jessica Dunn*	31
3. Relishing Portugal *Evanne Schmarder*	43
4. In Search of Tranquillity *John Hough*	57
5. A Simple, Rural Life *Sarah Gadd*	77
6. Discovering an Enchanted Land *Susi Rogol-Goodkind*	91
7. A Walker's Paradise *Johanna Bradley*	105
8. The Art of Wine – Quinta dos Vales *Karl Heinz Stock*	119
9. Ayurveda in Aljezur *Irina Adriaensen*	133
10. Raising a Family in the Algarve *Sue Englefield and family*	145
11. Figs on the Funcho *Cheryl Smith*	155
12. From the Swinging Sixties to the Present Day *BJ Boulter*	169
13. Under the Star-filled Sky *Uschi Kuhn*	183
14. The Healing Touch *Maryanne Sea*	193
15. Creating Safe Communities *David Thomas, MBE, BEM, CPM*	205
16. The Wedding Planner *Alisia Alao*	219

17. Almost an Artist – Possibly a Poet? *David Trubshaw*	227
18. Matching the Right Properties to the Right People *Susanna Gross*	239
19. The Inspirational Senior Solo Traveller *June Madilyn Jorgensen*	251
20. The Algarve – My Happy Place *Guida Pereira*	263
21. A Rewarding Life in Travel and Consular Service *Clive Jewell*	279
22. Living the Algarve Dream *Alyson Sheldrake*	295
Top Tips	311
Further Reading	329
Living the Dream – in the Algarve, Portugal	331
Living the Quieter Algarve Dream	333
Chasing the Dream – A new life abroad	335
We Love Memoirs	337
Contacts and Links	339
Acknowledgements and Dedication	341
Free Photo Album	343
Keeping in Touch	345
About the Author	347
Your Review	349

Foreword
CHRIS SAINTY, HER MAJESTY'S AMBASSADOR TO PORTUGAL

I was delighted and honoured to be asked to write a foreword for this lovely anthology, recording the wonderfully varied stories of twenty-two people who have made the Algarve their home and made such unique and distinctive contributions to their towns and communities.

Twelve of those stories are written by British people. As British

Ambassador to Portugal I am keenly aware of the allure and fascination that the Algarve has always held for the British. I can remember – as a schoolboy – learning about Henry the Navigator, Portugal's half-English prince, assembling mariners, shipbuilders, cartographers and instrument makers at his fort in Sagres in the fifteenth century to launch Portugal's great Age of Discoveries. As we all know there is a rich history of more than six centuries of unbroken alliance and friendship between Britain and Portugal that has created a very long-lasting and special bond between the two countries. And that is surely one of the reasons why the British feel so at home here.

But it's not just about the history. There are many other reasons why the British and other nationalities are drawn to Portugal and, in particular, to the Algarve. It is a region of astounding natural beauty: stunning rural landscapes, one of the most breath-taking coastlines in the world and hundreds of gorgeous towns and villages. For many the climate, the culture, the language, the music, the glorious cuisine and the traditional Portuguese way of life are also part of the draw. But perhaps more than all of this, it is the commonplace gestures of welcome and friendship that we, as outsiders, experience every day from Portuguese people which immediately give us that unmistakeably warm feeling that we belong here.

I have the good fortune to live in Lisbon – one of the loveliest cities in the world – and have no cause to complain. But driving down through the Alentejo to the south coast I invariably feel my spirit lift and the spell of the Algarve begin to work its magic.

That magic is captured in many different ways in this delightful book and I congratulate Alyson for assembling these stories, all very different but each in its own way communicating a deep affection for this enchanting place at the westernmost tip of continental Europe and its equally enchanting people.

Chris Sainty
Her Majesty's Ambassador to Portugal
February 2021

Introduction
ALYSON SHELDRAKE

"Why the Algarve?"

This is the question I have been asked more than any other, since we moved here to live ten years ago. We initially fell in love with the little fishing village of Ferragudo almost twenty years ago, first visiting there on holiday, then buying a house, and finally making the move to live permanently in the Algarve, Portugal.

In the intervening years, I have felt an immense sense of peace and contentment with our lives here. My husband, Dave, and I have had the chance to carve out new creative careers, explore and enjoy the wonderful coastline, beaches, and countryside of the Algarve, and discover for ourselves the warmth and generosity of the Portuguese people.

I tried my best to articulate our journey and feelings in two travel memoirs, written and published in 2020. *Living the Dream – in the Algarve, Portugal*, and the sequel, *Living the Quieter Algarve Dream* were initially created from the content of our blog about the Algarve. Our lives did not fit into the professional vibe of the blog, and so the books were borne.

I quickly realised that people were interested in our journey to a new life abroad, and knew that I had met so many other fascinating people who had also made the move to live here in the Algarve. They, too, have their own tale to tell, and I realised I wanted to bring those stories to life.

The result is this book. It was a project that was a real privilege to be a part of. So many people were willing to share their story, with such honesty that I was left humbled and amazed. All of us have a unique background, with experiences and consequences that lead us to where we are today, and each contributor to this book is no exception to this. They have carved out new lives that are both inspiring and fascinating, whether that is starting up a new business venture, setting up a charity, or working with animals or local families in need.

There are artists, writers and bloggers, charity workers, and owners of innovative magazines and news websites nestled in the pages. The owner of an award-winning wine farm, the couple who run a yurt farm, a wedding planner, an estate agent, the rural retreat owners, therapists, and the Vice-Consul to the British Embassy in Portugal all tell their unique story.

I purposefully sub-titled this book an anthology of life stories and wanted to use the term 'curated by' to illustrate how precious every person's narrative is. Like the exhibits in a museum, where each object is hand-selected, lovingly preserved, and beautifully displayed, I wanted to present these life stories in the same way.

Making the move to live abroad, often leaving homes, jobs, families, and friends behind, is not an easy decision to make. But it is a choice that can lead to wonderful new opportunities to live a different, often less stressful, more peaceful way of life. Maybe you will read these stories and be inspired too.

Please note that most of the chapters are written in British English. Two of the contributors, however, are American, and use US English. I have tried to stay faithful to the individual response of each person, whilst editing gently, and I hope their voices come through the pages for you.

I have been amazed and in awe of the work of the bombeiros firefighters here in Portugal, particularly when they respond to a forest fire. Sadly, these events occur too often, and we have sat and watched the rural landscape burn around us too many times, with its devastating consequences to lives, homes and livelihoods. It is my pleasure to donate ten percent of all revenue made from the sale of this book to the Associação para Alerta de Incêndio Florestal charity, to support the work of the bombeiros.

The book also serves as a testament to the wonderful Algarve, where we have all chosen to make our home. We have fallen in love with this magical place for different reasons, and I hope that in reading this, you will discover why each person who has contributed can answer, with great conviction and ease, the question, "Why the Algarve?".

Alyson Sheldrake
March 2021

1

Alerta - Supporting the Bombeiros
DEBBY BURTON, BEM

My birth certificate tells me I am fifty-something years old, but my brain refuses to believe it. I am originally from Wiltshire in the UK, where I grew up and lived and worked, until I came to live in Portugal.

My Grandfather was captain of the Boys' Brigade for over fifty years, and my parents were officers, so it was a family affair, although I had to join the Girls' Brigade, which was not as much fun. I was a bit of a tomboy.

In my youth I was a competitive swimmer and swam for Wiltshire county. I lived round the corner from an outdoor pool, so I spent most of my summers there. I completed my two miles' swimming badge on my seventh birthday; it took me two hours. I remember my mum coming to the pool to look for me, and I had my badge sewn on my costume with pride.

I loved horse riding and having fun, and I also played the bugle very badly in the Boys' and Girls' Brigade band.

I had a job on a bakery delivery round when I was at school, and in a café decorated to look like a cave when I was in college. They were both brilliant fun jobs, and the doughnuts and bread from the bakery were so good. Freshly baked hot bloomers—I can still taste them now.

I trained and worked as a mental health nurse and practised until I came to live here in Portugal. I started nursing in the early eighties, in what was the old county asylum, with over one thousand inpatients, and Florence Nightingale wards. I worked as a nursing auxiliary for a year on long-stay female geriatrics, then did my training as an SENM (state enrolled nurse, mental health), got married, and had children. Then I trained as an RMN (registered mental health nurse). By which time it had all changed and community care was the way to go. The grand old asylum gradually closed, and we all moved to a new purpose-built unit. I also did agency nursing, taking me all over the west country.

Now I am a reiki therapist, although Covid-19 has meant I can't practice at the moment.

I love cooking, sewing and crafting, horse riding, eating out, which is affordable in Portugal, exploring and trying new things.

One way or another, I have done fundraising and charity work for most of my adult life on and off. And I love a challenge. I have to do one constructive thing a day, not necessarily making something, but just so I know I am not wasting my life. A total sofa day is a waste—but half a day is ok! My motto is simple: 'Life is for living. We are a long time dead'.

My proudest moments in my life so far have been giving birth to my sons, qualifying as a nurse, being promoted to nursing sister, and receiving my British Empire Medal. And watching my Alerta charity volunteers all pulling together to achieve great support for the bombeiros (firefighters) and the community, especially in the years 2017 and 2018.

○ℰ✿ℛ○

So why Portugal? We used to go on holiday in our caravan with the kids to France or the UK, mostly Cornwall. I love to travel, but my hubby doesn't like flying, so to get him on a plane, I booked a golfing holiday for us twenty years ago. Purely randomly, we ended up in Alvor, in the Algarve. I didn't like it the first time we visited. I thought it was scruffy, and run down, and there were packs of dogs everywhere. But something got to me. The people are so friendly and helpful, we made friends with a family who owned a restaurant we used, and they are still our 'Portuguese family' today. They are lifelong friends and have helped us settle into the Portuguese way of life.

That scruffiness became its charm and character. From that first visit, I have always said Portugal is like England back in the sixties, there are still family values and respect here. Everyone is polite, the sun shines, and the food and wine are good.

When we decided to move here to live, we drove down with our caravan, and pitched at our friends' house in Vila do Bispo. It was initially to be for three months, but that turned into four months.

We started house hunting. We had no allegiance to any particular area, but wanted to be close to our Portuguese family in Alvor. We thought about other areas of Portugal, but we had already built up a social network whilst on our holidays, so it seemed daft to start again, without support from friends. So we house hunted in Silves and spread out from there.

We had sold our house in the UK, but lost a lot of money because it was the beginning of the recession. We looked at a lot of houses, but either we couldn't both agree, or what we liked was illegal, with extensions built without planning permission. We learnt this is a common problem here.

So we agreed to rent for six months, as it was getting too hot to live in the caravan. We found a place to rent in the small village of Odiáxere, and six months turned into five years, just because we got comfy.

Eventually, I decided I wanted our own place again, so we started searching, and after many ups and downs, we found our house, back in the Silves area. It was meant to be. It had been empty for eight years, and the gypsies had stripped it of anything of value. But we loved it and started to bring it back to life.

When we moved in, we had no bathroom, and the kitchen was very, very basic. The worktops and cupboards were just planks of wood balanced over cardboard boxes.

We knew we had to supplement our pensions, and would need to work. By accident we became property managers looking after holiday lets. But we quickly slipped back into the UK rat race of all work and no play.

We stopped and took check of why we had moved, and it was not to work ourselves to death. We reduced our commitments and re-addressed our work-life balance. I trained as a reiki therapist, something I was always interested in, but never had the time to pursue in the UK.

I don't think, unless you have an unlimited income, Portugal is the utopia people believe it is. We did our homework before coming here, and we were not blind to the actual situation financially. The secret to surviving is being flexible and adaptable. But life here is good. The people and the country are beautiful and welcoming.

When we moved here, we wanted to be part of the local

community and not live in 'Little Britain'. One thing that says you are accepted in the community is being invited to experience real Portuguese traditions, not the staged tourist ones.

Where we used to live, our house was on top of a hill and below us lived a couple of Portuguese farmers, with smallholdings. Hubby befriended them and often popped over the road for a beer with his new mates.

One day, they invited him to help 'bottle the medronho', and he trotted off like a kid going to a party. Coming home was not so easy. I stood at the kitchen window watching him take one step forward, one back, one to the right, and another somewhere in between. It took him ages to get home. And I was in hysterics watching his struggles.

The next time we were invited, we both went, and drove up into the hills off the tarmac roads, along tracks over rivers, into the cork forests. It was such a stunning part of the Algarve. We arrived at our destination, which was a small brick building. Inside was pretty bare, with a fire under a copper still. It had a copper pipe leading into a tank of water and out the other side. There was a mismatch of chairs and a few Formica tables, some old bikes, and garden tools.

Medronho is a Portuguese fruit brandy distilled from fermented berries picked from the Medronho, or wild strawberry tree. The drink is typically clear and strong and is mainly enjoyed neat, preferably as a digestif. It is also called *agua ardente*, which literally means 'burning water' in Portuguese. It is not for the faint-hearted!

The fire was alight under the still, and there were lots of fifty-gallon plastic tanks scattered around, with the fermenting berries inside.

Now I don't like medronho, so I am always the designated driver, which can be quite funny watching others getting merry. Hubby loves the stuff and likes to think he is a connoisseur.

Our friend gave us the education bit, and then the serious drinking started. Hubby positioned himself at the end product part of the still and became chief taster for every batch. We arrived at 6 p.m. and left around midnight.

On the embers of the fire, locally made sausage and chorizo was cooked, then squashed between fresh wood-oven baked bread which soaks up all the delicious juices. It is a meal made in heaven.

About every half hour, another cousin arrived with more chorizo and bread. All washed down with more medronho. Suddenly the room felt empty, and I realised about four cousins had left. Within the hour they were back, sporting a very fine rural delicacy. Being invited to these events is an honour, so you have to partake. They were carrying about six thrush, yes, songbirds. They proceeded to pluck them and cook them on the embers.

I sat there thinking, how can I not eat these without offending them?

They all got very excited when they were cooked. I had the tiniest piece possible, literally a sliver.

Before they could go off hunting again, I decided it was time to make our escape, and yes, hubby's legs did not work!

✧෨✧ଓ✧

Of all the things I have been involved in, I am most proud of my Alerta charity. In order to explain what we do and how we evolved, I need to take you back to 2003, when we were still only tourists. We were staying in a villa between Alvor and Monchique; it was August, and a Saharan dust cloud was shrouded over the region. For those that have never experienced this, they are horrible; they trap the heat in, and the air is oppressive. You cannot do anything because you are just exhausted and sapped of energy.

And a wildfire was burning in Monchique. We could see the fire from the villa, and during the day whole burnt leaves would float down into the pool. By night, we would sit on the roof terrace with our wine and watch the glow of the fire. It continued to burn for several days.

We had a vague understanding that the firefighters of Portugal were poor, and said to each other that when we lived here, we would try to help them. It was one of those throwaway statements. When the fire was over, we drove up to Monchique, which was our first real experience of the damage caused. We were shocked.

We eventually moved here to live in 2010, and discovered that, sadly, wildfires are a regular summer occurrence here in Portugal.

In 2013, a friend created the Facebook page *Alerta de Incêndio Florestal*, and I became an administrator in the group. It started out as a simple chit-chat type page, where people shared local information, like the helicopter has just flown over, or I can see smoke. The foreign community did not know where to get fire information, and the page was very useful. The friend eventually returned to the UK and left me in charge.

In June 2014, there was a large fire at the Autódromo near Portimão. We could see it from our house, and quickly enough word was filtering around Facebook that the local bombeiros needed help with supplies of food and water. We live just five minutes away, so we took supplies to the fire. Fortunately, our route was along a good wide road. The volume of traffic surprised us, with people taking supplies or simply being what we now call 'fire tourists'.

We decided we wanted to help, and that random statement we had uttered eleven years earlier, whilst on holiday, began to flourish.

The next day, Andrew, my husband, went to the commander of Lagos Fire Station, and told him we were willing to help them. After much discussion, they gave us a letter of authorisation, to enable us to go round the local supermarkets and collect donations on their behalf.

We went to the supermarkets, introduced ourselves to the managers, told them our plan, and they all agreed to help. A few weeks later, we had a phone call—Lagos Fire Station had three fires burning at the same time. One fire was very large, and could we help?

We dropped everything, drove to the station, got our instructions, and then went to the supermarkets. We collected bread, cheese, ham, water, fruit juices, and fruit. We took it all back to the station and helped make over one hundred packed meals which were delivered to the bombeiros at the site of the fire. We then helped organise the barracks to cater for feeding all the firefighters and emergency workers. They arranged for a local restaurant to prepare and deliver hot meals to the station.

This was the beginning of the Alerta work we do today.

Membership of the Facebook page increased each year, and in 2017, I decided I could no longer manage running it on my own. I persuaded friends and people who had offered to help to become admins with me, so one became four. By this time I had also discovered the national Civil Protection website, which now gives us all the information on wildfires. This means we can give much more accurate reports and the exact location of a fire. We still use this website today.

In 2017, we had three events that would change Alerta forever. In June, in central Portugal, there was the devastating fire in the Pedrógão Grande region. We donated 1,000 euros to the Red Cross to help with this tragedy. Sixty-six people lost their lives, many of them trapped in their homes, or cars as they tried to escape. It was the deadliest fire in Portuguese history.

We then experienced a large forest fire in Monchique at the beginning of September the same year. Alerta and our team of accumulated volunteers swung into action. We set up collection points in supermarkets. Our volunteers would be there waiting, and the donations of water, snacks, foods, and toiletries came thick and fast following our appeals all over Facebook.

Because of the terrain, and with only one road up and down the mountain, we used the Lagoa Fire Station station as a storage point. We did this for two reasons. The first is that people want to help but don't know how, so by giving them a list of items they can purchase and a location to drop them off, they can be of the most use. Secondly, and most importantly, by us collecting and delivering to a designated point, we keep those 'fire tourists' off the roads that need to be kept clear for emergency traffic.

The community maintained the donations for over a week, and the bombeiros wanted for nothing.

In October 2017, another devastating fire in the Coimbra region of Portugal, fanned by hurricane Ophelia, caused untold destruction, and more loss of life and livelihoods and homes. Ten days after this fire, I joined a team from across the Algarve, who drove to Arganil with donations of clothes and bedding for those who had lost everything in the fire.

I can never put into words what we witnessed. We drove for hours, through what had once been magnificent forests, and saw traditional granite houses reduced to charred shells. There was no vegetation, no fruit trees, no livestock, no bird song, no insects, not one bird of prey.

Electric cables, crash barriers, and road signs were all burnt and twisted on the side of the road. It was a still-smouldering route that seemed to stretch on forever. We drove for over 150 kilometres through the charred and barren landscape.

But the people still smiled. They still welcomed us. And humbled us.

✧෨✧ൟ✧

After these events, we were gaining support, so we became a registered charity, and the Associação para Alerta de Incêndio Florestal was born.

Our first official donation was to AFPOP, another local charity, that was running an appeal to buy every station in the Algarve a defibrillator machine. They cost around 1,000 euros each. We held a raffle at the 'Fatacil' Algarve fair one weekend with some fantastic donated prizes that raised well over 1,000 euros. From funds previously given to us, mainly five, ten, or twenty euros here and there, and money donated for fire relief, we supported the fundraising efforts of the appeal, aptly titled 'Operation Shock'. At the end of the campaign, all seventeen Fire Station Commands received a defibrillator machine.

In 2018 the Algarve was severely tested again. On 3 August at 1.32 p.m. a fire started in the hills behind Monchique that would burn for ten days and travel down to and beyond Silves. Over 27,000 hectares of land and seventy-four houses were destroyed, thirty of which were main residences. At its height there were 1,492 personnel involved in fighting the fire, all of whom needed supplying with essentials. Again we enlisted our trusted volunteers from all over the Algarve. Collection points old and new were pressed into service, and restaurants and supermarkets provided snacks and cooked food. Our volunteers would ring the bombeiros every morning for the latest shopping list and have it all at the Silves station by lunchtime.

You assume people know about the fire, however, I had a resident from Vale do Lobo ask me via Facebook, on the eighth day that the fires had been raging,

"Is there a fire in the Algarve, I have ash in my pool?"

To keep energy levels up, we provided cooked chickens and other meats as well as handheld food, such as energy bars and biscuits. Keeping the brave firefighters hydrated was obviously vitally important, so there was an almost inexhaustible need for bottled water and energy drinks, which we stored in specially purchased cool boxes.

We bought medical supplies on a large scale, including burn creams, pain killers, Ibuprofen creams and tablets, eye wash, dressings, bandages, and even ladies' sanitary products. As many bombeiros, particularly those from further afield, had been wearing the same clothes for days, we also supplied T-shirts and underwear.

As the fire grew and affected a range of properties, including smallholdings and animal rescue centres, we launched our animal rescue groups. Our brave volunteers were prepared to put themselves in danger to rescue a variety of animals, from cats and dogs to horses and donkeys.

We also created another branch of Alerta to liaise between the people who were being evacuated and those offering accommodation, meaning that many otherwise homeless families had a bed for the night. These are just a few examples of the work of the amazing volunteers who drop everything and help when the fires start.

None of this would be possible without charitable donations. Our fundraising team works hard throughout the year with events such as golf days, wine tasting evenings, coffee mornings, running the Lisbon marathon, sponsored walks, and auctions.

Raising money here is hard if we don't have a fire raging. If we have a large fire with smoke and flames that can be seen for miles, donations flow in faster than I can keep up with sending out thank you messages. We don't have sponsorship; it is all individuals who donate and fundraise, because they want to help. We have so many people that raise money for us including children who have given their pocket money.

One of the biggest contributions we have made to the bombeiros was after the 2018 fires when replacement uniforms were needed, as many had been burnt or damaged. Since that day we have bought 167 forest fire sets of kit in total at a cost of 350 euros each, distributed across every station in the Algarve and Odemira, Ourique, and Almodôvar.

Every summer we supply each station with water and energy bars, which go into their 'Fire Boxes'. Every engine now has an icebox which contains twenty-four hours supply of snack foods, to keep them going when on a job.

We have developed relationships and broken down barriers, so that between us we all have our own stations that we look after, ensuring they have the same face and contact point.

Since Covid-19 we have had to be creative, finding online and socially distanced ways of raising money. We have had a couple of online auctions, created a cookery book, and hosted a virtual Christmas fayre. As a result of the pandemic, we raised funds to buy 2,300 euros worth of much needed Personal Protection Equipment (PPE) for front-line workers. Many of our normal fundraising events, such as organising the car parking for the Silves Medieval festival, were cancelled. In spite of this, we still managed to purchase a further fifty-seven forest fire uniforms at a cost of 350 euros each.

I set myself a crazy challenge to raise money in 2020, deciding to swim the equivalent of walking from Vila do Bispo in the west to Vila Real Santo António in the east Algarve. A total of 147 kilometres, swimming a minimum of one kilometre a day. Except I only have an above ground plunge pool at home, that measures 4.5 metres in diameter. It meant I had to swim 225 widths every day, for the whole of the fire season, 122 days.

I am contemplating doing something similar again, but have not decided on my target yet.

We constantly fundraise so that we are ready for every eventuality during the critical fire season period. Our priority is to help with supplies, then food and toiletries, and with equipment out of season.

We have also used our contacts in the UK to secure decommissioned uniforms and equipment such as breathing apparatus and infrared cameras. Friends of Alerta, who know people in the UK, or follow our work, get in touch and liaise with the UK fire services to coordinate donations to us here. So far, Bristol, Devon, South Shields, London, and Derbyshire fire services have all helped us. They send a range of used equipment, urban uniforms, boots, breathing apparatus sets, and shoes. The kit is still good to use. Sometimes, if it is not suitable because of slight damage, it is used for training, saving the precious good kit for active duty. We share out all the donations from the UK on a needs-must basis. We have even sent some kit to Lisbon.

We use a local shipping company who donate their time and transport, and other people have organised and donated the cost of transport of the kit too. We are hoping this will not fall into the Brexit trap in the future, where we will have to pay import tax as it is for charity.

There is a two-tier system for the bombeiros in the Algarve. There are four municipal stations here and they get one hundred percent funding. The rest are Câmara-funded local stations. They get one third of their funding from the city hall, one third from Associação memberships and donations, and the rest from payment of work, like running the INEM (emergency ambulances), non-emergency ambulance work, and patient transport.

The stations have a quota of full-time bombeiros, who also have to work two days a month voluntarily, and the rest of the crews are volunteers. They are provided with basic uniforms, but if they want more, they usually have to buy it themselves. Twenty-three percent of firefighters are women. I know of many volunteer firefighters battling fires that wore only trainers and ordinary socks.

The crews function with very old engines, and they purchase most of their equipment through fundraising and donations. Funding to replace these, as they get damaged, is extremely slow to come, if at all.

We try to stay out of politics. We deal with the needs of the bombeiros. We provide on a needs-must basis. There are richer stations across the Algarve, and forgotten stations, like Messines and Alcoutim.

We have a team of nine people, from all walks of life, who form the legal requirements of the Associação. In normal times we meet once every six to eight weeks and also have an online chat group for urgent things. With Covid-19, our chat group has become our online meeting room, where we suggest, debate, and vote on any issues. We enlisted an accountant to help with the registration of the Associação, and she also manages our accounts and legislation.

Alerta has an amazing team from a wide variety of backgrounds, all with different skills and areas of responsibility, but we are always looking for new volunteers, both for our Facebook information page and for fundraising and the delivering of supplies.

Currently, we have a team of around twenty people who provide information on wildfires to our concerned members between May and October. They man the Facebook site from 8 a.m. to 10 p.m. every day, split into two-hour shifts. They all monitor the Civil Protection site and post alerts of any fires in our area, and watch and update the Facebook group until the fires are out. When we have a large fire, they double up, one concentrating on the fire statistics and the other covering the page and answering questions. Sometimes we have three on duty, one to cover the new member requests, which flood in when there is an active fire.

New helpers are always welcome, they just need a laptop, computer, or iPad and a reliable internet connection. Full training is given, and there is a great team on hand for support and advice.

In addition to our Facebook fire watch team, we are always pleased to hear from people who can provide practical support in any form, including those with access to land to house evacuated livestock, and empty properties for short-term emergency accommodation.

We have developed branch teams across the Algarve, who do shopping, collections, and deliveries when we have a fire. And we have more volunteers on standby for when we have a large fire. They help with extra collections and deliveries.

There are also more teams for re-homing people who have been evacuated, and two teams for animals, one for horses and large animals, and one for domestic animals. We have lists of people who offer spare bedrooms, empty holiday rentals, and fields, kennels, and stables.

It has taken several years to prove we are not just 'do-gooder' *estrangeiros* but that we are here to stay.

After the 2018 fire, the wife of a firefighter from up north contacted me. He had come down to Silves to help us with the fire effort. He spent several days here, and afterwards she said he had never been to a fire where there was so much community support and help for the bombeiros and how nice it was.

✧෨✧෬෯

When the British Ambassador to Portugal rang me to tell me I had been awarded the British Empire Medal (BEM) in the Queen's Birthday Honours list, I had literally just stumbled in the door of my house. I was carrying bags full of shopping, my dogs were vying for my attention, and the phone was ringing.

I just picked up the phone and said,

"Hello."

The very polite voice on the other end said,

"Hello Deborah," (only my mum calls me Deborah when I am in trouble), "This is the British Ambassador."

I thought, OK, this is a joke. I was trying to place the voice, and was about to tell him to P*** off, but something stopped me.

Phew, I'm glad I stopped. It really was the ambassador.

Later, I told him what I had nearly said, and thankfully he also found it funny.

I knew about my award in April 2019. The ambassador explained that someone had nominated me, (you are not allowed to know who), the committee and the prime minister had approved the application, and would I like to accept it?

Then the list goes to the queen to be rubber-stamped. They announced it in the London Gazette on the 8th June. It was so hard not to tell anyone, especially my family, before the official announcement. I expected to receive my medal in the September, then it was delayed until the October, and then delayed again due to Brexit. In the ensuing chaos, someone forgot to send it from London to Lisbon, so they finally set the date for January 2020.

It actually worked out really well. I invited my family to stay with me beforehand, and we celebrated my daughter-in-law's birthday. We went to one of our favourite restaurants, and ate enormous plates of *assadura à Monchique*, a traditional Portuguese dish made with pieces of grilled pork steak in olive oil, with garlic, lemon, and coriander. Chicken Piri-piri, homemade chips, and jugs of delicious Portuguese wine were also on the menu.

Eighteen of us travelled to Lisbon on the train. We arrived, and I tried to keep the rabble together, including my parents who are in their eighties. We had to get onto the metro and then locate our hotel. We were very much the typical tourist group, and all in very high spirits.

We got off the metro a station too early, so we were marching along the streets of Lisbon with Google maps on our phones, trying to find our way.

We arrived at the hotel, eighteen exuberant people en masse. We were early, (but not as early as if we had exited at the right station), and they had agreed via email that we could leave our luggage and go off for a few hours to explore. But I think we flustered the young girl on reception, with all eighteen of us arriving together, so they sat us down and served us cheese and wine while they sorted out our rooms.

So we shelved the sightseeing plans, and the party began!

My medal presentation was at the ambassador's residence, a five-minute drive from our hotel. I had to be there for 6 p.m. to have a chat with the ambassador beforehand. I had ordered taxis for everyone, with mine arriving fifteen minutes earlier.

Our taxi did not arrive. When I checked with reception, the poor girl had ordered all our taxis for the following morning, not that evening. We had to run out and hail a cab in rush-hour Lisbon, so I arrived late.

When I finally arrived, some of my other guests were already there, and I was very nervous. The ambassador appeared with his wife, and the first thing he did was offer me a drink.

Then we did a dummy run of the presentation ceremony, with his lovely P.A. helping me. By this time, everyone had arrived. The staff served drinks (mostly gin!) and delicious nibbles. Then the ambassador began his speech. I stood there next to him listening to his speech, thinking, My god, I did all that—and—oh, I had forgotten that!

He presented me with my medal.

Then he asked me to say a few words. I remember mumbling something, then started blubbing. The ambassador's wife handed me a tissue. I found it when I got home and put my jacket away.

It all felt very surreal. And emotional.

After my presentation, we all decided we needed to eat properly. We had all nibbled food and drank good wine and gins all day. So we found this little place in the back streets of Lisbon. Eighteen of us piled in. The owner was lovely and seemed delighted to see us and squeezed us all in. My uncle and I didn't want a full-on Portuguese meal, so we asked her if she could cook us egg and chips. She obliged, and they were so good.

I now have a framed certificate, and I keep my medal where I can see it every day. I have never worn it. I had some fundraising events I was going to wear it to, but Covid-19 put paid to those.

The BEM is for every single volunteer and donator, because none of this is possible without them. My citation reads: 'Deborah Ann

Burton. President Forest Fire Alert Association, the Algarve, Portugal. For services to the community in the Algarve, Portugal'.

I only use the title BEM when I am sending letters out to raise money for Alerta. My hubby keeps telling me off for not using it. My mum collects every news article about Alerta, and even BBC Radio Wiltshire follows us.

I am still me, I still like a good laugh, still like to drink probably too much wine. And I will still be out there, loading packs of water onto giant trolleys, begging cooked chickens from restaurants, asking for tills to be opened in supermarkets as I am in a hurry for the bombeiros. I will still stand in forty degrees heat, being bitten by mozzies, collecting car parking fees.

If I'm not busy working, you'll probably find me in a traditional Portuguese restaurant enjoying a meal with friends. The ones that look like a scruffy café from the outside, but once you are inside become a Tardis. They are the best places for lovingly cooked homemade Portuguese dishes. And the more times you return, the more local delicacies you get served. They offer you the food that is not written on the menu. The locals remember you; they welcome you back like old friends. For me, this is all part of the experience, as well as the good food.

I avoid beaches in the summer; they are too full, with too many beach balls and frisbees, and the sand is too hot to walk on. And we are always busy in the summer months.

Winter is my beach time. I love to stroll along the beach, especially when there are rough seas. I love blowing the cobwebs away. I like to get in the car, pick a town, Google the area, then explore. Portugal has so many beautiful places waiting to be discovered and enjoyed, people miss so much if they just stay at the beach.

There is a generation of Portuguese, who lived during the Salazar regime, who live a simple life. They make do and mend; the Portuguese are the kings of recycling. And they always have the most beautiful smiles.

Life in Portugal is not about material possessions, it is about family and community. Apart from my family, I don't really miss anything from the UK. Maybe shopping at Christmas. I don't miss the 'beating the Joneses' attitude to life, always having to have the latest TV, phone, or car, those designer shoes.

Life here is simple and refreshing.

✡⃝

To find out more about the work of the Associação para Alerta de Incêndio Florestal, including how to donate, visit their website: www.algarvefire.info

2

An Artist's Eye View
JESSICA DUNN

I am a British artist based in the Algarve. I am originally from London, born in Putney in 1963. I moved to live in the Algarve in my twenties. I have two children, Alice (25) and Lydia (22) and I live in Boliqueime where I have my studio. My sister Polly also lives in the same rural Algarve village.

I grew up in Barnes, South West London, in a showbiz household where the front door was always open. Usually someone was playing the piano or tap dancing in the front room, and every wall in the house was covered in art. My older sister, Polly, and I grew up with *Dad's Army*. My father, Clive Dunn, played Corporal Jones in the comedy TV series, and my mother, stage name Priscilla Morgan, was also an actress. We spent a lot of our childhood in and out of the BBC studios, various theatres in the West End, and at Christmas, we would go and stay wherever dad was doing panto.

My father was also a keen and talented artist. He would paint in our attic studio at the top of the house and often invite members of the cast of *Dad's Army* over to have their portrait drawn in our living room. He would put them in front of the TV to watch Wimbledon, which would keep them entertained and still for a decent length of time, long enough for him to get a good likeness. This was the norm for me, so my progression into becoming some kind of artist was inevitable.

Our move to Portugal was also a natural progression as our first home in the UK gradually became demoted to second home. My parents first came to Portugal in 1965 for a holiday. They chose Portugal after seeing the movie, *Queen Christina* starring Greta Garbo. At the end of the movie, Greta Garbo is at the bow of the ship heading for a new life in Portugal. Apparently, my father said,

"Well, if it's good enough for Greta Garbo, it's good enough for me!"

Our first Algarvian holiday was in an apartment in Albufeira when I was two years old. My parents fell in love with the place and from then on we returned every year for as long as possible during the summer holidays.

One summer our family shared a villa near the village of Porches, with my Dad's close friend John Le Mesurier (who played Sergeant

Wilson in the series *Dad's Army*) and his lovely wife Joan. My sister and I have fond memories of hot evening walks before dinner with John, wandering up a dusty *caminho* track and inevitably ending up at a bar for his G&T and our Coca-Colas. Actually, my mother told me recently that it wasn't even a bar, but a restaurant called O Leão, where the owners constantly tried to explain to John that the tables were reserved for diners only and not drinks. Anyway, he took no notice at all and each time continued to order his apéritif in his charming and nonchalant manner.

It seems so unlikely now as he was such a gent, but my sister and I used to jump on him in the swimming pool and he was heard to shout,

"I haven't come here to have my holiday ruined by bits of kids!"

Year after year we returned, and took literally every possible opportunity to come back, until gradually we all moved out here permanently. Although we had always holidayed on the strip of coastline between Armação de Pera and Olhos de Água, my parents eventually bought a holiday home fifteen minutes inland, in the little village of Boliqueime. This is where we have ended up, all living within five minutes of each other.

After a few years, my dad built a lovely art studio/gallery on his land. His idea was that we would paint there together, which we did many times. Apart from painting and exhibiting, the studio has had numerous uses over the years. It was used for piano lessons, yoga classes, my father's Portuguese lessons, and my mother held rehearsals for her shows that she would put on in various venues around the Algarve with her actors from the 'A Portada Theatre' group.

These days it's the venue for my annual open studio exhibitions.

✿❀✿❀✿

During my first few years in Portugal I worked as a jobbing artist, doing sign-writing for local businesses, painting murals, taking commissions for portraits: children, dogs, horses and even a donkey. You name it, I painted it!

One day I was painting a mural at a leisure centre in the resort of Vilamoura, when a small child asked me if I had painted it. When I confirmed to her that yes, I had, she replied,

"Oh! You don't look clever enough to do that."

(I'm still figuring that one out!)

We then opened a restaurant in Quarteira, where my sister was the chef. My mother with her great gardening skills supplied her with wonderful home-grown vegetables while my dad brought in the punters! I began helping out, greeting the customers, taking orders, and being a pleasant but not very good waitress.

During this time, I continued to paint during the daytime, bringing my paintings to hang in the restaurant, serving customers, and selling my paintings (mostly nudes at one point!) to a captive audience.

We had great fun in that restaurant, as all sorts of colourful characters used to come in. The lovely Ronnie Corbett came with his family for dinner and spent the whole time pushing his baby granddaughter around in a pram. We also had some of the cast of *'Allo 'Allo!*, Bob Carolgees of *Spit The Dog*, and even the Labour politician, Neil Kinnock, showed up one evening. He sat at the bar and made jokes about having short legs. He said,

"You'll notice when I stand up, I'm the same height as when I'm sitting down!"

The artist, Damien Hirst, was also one of our customers for a few days before he became extremely famous just a year later. He would come in very late for dinner and polish off a few bottles of wine with us after-hours. I would sit and listen to all his very funny stories.

He realised I was an artist because of all my paintings on the walls, so we had some good chats about the art world, and he told me an amazing story about Saatchi coming to check out his work. He had already begun his project with the dead cow in a tank and he told me all about it, in fascinating detail.

About a year later I was reading Blitz magazine, and his name was mentioned alongside a very familiar description of this formaldehyde cow. I couldn't believe what I was reading—this was the same guy!

We did not stay in touch, but I get great satisfaction from retelling the story to anyone who will listen. Especially as there was a funny moment one evening when he said to me,

"I can draw, you know!"

Who knew he was on the verge of something so huge? He is now the world's richest living artist! Shame I never got his phone number.

My time exhibiting my work at the restaurant was very encouraging, and after a couple of years I decided to quit working as a waitress, and just paint full time. At that stage I lived with my partner in Olhos de Água. He was also the manager of my sister's restaurant, and it was two weeks before expecting our first child that we moved up to Boliqueime for more space and to be near my parents.

That first year of motherhood was my most productive artistically. Ann Croft, the wife of David Croft (writer of *Dad's Army and 'Allo 'Allo!* among others) was a collector of my work and she decided I should exhibit in London, so, much to my surprise, she organised an exhibition at the Eaton Gallery in Piccadilly. This was a big deal for me. There was a huge turn-out, the Anglo-Portuguese Society came, there were Fado musicians playing, TV cameras, and several celebrities.

There were many sales, including my main piece featuring Portuguese folkloric dancers, which went to the home of Ian Gillan, the lead singer of Deep Purple, who incidentally was also a regular visitor to the Algarve.

That same year, my dad wrote a book of jokes and anecdotes, which I illustrated, so it was a very productive year.

✡❀✡೧✡

I have never found anywhere more welcoming or inspiring than Portugal, where I feel so at home. There are the obvious things which make Portugal special ... the sun, sea, sky, and the people, the food, and the laid-back pace of life. I have always found the Portuguese, and particularly Algarvians, to be a very gentle and tolerant people, putting up with us foreigners with great humour and generosity.

Luckily for us, most people in the world appear to be oblivious that Portugal exists, so we tend to enjoy an exclusivity to this beautiful country. As my mother points out, Portugal is hardly ever mentioned on the news and even watching the weather report on TV, the presenter often stands right in front of Portugal on the map.

When we first moved to Boliqueime, we were very aware of how different the culture was compared to the coastal towns. The locals had quite a different view of foreigners in those days and were just not used to us. However, they were still very accepting and patient with our lack of Portuguese language and foreign ways.

My sister, Polly, recently reminded me of a day when my father walked down the lane from the house to the communal bins near Boliqueime cemetery, pushing a wheelbarrow full of rubbish to dump. This would have been fine except that he was only wearing a tiny pair of black speedos, a hat, and sandals (his usual daily attire) and there happened to be a funeral going on. Amazingly, no one blinked an eyelid as he nodded good morning, and everyone continued with the procession. Well, at least he was wearing black, I suppose!

In the early days, before mobile phones, if the post office was closed, the only place to make a phone call was a small bar in the centre of the village which we called Ants' Bar. They had a tiny back room with a phone and a terrifyingly expensive meter, which clicked rapidly as we shouted down the crackly line. There was always a long line of ants making their way across the wall, over the phone and up your arm, so conversations were quick!

Apart from the obvious … the beautiful landscapes, the fabulous light, the sun, and the laid-back pace of life, this is a perfect place for an artist to work. My work has almost always been influenced by the Algarve, and I've been through different stages artistically. After my nude phase, my paintings depicted Portuguese scenes of fishermen mending their nets, old locals sitting in the streets playing cards or *petanca*, old ladies dressed in black, and the daily customs and traditions of the Algarve and its people. I would go to folkloric festivals to get material for my work. I enjoyed painting local Algarvians and their way of life and their customs, which were rapidly disappearing.

I think a younger generation in Portugal is starting to acknowledge the rapid disappearance of these precious traditions and they are beginning to revive them. I'm very happy to see new projects appearing all over the Algarve where they are starting to re-generate old artisan traditions.

In my early days in the Algarve, there were very few artists living here and I have to admit there wasn't much going on in the art scene. However, these days there are lots of great galleries in which to exhibit, and many good Portuguese and international artists to collaborate with. It is now a spectacular place for an artist to be.

One local gallery, which I have a great fondness for, is Galeria Côrte-Real, a beautiful little gem of a place hidden in the hills near Paderne. They were great to work with. At one point they took over Boliqueime train station for a couple of seasons and we had some fantastic exhibitions there in an enormous warehouse right next to the railway. These days the gallery in Paderne is still worth a visit.

For several years I was part of an artists' group called the Algarve Artists Network, started by artist Charlie Holt. This kind of networking proved extremely beneficial socially and professionally, as the artist's life can be rather solitary. Now I am part of a new project called Quinta Art Collective. We are a group of like-minded women artists, living close to each other in and around Boliqueime, producing very diverse styles of art and best of all, we happen to be great friends.

Over the years, I have been lucky enough to exhibit in many galleries throughout Portugal. Years ago, I spent some time in Setúbal, and devoted a whole exhibition to the city and its inhabitants. The exhibition was shown in a lovely gallery there in the centre of town.

Another highlight of my artistic career was an invitation to take part in an International Art Symposium in the city of Guarda, which is the highest city in Portugal. I was one of twelve international artists who spent two weeks creating their work in public, which culminated in an exhibition in the Guarda Museum.

I was lucky enough to be invited back the following year, however due to the pandemic this was unfortunately cancelled.

In 2020, despite the obvious complications, I exhibited in two galleries in the Algarve, the Fresco Gallery in Almancil and the Adérita Artística Space in Vale do Lobo, so the art scene is still defiantly alive and kicking!

I'm also very lucky to have my own little studio/gallery in Boliqueime, which we have named the Dunn Studio. Whatever else is going on, I have my own means of exhibiting independently, which I do at least once a year.

I show my latest abstract landscapes, a selection of figurative works, and some limited-edition prints. I also collaborate with an American print company to create custom printed items, such as scarves, cushions, and jewellery.

Strangely enough, the company contacted me in May 2020 to say that one of my images had been chosen for their limited-edition masks, which are selling in the US. These days, bizarrely, I can be seen wearing one of my paintings on my face along with hundreds of Americans across the pond! Strange times indeed.

✧ಸಿ✧ಅ✧

Even while living in Portugal, I've always enjoyed travelling. It seems mad to live in a tourist destination and to go and be a tourist somewhere else, but a change of scenery is valuable to me. I have spent time in Cuba, and India, which was a great inspiration for my figurative work at the time. I would paint a whole series inspired by that journey and then hold an exhibition the following season.

Later I visited Italy and Corsica several times with my family, and I've done many paintings of my father in his very recognisable stance and Panama hat posing at a lake or on a beach with his granddaughters, my daughters, Alice and Lydia.

After starting a family, my subject matter shifted and my children were my muses. With inspiration from David Hockney's work, I began painting large canvases depicting swimmers in pools and on beaches. This became an obsession for some years until my girls grew up. I then started to focus less on the figure and more on the sun-drenched backdrop of the land or seascape, until eventually I completely removed the figurative aspect of my work. Now my work is abstract but still very much influenced by my surroundings. My paintings are a direct emotional response to the light, the land, the sea, and the sky. I am never without inspiration living here.

I think like most mothers, I'm proud of my children and the way they have grown into such intelligent and caring human beings. They are a mix of Portuguese and English and have a very rounded perspective on life, with an awareness of two cultures and two languages, and I believe this gives them some kind of superpower! They both have a broad outlook and an empathetic view of the world.

It took me a long time to get to grips with the Portuguese language, but my biggest leap was when I had children. In our household we kept to a pretty strict rule of me speaking English to them and my husband speaking Portuguese. This is what we had been advised to do to get the best of both worlds and not confuse them.

I would hear my young children speaking day-to-day Portuguese, and I appear to have absorbed a lot of the language unknowingly. I suddenly realised that I could understand what everyone was talking about and I was able to hold a normal conversation. My Portuguese is pretty good on the whole, although I really feel that my grammar is lacking. And I still like to brush up on it through reading, and sometimes while I'm painting I listen to a podcast called simply 'Practise Portuguese', which is very entertaining and educational at the same time. We have a problem here in the Algarve in that everybody speaks English to us, which makes some of us even lazier and more self-conscious than we already are.

We British often have difficulty speaking foreign languages. I guess we don't like to risk getting it wrong and being laughed at. It puts us in a vulnerable position, which is very inconvenient when you're trying to be superior!

But seriously, what I have found is that the Portuguese are usually very patient and really appreciate it when you make the effort.

My own daughters offer this advice: give your children a fighting chance at speaking the language. If they are still young enough, perhaps less than ten years old, put them into a Portuguese speaking school. This will help them integrate and you too. If they are older than ten, then it may be too traumatic for them unless they happen to be really good at languages.

Another piece of advice I always give is we have to accept that there are differences here and things might be moving at a slower pace at times, which some people find very frustrating. You have to remember why you wanted to come and live here in the first place. When you're queuing up at the cashpoint in your shorts and flip-flops, will you really be reminiscing on the wonderful speed and efficiency of your UK High Street branch with a nostalgic tear in your eye?

We always laugh about my youngest daughter Lydia's journey to school from Boliqueime to Loulé, when the bus would be stuck behind a mule and cart for about fifteen minutes going at a snail's pace. Everyone took it in their stride, no point in stressing, and we accepted this was just one of the glorious perks of living in the Algarve.

I spent ten years in Olhos de Água, down by the sea, so I really have a strong connection and deep nostalgia for the place. When I go back there, I'm always shocked at the way it's been developed, but once I'm down on the beach, looking out to sea, I just don't look behind me and it feels like time has stood still.

It was one of the first beaches we used to go to when I was a kid. I remember making friends with various families who we reconnected with every summer. They were very carefree times. In the evenings, the adults would all sit up in the restaurant overlooking the beach while we kids would run wild climbing up an enormous rock and jumping off it.

Later there were times when the local fishermen would take us on boat rides and then cook up a *sardinhada* on the beach where much wine would be consumed out of five-litre *garafes*. This was my first experience of witnessing a teenager spewing up pink vomit due to an excess consumption of sangria. A revelation!

We continued to go there every year throughout my teens. I did a lot of my growing up in that village. This was where I discovered smoking fags, sitting on a cliff top with my best friend Ceri, coughing, spluttering, and laughing in the scorching heat. It's strange, but I still experience a wave of nostalgic pleasure when I get a whiff of someone's cigarette smoke.

We made lifelong friends with Portuguese boys and girls from Lisbon, who also returned every year. Some would camp on the cliff tops in the days when you were allowed to, and we would all trek off to the bars and clubs in Albufeira, often hitchhiking around as it was the only way of getting about in those days. We would then stumble back to Olhos de Água as the sun came up, find the nearest tent to occupy for a couple of hours' kip before it got too hot, and then wander down to the sea for a refreshing swim. Bliss! We never seemed to get much sleep back then, but we obviously didn't need it.

Many years later, when I was living there, I did lots of artwork for various restaurants and bars in the area, so I have a connection to it in that sense too. Whenever I visit there, I seek out all the places where I've left my mark.

My father and I often used to paint Olhos de Água seascapes featuring an infamous giant rock which jutted out of the sea. Sadly, it has disappeared after years of erosion from the waves and I'm always still surprised to see that it has gone.

However, when the tide is out, I am guaranteed the satisfaction of taking people down to the beach and showing them the 'Eyes of the Water', a direct translation of *'Olhos de Água'*, which are small freshwater springs in the rock pools. They are always fascinating. Once you've spotted the spiralling rings in the sand under the shallow water, you can put in your hand or foot and watch it disappear into the freezing and apparently bottomless well and taste the sweetness of fresh water contrasting with the saltiness of the sea.

Another high point is to walk along the rugged cliff tops over to Praia da Falésia and enjoy the beautiful expanse of white sands and the horizon glistening on the sea. Out of season, you might be the only person in that landscape.

The visualisation of these experiences are imprinted on my memory like a series of paintings, to be recreated in the studio. Full of light and colour, they conjure a feeling of freedom, lifting the spirits!

✧೫✧ଔ✧

To view Jessica's art work, and subscribe to her newsletter, visit her website:
www.jessicadunnart.com

3

Relishing Portugal
EVANNE SCHMARDER

The wedding took place on Fort Lauderdale Beach at sunrise, 1989. An intimate gathering of close family and friends, our ten guests were instructed to join us barefooted. A dear friend of ours—a newly appointed Public Notary—presided over the ceremony, her back to the crashing waves while we sleepily whispered our vows to one another. Back at another friend's oceanfront condo, aside from the teary goodbye to my mom and dad, the lopsided leaning wedding cake is what we remember most. A group of girlfriends stayed up all night making that cake for us and, while we don't recall what it tasted like, it always makes us laugh.

We glowed as we set off on life's adventure together, tin cans and streamers attached to our back bumper, 'Just Married' written all over our windows. Working situations resigned, notices served on apartments, and most of our belongings given away, we made our way into a bright, unknown future together. For three exciting months, we camped across the United States, east to west, with our six-man dome tent and our trusty black labrador mix called Jim Snout. We settled in Portland, Oregon, initially in the park blocks, in the city center. Portland was a sleepy city back then. You'd be hard-pressed to find a place open for Sunday morning breakfast. Eventually, we bought a floating home on the Columbia River. Those were good years—with great friends, new experiences, and upward career mobility.

As a union stagehand, Ray worked everything from rock shows —think Bruce Springsteen, The Eagles, The Rolling Stones, and singing onstage with Jackson Brown—to opera and dance, including The Phantom of the Opera and other such musicals, lectures, including Maya Angelo, and even the NBA draft. Later he worked as the stage manager for the Oregon Symphony Orchestra.

I settled into the 9-5 world of corporate travel management, overseeing multi-million-dollar travel programs with staff around the country. Our jobs required long hours and excessive travel. We counted ourselves fortunate when we had a weekend at home together.

The breaking point (and in the years since, we've learned there's always a moment or event that delineates before and after big decisions) came when we arrived home from a lovely ten-day Caribbean cruise. Transported from warm tropical sunshine to dreary Oregon drizzle, we'd had enough. Enough of the wet weather (which, by the way, is what makes Portland so amazingly green); enough of being apart from one another for our jobs; and enough of trying to build what we'd been spoon-fed as the 'American Dream'. As it turns out, we had a completely different dream.

So, in 2000, for the second time in our married life, we chucked out nearly everything—careers, house, possessions, outdated ideas—and hit the road. For the next eighteen years, we were what are referred to as full-time RVers, living in our efficiently designed two-hundred-square-foot road abode. We traveled coast-to-coast and north to south with our trusty fifth wheel. We were snowbirds of the rolling variety. From national parks—obscure to overrun—to historic hot springs, ghost towns, architectural gems, and famous flyways, we made up for the lost time.

It didn't take long, however, to realize that there is a myth surrounding a carefree life—the need for a purpose. We'd joke, "another beautiful waterfall, another interesting museum." We needed purpose. That manifested itself in several ways, through some chosen passion projects, and some work opportunities. Over the years, rockstar Ray—bass player and vocalist extraordinaire—reconnected with band mates. We enjoyed a string of band reunions in the form of jams, gigs, and festivals.

I put my tech-curiosity to work as a digital marketing consultant, speaking, writing, and guiding clients. Together we created an online cooking show that was picked up by broadcast television in the United States.

When an opportunity to tour eastern Australia in a campervan presented itself, we jumped at it. RVing friends recommended a storage facility near the little central California coast town that had become our home base, and in no time we were on a Virgin Australia flight to Melbourne. When our three-month adventure ended, we returned home, picked up our RV, and pinched ourselves. It had been a dream come true. We also realized we hadn't missed the RV one bit.

As we settled back into a routine, we wondered what was next for us. It was becoming painfully obvious that after all our years traveling across the United States we had seen and done most of what we wanted to and, after always keeping an eye out, hadn't found a single place we wanted to settle down in. When it became more trouble than adventure to pick up sticks and travel from point A to point B, we knew it was time to make another change.

✪৯✪ଓ✪

For reasons that are still a mystery to us, Europe was never on our 'move to' radar. Aside from brief, but illuminating, speaking gigs in Europe for me, neither of us had ever crossed the pond for pleasure before. That all changed in early 2016. Through a series of coincidences (thank you Universe), Portugal began to get a lot of buzz in our humble home. A Portuguese-American friend raved about his homeland, rapturous in describing seafood rice among other Portuguese culinary delights. With that seed planted, everything was coming up in favor of Portugal. We read about Lisbon as a retirement haven, and that further piqued our interest. What was this mecca we were missing out on, we asked ourselves?

The RV went back into storage and we flew across the Atlantic for another three-month whirlwind adventure. We visited friends in Germany, Austria, and France. We spent a spectacular month in Paris. Our next destination was Lisbon, where we aimed to determine if a move to Portugal was for us. We spent a wonderful month in Principe Real, chosen because of its proximity to the weekly bio farm market. That was nearly the extent of what we knew about the city and the country. We wrapped that trip up with two weeks in the Algarve, staying in Lagos, then Faro. During those six weeks in Portugal, we came to love the culture, the things that the Portuguese people held dear, the ways they spent their time, their kindness, and their quirks. Their pride was, and is, palpable when listening to our appreciative response to a frequent question, "How do you like Portugal?" The European culture was so different from anything we'd ever known before. We loved it.

In true form, it wasn't a difficult decision. We have always been very aware of when it's been time to make a change. We're lucky that way. As usual, when we returned to the California coast, our small circle of friends gathered. They had been following along and were eager to hear about the possibility of us moving to Portugal. It must have seemed like such an eccentric thing to do, but with smiles on our faces and quickening hearts, we gave them the news.

We would once again up-end our lives to experience something new. By the spring of 2017, again dispossessed of most of the trappings of the past eighteen years, we arrived at the Portugal Embassy in Washington, DC, to apply for our D7 visas. We had carefully assembled the required paperwork for each of us. Our appointment was at 10 a.m. Staying with friends in Annapolis, we drove into DC, found a parking spot right across the street from the embassy, and presented ourselves at the door around 9.30 a.m. It was 10 a.m. on the dot that they called us up to the desk. In less than fifteen minutes we had presented our paperwork, paid the fees, listened to the next steps, asked a few questions, and were on our way.

We expected the visa approval decision to take two to three months. We waited it out in the vibrant city of Montreal, Canada (or as some call it, Europe-light). Sitting in our back garden, eating Lebanese mezze from the neighborhood takeaway, we got the news from the Portuguese Embassy—we were in. Joy ensued!

Our plan was simple. We'd move to the gorgeous capital city, Lisbon, and experience everything that it had to offer for two or three years. At that point, we reasoned, we'd be priced out of the real estate market and ready to get back to nature. And that's exactly what happened.

We spent our first six weeks in Mouraria, finding our way around and figuring out how to secure appointments with the SEF office for our first temporary resident permits. While we arrived in September, our appointments were set for the following March. We printed the official appointment paperwork out and kept it in our passports with our affixed D7 visas. (We're thrilled to report that our initial SEF appointment, as well as our next, went off without a hitch).

Knowing we needed to make a move in a matter of weeks, we visited a local real estate agency. They welcomed us in and we sat down. After general pleasantries, the fellow asked us where we were currently living.

"Mouraria," we replied.

"I'm sorry, where?" he asked.

Slower this time, we replied, "Mouraria."

With a puzzled look on his face, he asked the receptionist to help.

We looked at her and said,

"We are living in the *bairro* of Mouraria." (the Mouraria district).

"Oh," she said, nodding to the fellow with understanding.

Then they both smiled, with more nodding, and said "Mouraria!" in unison.

Once we wrapped up that quick meeting, we headed down the road to a funky little Middle Eastern hole-in-the-wall, called Ink Farm Foods, and had the best Israeli falafel balls we'd ever eaten.

It didn't work out with that agency—or any other, actually. Yet despite the tight rental market, we secured a large flat (unusual for the neighborhood) in the historic Alfama district from an absolutely delightful Portuguese gal, a filmmaker that spends half her year in Brooklyn, New York. We stayed seven months, soaking in everything that was happening around us before taking off for an extended summer holiday in Italy, a stopover in Dublin, and a few fun Ray-rock gigs back in the United States.

As luck would have it, the across-the-hall neighbor in our old Mouraria building was moving into a new flat and looking for renters right around the time we planned to return to Portugal. One wonderful thing led to another. We moved into her beautifully cared-for flat and made a great friend in the process. In fact, we have built our Portuguese circle of friends in this manner. We are close to the couple that owned our first Mouraria place and also developed a friendship with their apartment manager. Our Alfama landlady has become a dear friend and we enjoy the commonality of countries.

The connections and generous nature of the local people are

things that always stand out to us. For Ray's first birthday in Portugal, we took a day trip to Setúbal. We had heard about their fabulous fish and farm market, and it seemed like it would be a charming city to explore. We boarded the ferry that took us to the train which took us to Setúbal, though we got off the train one stop too early and had to wander around and walk our way to the heart of town. We easily found the market and after all that travel and traipsing around we were hungry. Like many markets, the perimeter was a useful collection of meat markets, cheese stands, and snack bars. Ray spotted one that specialized in *bifanas*, a new-to-us taste sensation, so we headed over to sample their wares. A *bifana* is simply a pork steak, seasoned with garlic and spices, then placed inside a bread roll.

With our limited Portuguese language skills but open hearts, we were able to communicate to the folks behind the counter that we had just come from Montreal. It turned out that the fellow behind the counter, who was the owner and husband of his coworker, had spent time in Montreal on a military ship. He must've had quite a colorful time there because before you knew it, everyone was joking and laughing. The dozen or so individuals in the snack bar couldn't seem to get enough. Finished with our delicious *bifanas*, somehow it slipped that it was Ray's birthday. It was everyone's lucky day then. They set up the shot glasses and the *ginjinha*, a Portuguese liqueur, poured freely. There were toasts. There were laughs and more shots of *ginjinha*. There were selfies and warm wishes all around. It was a fabulous introduction to these wonderful people and a birthday memory that will last forever.

✥❀✥❀✥

Just as predicted and again true to form, we were now ready to try something new. After having observed the real estate market and feeling ready to make Portugal our true home, it was time to buy a place of our own. Sure, we could find a place in Lisbon within our budget, but it would be a shoebox. As much as we loved the capital city, we needed room to grow and were yearning for a bit more nature. Having always been ocean people, we began to explore Portugal's ample shorelines. We looked to the north and loved what we saw but remembered the cold, rainy Portland winters. No can do. The Silver Coast was very alluring but dedicated to being car-free, we couldn't live with its limited public transportation options. Setúbal was in play for a while, but without an easy walk to the ocean, we felt that, even though we loved the small city vibe and everything that it brought, it was too similar to Lisbon. That left the Algarve to explore.

Digging deeper, we created a checklist of everything important to us in a hometown. We wanted to be within walking distance to the ocean, with pleasant weather, good grocery options, a fresh market nearby, international dining options and neighborhoods, and easy to access public transportation. The infrastructure was first, but equally important, we wanted to love where we lived, the town, the community, and yes, the home itself. We looked from Tavira to Aljezur. Each had a lot of 'something specials' and were worthy of deep consideration, but from our list of personal needs, they each missed a tick or two. Finally, swayed by the embarrassment of coastal riches combined with a pleasant walking city, an international community, a reasonable transportation hub, and great food, Lagos ticked all the boxes. That's where we set our sights.

We joined every Portuguese-selling real estate site known to man (at least it felt that way) and poured over the daily listing updates. Maybe this one would work, maybe we should consider this other one? We had to head down there and get a feel for what was on offer. The couple of places we looked at did not set our hearts aflutter. That's when, during an exploratory trip in October 2019, our Airbnb host told us about a neighborhood in Lagos that might meet our needs. We took a walk, had a look, and fell hard. We kept our eyes peeled for a listing in that neighborhood but, because it's a mostly Portuguese community that uses different (mainly Portuguese-serving) realtors, we didn't find anything on the standard sites normally used by expats to find real estate.

In a passing conversation, new Lagos-loving, California-RVing friends we had recently met, Dave and Phyllis Johnson, mentioned a realtor that they clicked with, Joey Decoz at Abacoz Algarve, and suggested we give her a call. We figured there was nothing to lose and so scheduled a call with her. After really listening to our likes, dislikes, and specific needs and asking questions, she promised to scour the market and send us anything that she felt was a match. After we hung up and just for fun, we sent her some photographs we had taken of the community we'd fallen in love with six months earlier. Lo and behold, we kid you not, the next morning Joey sent us a listing that was being handled by an agency she frequently partnered with. It was exactly what we were looking for! Exactly.

By now, April 2020, Covid-19 was rearing its ugly head. But buying a house in the time of Covid turned out to be surprisingly easy. The listing remained open on our computer. We looked at it every day and had calls and written questions answered. We developed a relationship with a banker and received pre-approval on a loan. They treated us to a video tour and as the stars were aligning, we scheduled a masked and socially distanced viewing. We knew that if the property lived up to what we'd seen and heard so far, we'd make an offer.

Unlike a home purchase in the States, the seller wanted—no required—the furnishings to be part of the deal. Though not what we would have chosen ourselves, this would make the property move-in ready the day we closed. We negotiated hard. Both parties were ready to walk away from a possible sale. We were clear that if Joey didn't sell us this house, she'd sell us another in Lagos (but we hoped it would be this one). Super-close on an agreement, we let things ride overnight. The next morning a price agreement appeared in our email inbox. It was right on the money and we committed.

Working with a professional and caring team that included a bilingual, experienced lawyer (Juanita Rodrigues is not the least expensive in Lagos but she certainly is trustworthy, thorough, and knows her business inside and out—we were in great hands), together with Pedro Monteiro at Bankinter, and Joey, we closed on the house of our Lagos dreams in less than three months, and moved to the beach that very day.

Since moving to the Algarve, it has been an odd roller coaster of

Covid living. We've gingerly enjoyed favorite dining spots—including The Garden, The Green Room, and Pizza do Francês. We've shopped at all the major grocery stores, markets, and hardware stores in town. And like everyone else, we are eagerly awaiting broader freedom and a future that a vaccine will bring. But the beach, ocean, and cliffs are always open and since they are just a hop, skip, and a jump away from home, you'll find us there—on any one of the many beautiful ocean fronts—most days.

✿ℬ✪ᘄ✿

Book and magazine exchanges were one of the perks of living and traveling in an RV. Sometimes you'd pull into a campground to find a cozy library with books on the shelves and instructions to 'take one and leave one'. Other times you'd find stacks of magazines and a few dog-eared books in the laundry room. Those were my favorites. I was known for always having a selection of diverse magazines on my back table. Many an interesting food or travel tidbit came from those pages. When we moved to Portugal, even though we were busy living the life, I was always on the lookout for interesting magazines. Passing a newsstand, the offerings always caught my eye but, unfortunately, they were all in Portuguese. I can easily enjoy the pictures and, with a little concentration and an occasional error, make out the recipes, but the fun of flipping through the glossy pages in search of a gem of insight was missing.

It was also strikingly clear that as the dedicated food lovers, teachers, writers, photographers, speakers, and home cooks that we are, Portugal was indeed a different ball of wax. Certainly, several things were familiar, but many things were new to us, too. For all the hullabaloo about the emerging food scene and the fresh and/or different ingredients found in stores and markets here, we needed something to help us navigate our daily food lives. And we wanted that necessary information delivered in an entertaining, educational, full-color English-language magazine. Good luck with that.

Suddenly it became obvious. We could combine our writing, cooking, and communication skills with our insatiable curiosity and interest in all things food and Portugal, and simply start one. That's how *Relish Portugal*, the English-language food and culture magazine for Portugal lovers everywhere, was born. It's a free, online, subscription-only magazine for Portugal-curious home cooks, delivered to subscribers' email boxes quarterly. Not to be confused with a 'What's On' type of magazine, inside each issue's nearly fifty pages we share stories from expats and those of Portuguese heritage —often small business owners, bloggers, tour operators, or authors —that are equally in love with the flavors of this beautiful country.

We always open with Food For Thought, a piece penned by a food luminary. We close with a Perspective piece about life and food in Portugal. In between those pages, we explore the world of natural, organic Portuguese wines, pick up some European Portuguese kitchen and cooking terms, and talk to locals about their adopted towns. We feature a non-Portuguese eating establishment in our Not From Around Here section, take a closer look at a philanthropic food-related organization, serve up a couple of interesting feature stories, spotlight an ingredient, share the work of talented artists, and more.

There's also a virtual cookbook shelf since many of our contributors are published cookbook authors, and we ask each contributor to share a recipe that they love. Sometimes they are Portuguese specialties, other times they are simply what our contributors love preparing at home. In tandem with the magazine, we publish a playlist on Spotify called What's Playing In Your Kitchen, composed of contributor picks. The songs run the gambit from fado and country and western to show tunes and rock ballads. The playlists are one of my favorite features of *Relish Portugal*. We play one of them every Saturday or Sunday morning as we make blueberry spelt pancakes.

Our first issue came out on January 7, 2020, with three more issues delivered quarterly over our first publishing year. *Relish Portugal* has attracted subscribers from around the world, and we're always thrilled to connect like-minded readers, writers, and businesses. We know we're doing something right because at the end of 2020 we were honored with a national competition Gourmand

World Cookbook Award, voted the best Portugal food magazine. In January 2021, we received the news that our magazine was honored with a Gourmand Best In The World award. We were thrilled and humbled.

✿ℬ✪ℰ✿

Oh, Portuguese, why do you taunt us so?

Any, no, make that every, self-respecting Portuguese person will tell you that Portuguese is not Spanish. However, Ray's high school Spanish has been extremely useful in understanding the written language. We've picked up tons of words through the food world, including the grocery store, markets, and restaurants. A little game we play with ourselves involves calling each grocery item by its Portuguese name as we unpack the bags. We also make an effort to scan the store receipts, reading the names, and trying to remember exactly what and how much of each item we bought.

When communicating, especially with the older generation, we have found hand gestures to be very effective. And be careful how you ask a younger person if they speak English, as it may offend them. We've known many to say, "of course I speak English as well as German, Italian, French, Russian, etc. etc." We learned that particular lesson at our local Pingo Doce supermarket. The young fellow behind the checkout was incredulous that we'd even doubt his ability to speak classroom-perfect English. We then received a friendly lecture about how Portuguese children are schooled in the language arts. He closed by asking Evanne, "Now, am I handsome?" What a hoot! He is kinda cute, but we're guessing something was lost in translation.

Aside from casual language learning, we've decided that when we receive our last temporary residency renewal in 2021, we will enroll in some in-person Portuguese language classes with the goal of passing the CIPLE Portuguese proficiency test. With an A2 language competency certificate in hand, we will be one step closer to Portuguese citizenship. Wish us luck!

One of the biggest concerns from American expats is health

insurance because, let's face it, those coming over to Portugal on D7 visas are usually of the retirement-class. We were, too, and also had pre-existing conditions to take into account. After some research, we found that joining the expat organization called Afpop and securing private health insurance with Allianz through their broker Medal, was not only easy but also affordable. In fact, their annual premiums are based on age-brackets, not previous health issues or insurance claims. How refreshing. Then came time to use it.

It was time for our annual medical checkup, complete with a full slate of tests and visits. We could choose our own specialists. We had to make a new patient appointment (we did so in person) and the girl at the desk frowned, looked up at us, and told us they were slightly backlogged. There would be a wait. Would it be acceptable for us to book an appointment three weeks out? Are you kidding? In the States, six-plus months is considered the standard. The appointment days came, everything was well, we paid our modest ten percent upfront payment as required by the insurance policy and headed home. We won't fool you; these visits aren't just a blood pressure and stethoscope check. They are expensive tests and entail visits to specialists. We were slightly concerned about how much the eventual bill would be.

About a month later, the inevitable happened. We opened our mailbox and had an envelope from Allianz. Bracing ourselves for a big bill, we sat down and opened the envelope, nervously removing the enclosed letter. Remember that in the States people go bankrupt over the cost of medical care. Yeah, we were anxious. We unfolded the letter, and to our absolute shock, read the first couple of lines. They went something like this: 'Dear Insured Client. Thank you for allowing Allianz to serve your medical insurance needs. We have paid the non-co-pay balance in full. Again, it is our pleasure to serve you, thank you for the opportunity.' And that has been our experience with them again and again.

One day over coffee we were discussing the many things we love about the Portuguese people. We challenged each other, based on our experiences, to come up with a one-word descriptor. The result was fascinating. One of us used the word genuine. The other used the word authentic.

And kindness—you'll hear it again and again. What constitutes kindness in our eyes? The young fellow who stops on the way to an appointment to offer his arm to an elder trying to cross a street. Meeting a neighbor for the first time and being offered some of her dinner. A busy restaurant host offering to watch our moving boxes as we scampered down the street to retrieve more of our belongings. The Uber driver that tells us about the best neighborhood in town (which incidentally happens to be his).

They are proud people and they love that you find joy, beauty, and value in their country, customs, and food. There's never any doubt about it, yes indeed, they ARE handsome.

✿ℬ✿ℛ✿

To find out more about the Relish Portugal magazine, including how to subscribe free online, visit their website: www.relishportugal.com

4

In Search of Tranquillity
JOHN HOUGH

I was born in Limerick, Ireland, the youngest of four children. My position in the pecking order was fortunate in that I learnt to avoid repeating my elder siblings' mistakes whilst making the most of presumed innocence as the junior member of the tribe. My very hard-working parents provided a comfortable middle-class upbringing for us, with little left over for their own self-indulgence once we had benefited from the lion's share. After an average performance in school, the local university beckoned, providing a plethora of opportunities to indulge in lots of questionable activities and to dabble in student politics.

Despite the distractions of a busy student social life, pub crawls, and involvement in the students' union, (all designed to avoid academic work), I earned a respectable degree. The result of this meant I was now looking for employment. With little prospect of an immediate job, I wangled a scholarship to study for an MBA at a college in upstate New York. The fact that I was still a student member of the university's governing body may have helped in negotiations.

After my stint in the US, I headed back home to take up teaching at the alma mater. Fortuitously, in making the appointment, the powers that be decided that both they and I would have had enough of each other after two years, so I would have to find something else to do rather than becoming a permanent fixture. With academic opportunities thin on the ground, I applied for a lectureship at an international college in London. The stars must have been aligned that particular year as I was successful in securing the job and started on the next chapter of my career.

Richmond, The American International University in London was a world away from my humble beginnings. With a campus in leafy Richmond overlooking the Thames, and another in bustling Kensington, the contrast could not have been more startling. The student population of some 1,200 seemed to represent the United Nations, with the bulk of them coming from some of the most affluent families around the world.

When not dodging Ferraris and Lamborghinis jostling for space in the car park, I spent a great deal of time prepping and delivering endless numbers of courses in marketing and international business. How I found time to volunteer at MENCAP and to accommodate a daily swimming addiction is a wonder. Taking a further degree at the University of Westminster also kept me busy. I must have enjoyed it as I stayed put for nearly twenty years, becoming a professor, and then a Dean of the Business School.

Living in London was a wonderful experience. Not only did my job send me around the world to promote our post-graduate programmes, I had the good fortune to lecture as a visiting professor in different countries too. But as I lived in the heart of the city with endless opportunities for entertainment and excess, London was the magnet that kept me grounded.

One fortunate development occurred while I was putting together a course on luxury brand marketing. Some French acquaintances I had made in Ireland invited me to visit them in the Champagne region outside of Paris. Whilst there, I realised this would make an excellent field study location for my students. With some helpful pointers from my friends, I put together an immersion experience that included trips to many Champagne houses, both large and small; with lectures from the Ruinart brothers of the eponymous Champagne brand owned by Moët et Chandon and LVMH. Most of my time was taken up with quality assurance, as I was invariably first in line with a Champagne flute when it came to the tasting room.

I was very lucky to have also become involved with several wine merchants in London who had an avid interest in both Champagne and having a good time. They introduced me to the L'Ordre des Coteaux de Champagne, and after several expensive dinners over many years, I was intronised (inducted) as a Chevalier and subsequently as an Officier of the Order. It was all very nice, but a bit stuffy, and the paucity of Champagne at the events led the London contingent to look for something with a bit more panache and style.

Luckily, a second 'Brotherhood' or Order existed in Champagne. Though not actively promoted by the main Champagne houses, the Confrérie du Sabre d'Or was very much dedicated to promoting the celebration of Champagne, and in particular, having as much fun as possible while opening your Champagne bottle with a sabre. The sweep of a sword up the side of the bottle and removing the cork with the glass ring intact is known as sabrage. All very easy when you know how. From an initial recce to Reims and Épernay, we established a new Embassy of the Ordre in the UK and soon sabres were flashing and liberating bottles at some of the most fashionable hotels and restaurants across the country. Twice-yearly Gala Balls kept us busy, with members of the French Council always insisting on being present to show their support. Obviously we knew how to throw a good party.

One memorable experience with the Confrérie was our annual outing to Press Day at the Chelsea Flower Show, where the great and the good had the chance to turn their hand to sabering a bottle. Little did I expect to hit the front page of the Daily Telegraph when Jerry Hall agreed to sabrage a bottle of rosé.

My career in academia continued alongside my love of Champagne and included a stint working for the Aga Khan as the Head of Administration in his then newly opened post-graduate institute in London in 2005. From there I moved to a local higher education college in Kent but with several family bereavements that year and government funding threatening the job, it felt appropriate to take a change of direction. My partner and I had set up a recruitment business which was performing exceptionally well, so I focussed my attention on this and took advantage of more free time to have a hip replacement. A subsequent trip to the Maldives had me back in hospital, this time dealing with a herniated disc and other complications. Luckily the procedure was swift, and the stay in The Blackheath private hospital very short-lived, with instructions from my consultant to "take it easy".

✧ℬ✧ℛ✧

What better place to recuperate than Portugal. We had travelled to the Algarve many, many times over a period of about twenty years. The western Algarve for me was the most special of places. The raw and wild coastline along with endless beaches reminded me of the west of Ireland, but with sunshine and blue skies in abundance. Although we explored the central and eastern region, we set our hearts on staying in the west, where it is far less crowded or busy. A trip from Burgau to Salema on an unmade road brought us to a beach called Cabanas Velhas and to a newish development of quirky looking houses with curved roofs. They were all perched on the side of a hill with spectacular sea views. Quinta da Fortaleza was quite unique.

We came back that evening to look at the stars from the Fortaleza de Almádena, which teeters on the edge of the cliff above the beach. With no light pollution and a cloud-free sky, you could almost touch the heavens. The sea air along with the smell of the nearby pine forest and sticky cistus growing on the hillside was an intoxicating mix. It definitely must have captivated us as we looked at each other and agreed that to live here would indeed be living the dream.

Back in London a week or two later, curiosity got the better of us and I checked out the cost of local property. To my surprise, thanks to the fallout from the 2008 economic crisis, villas that had originally sold for well over 1.5 million euros in the noughties, were now on the market for less than 700,000 euros. This was definitely food for thought. Neither of us had contemplated living outside of the UK. Sure, Cape Town and California were wonderful places to visit, and we had discussed making an investment there, but the complexities, risks, and cost of such a move seemed prohibitive. Suddenly, Portugal seemed like a real possibility to get away from the hustle and bustle of London, but still allow for easy access to the city if we needed to get back in a hurry.

Sometimes you have to jump into the abyss. Without a huge amount of thought to how we would manage to run our UK business and its hundred-plus employees, we stuck a toe in the water and made a cheeky offer on one of the large 'Teletubby-style' houses at Cabanhas Velhas. After a great deal of soul searching and considerable wrangling, they accepted our offer. Reality soon set in as we had to decide how to pay for the villa and how best to manage a move from our home. We raided the bank accounts and piggy banks to get the total sum together. This was heavily influenced by the exchange rate at the time. We were very fortunate to buy the villa just as the British pound hit 1.28 euros. A nervous week of watching fluctuations was managed by a company called Currencies Direct, who made the process very easy. We locked in the rate and combined with other currency buyers to get the best deal possible.

Twenty-five years of accumulated possessions, junk, and a large library made a great excuse for a thorough life laundry. By December 2012, we had packed everything, rented out our UK home, and made the move to Portugal. It all seemed surreal as we spent the first few nights staying at the Vila Luz Aparthotel in Luz while the paperwork and transfer of deed was sorted. Finally, the day arrived, and we managed to dovetail with the removal company just in time to unpack the teapot and bedding to settle in.

A few days later we picked up our ageing Miniature Schnauzer. The pet transport company had driven all the way from the UK and despite the length of the journey, Holly seemed pleased to see us.

Having settled in and come to terms with one of us commuting back and forth to London to run the business, while the other (me) stayed in the Algarve to manage the fort and phone from a distance, a routine of sorts took shape. I spent many hours toing and froing to Faro airport in that first year. Thankfully, by then the A22 motorway was open and the journey could be done in an hour.

On one return trip I arrived home much later than expected and was met with a torrent of water gushing out of the front wall of the villa. A feed pipe from the mains into our deposit had ruptured and was flooding the front garden. I was astonished at the pressure behind the water. It had never been very impressive indoors. I later discovered that the system in Portugal is pressurised. Typically, something like 7 bars of pressure can be coming into the house. My neighbour came to my rescue and located the stopcock to turn off the offending pipe. Next day he got his revenge for the late hour wake-up call as he managed to drop a manhole cover on my fingers while we investigated what could have caused the problem. A very efficient plumber put matters right and fitted a pressure limiter to avoid any further problems inside the villa.

Fun with the water supply was not the only headache we had. Our attempts to get a telephone line installed along with some sort of TV and internet was a feat almost as difficult as trying to get a Brexit deal. Having signed up to a company who assured us we would have high-speed connectivity, the result was anything but. A year into our contract and several dongles later, we cancelled the contract through lack of service provision. The lesson learnt was 'believe nothing and you are already halfway to the truth'.

Speaking of lessons, I spent a good deal of time trying to come to grips with the Portuguese language. Having studied French at both school and university, I had achieved a degree of fluency and assumed that the migration to Portuguese would be straightforward. Hmmm, definitely not the case. One amusing episode with linguistic confusion happened on a memorable trip to Vila Real de Santo António. We were with some Portuguese friends to watch their son play in a local football league match. Lots of parents and children crowded the stands, and a curiously large presence of local police bordered the pitch. It must have been a quiet weekend!

Deciding to throw myself into the spirit of the game and to add a bit of vocal excitement, I roared loudly at every opportunity if a foul or a decent shot at goal stirred the crowd. What I could not understand was the sea of faces who turned and stared at me every time I shouted "CORNER" for this obvious infraction. Our Portuguese friends dissolved in laughter, but did nothing until after a particularly loud episode, when two burly members of the GNR police approached our area. I was firmly pulled down into my seat and told to look innocent. Luckily we were ignored, and I was quietly informed that my outbursts were causing upset to the other people around us. Apparently, the word I had been shouting so loudly closely resembles a hugely vulgar term for a very intimate part of the female anatomy. Duly informed, I stayed glued to my seat for the rest of the match and tried not to look like a beetroot as we made our way to the exit when the game was over.

Back to reality and with time on my hands and feeling that a large villa on the side of a hill was too much for one person, we decided to test the market for summer rentals. I was stunned that in our first year we managed to rent our villa out for fourteen weeks. Luckily, I found a small flat to rent in Burgau, so I was on hand to deal with the check-ins, cleaning, laundry, troubleshooting, check-outs, and anything else that cropped up. Oh, and did I mention the endless cleaning and laundry? It was hard work and totally different to anything I had done before. The pay-off made it all worthwhile, and we even had repeat business from happy punters the following year.

While all of this was going on, my partner had grown very tired of flying back and forth to London. Some forty journeys in one year. We decided to sell the business and see what we could turn our hands to in Portugal. After a tense few months of negotiations, the deal was completed, and we finessed our commitment to Portugal by selling our UK property too.

With a reasonable amount in the bank and with time on our hands after our first foray into the rental market, we agreed to set up a property management business called Plum. I took care of the marketing and we tested the market by advertising in the local media to see if we would get any interest. I recall we had only one enquiry after about eight weeks, so we were not going anywhere fast with this approach. As we considered our options and how to drum up business, we took a flight back to London so that my partner could have some medical tests completed for recurring vertigo and blurred vision.

Several MRI scans and consultants later, we were horrified to learn that my partner had a rare type of diffused brain tumour which was inoperable. Radiotherapy and chemotherapy treatment could be given, but the prognosis was very uncertain as the condition was usually terminal in adults. Reeling from this bombshell, we headed back to Portugal and onwards to Seville for a long-planned break. Obviously, our plans for the business venture went up in smoke as we tried to come to terms with what would be the best way to treat the condition. While in Spain, we spoke to an eminent London consultant who agreed to provide treatment. She advised holding off on any therapy for as long as possible to give the treatment the best possibility of working only when it became absolutely necessary. It was all very stressful and nerve-wracking.

To add to the mix, I decided it was time to propose marriage and was very grateful to receive a positive reply. What better way to take your mind off something worrying, than to have something else almost as stressful to engage with. We returned to Portugal and set about a whirlwind of organisation to get the 'Big Day' planned.

'Wedding Central', as it became known, had us looking for a venue and fortunately we hit upon the newly opened Clubhouse at Espiche Golf Club. A wonderful contemporary South African inspired structure with personality and style that enjoys sweeping views in all directions across the hills and fairways of the course.

As we planned everything down to the nth degree, it became apparent that my partner needed support to come to terms with his medical condition. Being told you are terminally ill and that your consultants have no idea what direction the tumour might take is a very difficult concept to deal with. Friends of ours mentioned a local charity called Madrugada that helps people facing a life-limiting illness. I got in touch and was hugely relieved and grateful that the Clinical Lead was a counsellor and offered to provide support. Over a period of six months a huge burden was lifted, as the counselling sessions gradually turned my partner's negativity into a more positive outlook.

Back on the wedding front, we were bemused by the bureaucracy and officiousness of the Registry Office (*Conservatoire*) in Lagos. The wedding ceremony is treated like a contract with the parents' names of both parties read out along with identification numbers, dates of birth, and the names of the intendeds. That done, as long as there are no objections, you are declared married and sign the certificate, all of which takes about five minutes. With such an uninspiring and perfunctory approach, there seemed little hope that we could have the ceremony we wanted. Luckily we met a very helpful official who agreed to travel to the golf club and work with us and our plans for the event.

Organising the party of a lifetime for sixty people certainly took up a huge amount of time and effort. Taking account of the fact that we were effectively retired, (Ha!) and in spite of the continuing very busy rentals, we decided to do a DIY wedding and make pretty much everything ourselves. Weeks of sourcing materials, printing, cutting and glueing had the flat looking like an art room in a primary school. Nonetheless, the results were acceptable, and we sent invitations and reply cards out in a speedy fashion. I bought all the components for the table centre pieces and table decorations online and waited nervously for deliveries to arrive. We had agreed on a date in early October for the ceremony, and once back in our own villa, our attention focused on the legal paperwork requirements for the Registry Office.

A trip to the Irish Embassy in Lisbon became necessary as the registrar required a *Certificado de Coutume* or 'Certificate of Freedom to Marry' from the Department of Foreign Affairs. Once armed with all the relevant papers, we managed to confirm the date and timing with the registrar.

Our wedding 'Bake-Off' moment came when we realised it would be better to have a wedding cake made in the Algarve rather than engaging in a diplomatic dance between friends and family in the UK and Ireland about who might make what. We were blessed that a local expat, Ruth Jackson, lived near the golf club and was a wedding cake specialist and delivered cake decorating classes too. Rather than getting stuck in ourselves, we opted for Ruth to bake and decorate a seven-tiered monolith. The result was a splendid-looking tower finished off with top hats and stars. It's not who you know: it's who you know who knows whom! The rule of thumb in the Algarve is if you think you cannot find something, think again, as someone, somewhere will be able to help.

With the venue, entertainment, menu, and invitations all done, we braced ourselves for the big day. Of course with so many people travelling from overseas to attend we had to do more than offer just the one showstopper. A wedding eve dinner and entertainment took place at a local restaurant in Espiche, which presented a challenge in that we didn't want people to have too much 'fun' the night before the big day. Luckily we got home from a splendid meal at a reasonable hour and endeavoured to get some sleep.

My stress levels peaked at about one hundred percent on the morning of the wedding day. When we arrived at the golf club to decorate the space and layout the seating, we discovered they had not set the room up with the extra-large round tables we had hired. Luckily, some close friends were on hand to pull, drag, and lift to get everything in place. Specially acquired white carpet and white chair bows along with lots of diamanté and white flowers made for a magical transformation to the room and to the outdoor area where the wedding would take place. By the time I was satisfied that no more could be done, I realised I was cutting things very fine to be able to get home, changed, and back in time for the ceremony.

Needless to say, a wonderful time was had by all, with many magnums of Champagne sabraged too, just to prove we hadn't lost the knack. We were truly fortunate to have discovered a professional singer who provided all the music throughout the ceremony and into the early hours of the morning. She is now a firm friend who has made many more occasions extra special with her upbeat vocals and willingness to perform at the drop of a hat.

The following day the parting shot with friends and family was a somewhat bleary-eyed round of golf at Espiche followed by an early evening pizza for everyone at Casa Padaria in Burgau. In spite of the excesses of the previous day, there was much effort expended on trying to match the dizzy heights of the main event with yet another late night of carousing notched on the bedpost. It was a bit of a relief when everyone finally took themselves home.

After a brief trip (aka honeymoon) to the UK, Belgium, and Porto, we settled into life back in Burgau. A steady stream of visitors had us busy playing host, but our thoughts were never too far away from the demon brain tumour and what might happen next.

Not being ones to stand still for very long, and having grown somewhat tired of the 'Tellytubby' house, but not its magnificent views, we decided to put it on the market and see what we could get for it. Many estate agents professed to have buyers ready and waiting and all were entirely straight-faced when they asked for four percent or five percent commission plus VAT if they could make the sale. On a million euro sale that amounts to some 60,000 euros. Even though this staggering figure can be deducted from any calculation for capital gains, it still represents a huge charge for what seems like very little done by the agents. We were so underwhelmed by the images and 'storyboard' produced by several of them we got in touch with a professional photographer to create an appropriately appealing set of images offering a true reflection of the villa's best assets. After many months of show-rounds and tidying up to make sure the villa looked its best, we were delighted to sell with almost everything in it. We decamped back to Burgau and took up residence as house-sitters for friends who had moved back to Scotland.

We made several trips back to the UK for scans. Our hearts sank when the consultant informed us that the tumour appeared to be active and that treatment would be necessary. My partner stayed in London for intensive radiotherapy over a period of nine weeks while I returned to the Algarve to deal with issues here. Sadly, our ageing Miniature Schnauzer was clearly very ill too, and eventually we had to make the difficult but merciful decision to have her put to sleep. All of this was quite emotional and as I made my way back to London to provide support, I wondered what life might throw at us next. After the radiotherapy, the consultant recommended a switch to chemotherapy, so we spent several months working out which poison was the least unpleasant and could be reasonably tolerated. After several challenging experiences, we found a bearable regime and came back to Portugal to recuperate.

Post-diagnosis, one of the first things my partner had done to cope with stress was to take up Reiki and also to visit a therapist called Marion Saraswati in Figueira, near Salema. Marion specialises in craniosacral treatments, which seem to be particularly effective in supporting the healing process of chronic illness conditions. Six years on and she continues to play an important part in maintaining my partner's equilibrium and well-being.

To keep my mind from wandering too often to negative thoughts, I had volunteered to join the Management Board at Madrugada. I was so impressed by what the charity had achieved in a few short years, I felt it important to give something back for all the support they provide. When it was founded in 2010, there was little or no end-of-life palliative care for patients in the Algarve. The purpose of the charity is to give patients the choice about where and how they would like to spend their final days. Madrugada provides free of charge end-of-life care in the home, with all the equipment, nursing, and emotional support the patient and their loved ones might need at an incredibly difficult time. Effectively, this 'hospice-at-home' initiative replaces the need for hugely expensive to run care homes. It also assures patients that their wishes at the end of their life will be respected and that they can pass on with dignity, surrounded by those most important to them.

If I thought we had faced many obstacles and challenges in our Portuguese journey, the stories and the reality for many of Madrugada's patients was extremely sobering. What I found very uplifting was the positivity people demonstrated despite their illnesses and debilitating conditions. The charity provides art classes, counselling, and other complementary therapies at its support centre in Luz for anyone who wants a break from home and too much time spent looking at the four walls. These very simple and ordinary activities make a substantial difference to many patients who appreciate the support and company of others while having the opportunity to focus on something other than their illness.

Of course, providing these services free of charge means that the charity has to raise funds in as many ways as possible to cover the cost of care and its other activities. Being somewhat naïve in terms of the state of philanthropy in the Algarve, I assumed that the many deep pockets living in the region would be happy to support such a worthy cause. The notion that all foreigners who have settled in the Algarve are flush with funds is erroneous. Also, the average

Portuguese income is very low by comparison to its northern European neighbours. This explains why so many people hold down two or even three jobs to try to make ends meet.

What became apparent to me over time is that many other charities and causes raising funds for animal welfare, children's support, and the adequate provision of local services such as the fire brigade were all drawing from the same limited pot. However, what people do have is time and enthusiasm to throw themselves into a good cause. Madrugada is fortunate to have a great team of volunteers who provide support to run its charity shops, fundraising events, and craft fairs, along with help for the clinical team to deliver and collect care equipment to and from patients as the need arises.

✧ഌ✧ଊ✧

A post-chemo restorative trip to Aruba got us thinking about buying our next home. We were keen to invest in a property we had designed and built ourselves, so we set about looking for a project. Having moved into our friends' much smaller villa in Burgau, we decided that something of a similar size would suit us, but hopefully with the added benefit of a sea view. We found a small unoccupied house in Salema that needed updating and set about trying to buy it. At the same time, our friends announced they had decided to stay in Scotland so they too would be selling. A frustrating exchange between our lawyer and the vendor in Salema had us eventually pulling out of the deal, even after we had agreed terms. The vendor refused to agree to an early completion date that would allow us time to refurbish and move in before the villa in Burgau was sold. In the end, to make life easier, we decided to buy our friends' Burgau property and look for the build project elsewhere.

Our search took us to Parque da Floresta, a golf resort in nearby Budens which had been built by Vigia, the parent company who had constructed our original villa at Quinta da Fortaleza. Like so many stories across Portugal and Spain, the developers had over-extended themselves, which resulted in bankruptcy. Although the course and development looked splendid, quite a few villas were left unfinished and others unoccupied as the banks foreclosed on unpaid mortgages. We drove around the estate and discovered a very traditional-looking villa that was about thirty percent built, situated between two completely finished properties. It had wonderful views of Monchique and the surrounding countryside and its position on a thousand-square-metre plot allowed for lots of creative thinking about how it could be re-imagined. We made enquiries about the price from the bank and with our trusty architect back in tow; we conceived a very different large modern villa from the bones of the original structure.

Friends and family did ask us why we would move to a golf course when we don't play golf. The truth is, my frustrating experience with the game had put me off and I suspect my past history of rearranging quite a few courses would have encouraged Parque da Floresta to pay me not to play. In reality, neither the golf club nor its facilities were of particular interest. What had won us over were the views and the peace and quiet of the location where the villa was situated.

Somewhat older and wiser, we headed back to the Câmara with our new plans and a builder lined up to take on the work. After what seemed like an eternity, we were given planning approval. The project was treated as a completely new build because the original had never been finished and no habitation licence had been issued.

Work started on clearing the site and we were surprised and grateful that the structure of the original villa, which had been completely open to the elements for ten years, was in quite good shape. Our goal in building the villa was to achieve an A+ energy rating and to have as green and efficient a property as possible. We spent many months investigating different solar energy options and finally settled on installing an array of eighteen solar panels on our flat roof. After twelve months living in the property, we are still waiting on the EDP renewable energy company to visit the villa to approve the installation and confirm that our brand-new system and meter is fit for purpose.

Notwithstanding the stress all of this caused, we decided to adopt a small dog to keep us on our toes and to get us away from the endless round of emails, negotiations, and decisions which had to be made with the project. We found Olive, a Miniature Pinscher puppy posted on a dog rescue and fostering Facebook site called PRAVI. One look at her melted our hearts, and we decided that a trip to Faro the following day was imperative in order to see her. We agreed to meet with the fosterer at a vet's surgery in Faro, and only then did we realise the dog had been seriously injured before being rescued. We were appalled to learn that she had been used as bait in illegal dog fighting, which had caused a huge open wound on her back. Not that this deterred her enthusiasm for life. She was like a kangaroo bouncing around the surgery with huge excitement at meeting new faces. The vet had spayed the dog ten days before, so the visit was simply to remove any remaining stitches and check her over. We paid for her treatment and registered with PRAVI as the official, very proud, and somewhat nervous new owners.

We particularly like the PRAVI model because its volunteers act as foster carers for abandoned pets and look after them in their own homes until an adoption takes place. There are none of the costs associated with running a kennel, and volunteers work tirelessly to find new owners for pets so that the animals can settle as quickly as possible into a permanent home. Along with their Facebook advertising, the charity attends several markets in the Faro area every two weeks to showcase the pets up for adoption.

Once home with our new addition, it took a few weeks for her to settle in. Soon, Olive became better known in the village than us as her incredibly cute face and antics charmed everyone who met her. To say she was a blessing is an understatement. Her huge personality and almost human interaction captivated us, and she is now an integral part of our lives.

Our go-to location for long beach walks with Olive has to be one or other of two favourites. The twin beaches of Castelejo and Cordoama are a short distance from Vila do Bispo and have spectacular rock formations both onshore and jutting out of the sea. The two beaches join at low tide and to walk from end to end and back again takes about an hour. Monitoring the tide is important, as it can be surprisingly quick coming in.

Further up the coast is the glorious headland loop at Carapateira which stretches from Amado beach to the endless sweep of Bordeira, which has a lagoon at the back of the beach that in summer is like a warm bath to swim in. There are viewing points along the coastal loop road which give amazing views of the cliffs and beaches and of course the myriad number of seabirds which nest in the rocks. What is terrifying to watch are the local fishermen perched on precarious precipices trying to catch anything that will bite, even with the risk of huge waves coming in that can snatch them off the cliff face. Closer to the shoreline, incredibly brave (or foolhardy) locals scavenge for goose barnacles or *perçeves*, a much sought-after delicacy.

Venturing closer to Aljezur is the stretch of coast that includes Arrifana and Monte Clérigo. Both are exceptional beaches with huge numbers of surfers vying to catch the biggest waves. A favourite low season expedition often sees us travelling to Arrifana for lunch at a small family-run restaurant called Sol e Mar. There is nothing fancy about the place apart from the fact that you can sit outside in the sunshine and enjoy the spectacular views of the coastline while eating the most reasonably priced fish and salad in the Algarve. If we are feeling adventurous, a drive beyond Aljezur includes Odeceixe, and Zambujeira do Mar, which has a beautiful beach and is a pretty village on the clifftop.

The Algarve is blessed with an abundance of excellent restaurants. The inevitable impact of tourism on Portuguese menu authenticity has reduced some offerings, but it has also brought lots of new flavours and creativity to the region as well. Our go-to restaurant for extra special occasions is Dos Artistas in the centre of Lagos. The creative menu is exciting and the venue a delight. For more day-to-day entertaining Tasca do Kiko at the end of Lagos marina is a contemporary gem. Closer to home, there is only one Indian restaurant for us: Spice Cottage, located between Burgau and Cabanas Velhas, which offers the most authentic flavours and quality. If we need a fish fix, then either Restaurante Ancora in Burgau or A Boia in Salema are a must, with O Lourenço in Salema topping the list for freshness and value.

On average, the Algarve enjoys over three hundred days of sunshine per year. However, the west coast can be a bit more unpredictable and definitely cooler in the low season than the central or eastern Algarve hotspots. We check out the forecast every day on the very reliable IPMA website which is run by the Portuguese Meteorological Institute. This gives really accurate hourly forecasts along with sea temperatures, wind speed, wave height, and much, much more. If the day is looking a bit dull, we take ourselves off to Meia Praia in Lagos, Rocha Brava near Carvoeiro, or further along the coast to Armação de Pera and the vast beach called Praia Grande. This is in fact three or four beaches that all form part of one amazing long stretch of sand.

Throughout our time visiting and living in Portugal, its wine industry has gone through a revolution with an exponential leap in both the quality and variety of what is produced. Our early experiences of table wine had been underwhelming, and I have memories of too many thick heads from overindulgence of port to drink it more than a few times a year. Nowadays, the country has so much to offer, and it is a full-time job keeping up with the releases and accolades being heaped on red, white, rosé, and green wines. The biggest surprise has been how affordable good wine is, and in particular, how well Portuguese Espumante has come on. We were delighted to find a very nice sparkling rosé called Terras do Demo to serve at our wedding. This came in at under eight euros a bottle and the choice of so many others on offer for under ten euros is very exciting when you have a sabre near to hand.

What can be a bit confusing is how little difference there appears to be between some of the cheapest wines and their much more expensive cousins. Obviously this calls for us to continue with much deeper and more focussed research! A Portuguese friend regularly advises me that for internal and external whole body cleansing, a shot or two of local *medronho* (Portuguese Firewater) made from the fruit of the Arbutus tree will kill or cure most germs and ailments. His eighty-five-year-old father swears he has conquered Covid-19 by drinking a shot every two hours, every day.

Our move to the Algarve has had its ups and downs. My

partner's condition is stable, and we are thankful that the peace and tranquillity of the countryside around us keeps us grounded. Every so often we experience wobbles, so a further scan becomes necessary to reassure us that everything is okay. Our day-to-day lives are busy with something always needing attention around the house, or there's yet another beach or village to be explored with the dog leading the way. The thought of moving back to the UK, or elsewhere, never crosses our minds as we know our home and lives are now firmly rooted here in Portugal.

✿ഔ✿ഩ✿

To find out more about the work of the Madrugada charity, including how to donate, visit their website: www.madrugada-portugal.com

5

A Simple, Rural Life
SARAH GADD

I grew up on a farm in Nottinghamshire, which is probably why we ended up living somewhere rural. I can't settle in a town or city, well not yet. I have a dislike of crowds that has got worse over the years, preferring small groups where conversation is possible. My partner Phil is originally from the London suburbs and also has a love of the countryside. We have three grown-up children between us, Phil has a daughter and a son, and I have a daughter. We are immensely proud of them; they are hardworking, respectful, decent people making their way in the world.

Phil and I both have a love of travelling, and enjoy exploring new places rather than lying on a beach. As keen photographers, new is always good, though we do have favourite destinations we have visited many times, Sorrento being mine and Rhodes being his, and we would swap between the two for summer breaks. It has been wonderful to share and explore places together, showing each other the best of what we love. We both have a love of photography but with different styles, Phil orientates toward the technical side whereas I opt for the more artistic shots. For one of Phil's birthdays we were supposed to go to the Isle of Wight—somehow we ended up in Barcelona, as it was actually cheaper. We had an amazing time as we were very close to La Rambla for Halloween, a spectacular sight, the living statues were amazing. We had a couple of excursions into North Africa, one better than the other, and hopefully we will travel again in the future.

We currently run a small *alojamento local*, a micro-tourism business with two yurts. The work is hard and mostly rewarding; we moved to Portugal to live longer, not make our fortunes. The land we bought with the house was large enough to turn into a lovely garden without being too big. The garden is not without problems though; we had to do a complete re-design over the winter last year as we lost all the grass following two years of drought. We had envisioned being popular with UK tourists; but we were pleasantly surprised to find we have mostly Portuguese clients. This has, at least, pushed my Portuguese vocabulary further forward, despite many of our guests wanting to practise their English with us. Covid-19 hit us as it did everyone else, reducing our income, but we battle on regardless.

I have worked in many different areas from riding stables to a university, and Phil is an electrical engineer. We are both well versed in dealing with the public, which has proved useful in running our current business. Luckily we are both good with people and we are fairly flexible in our approach to problems.

I loved my last job, which I had for fifteen years, training students in all areas of practical media. Sadly, things change, and you take the decision that it is time to move on before your love for it completely fades. I enjoyed meeting new students year by year, watching them grow as people. Via Facebook, I am still in contact with many of them today.

I would say I am most proud of my daughter, a fine young woman with great morals and values. My pet hates? Racism, bigotry, sexism, homophobia, and any kind of discrimination against others. My mother always said I was a champion of the underdog. I guess that is something I am very proud of and will continue until my last breath. I have no time for those who are cruel for the sake of it, who use words or deeds to hurt, simply because they can.

It probably goes without saying that animal cruelty is on the list. From our starting point of declaring that we would not have any pets when we moved to Portugal, we currently have three house cats, and an old stray whom we feed who lives outdoors with plenty of comfy places to sleep. All of them are rescues in their own way.

I am amazed by current politics across certain parts of the globe. I'm happy I can enjoy the relative calm and security of Portugal despite not being able to vote in major elections. Oh, and hypocrisy, I forgot about that one! A particular pet peeve of mine is immigrants to the EU who voted to leave in the referendum, they like to call themselves expats, a term I dislike immensely.

○෨✧ൠ○

Our first visit to Portugal was a potential disaster. We booked a very cheap break in Albufeira in the Algarve in a huge hotel. It was not our usual choice, but our aim was to find something cheap and cheerful. We arrived at the airport to find no transfer had been allotted to us; undeterred we found a taxi and arrived at the hotel. At the desk they said they had no record of our booking. I couldn't call the agency as it was an 0800 number, so I had to phone my daughter. It turned out the booking had been moved around and eventually everything was sorted out, and we actually got into our room before any of the other recent arrivals.

We decided we didn't want to eat at the hotel as the buffet food looked unappealing. Luckily, just outside the gates we found a traditional Portuguese restaurant and discovered the wonderful kindness of the Portuguese. The young waiter chased me up the street two or three times as I had forgotten my pashmina, having left it on the back of a chair. I also asked to buy a bottle of wine to take back to the hotel, they filled a bottle with the house red and charged me two euros, the next bottle I was given free, and on our last night they gave me a lovely bottle of red to take home.

Our second visit was to Alvor. It was quieter, smaller, and where our true love affair with Portugal and its people began. As is our habit, we found a restaurant we liked and ate there most nights. Sadly, it had to close due to the crash in the economy. We are still in touch with the old owner though, which is lovely.

We decided to leave the UK years before we actually made the move. Our search for the right property went on for five or more years. Oddly, the house we bought in the end was one I had seen online but rejected. We are living just over the border from the Algarve in the Alentejo region, a couple of miles from the coast in a national park. We chose our location because there were very few British people living there. We wanted to immerse ourselves in the local way of life. That said, we have a few British friends who we see from time to time, but we do not live in each other's pockets. As they say here: *'sempre um prazer'*, it's always a pleasure when we meet up. We have made some wonderful friendships within our local community, despite our poor language skills.

Portugal is special to us because of the people, the slower pace of life, the nature of community, people giving and helping and expecting nothing in return. Oh, and the vegetables. We receive mountains of vegetables and eggs from our neighbours, which we always try to reciprocate if we manage to grow any ourselves. Portugal is full of long hot summers and short winters.

I love walking down a street you've walked down many times before and finding that behind an anonymous-looking door there is a 'man cave' or hardware shop as most people call them. It is the simple pleasures here that are special, like walking into your local shop and being greeted by one and all.

Some nights when sleep eludes me, I stand on the veranda and listen to the distant roar of the sea, and watch our local lighthouse light up. Our lighthouse is a little different to others. They built it with the plans upside down so the light flashes twice inland and once out to sea. By the time the authorities came to oversee the work, it was already finished. The interior of the construction is quite something to see, there is so much brass. I am not an engineer, but I can appreciate the beauty of the work.

It is on these nights and indeed days too when I wonder how I coped with the stresses of the UK. The forty-minute (if I was lucky) drive to work on the M1, the demands of other people both at work and socially, other people's expectations, and being judged by what you do, wear, own, or drive. I find none of that here, except occasionally when I visit some shopping malls in the Algarve in my scruffy clothes because we are there to buy practical materials, not just to browse for garden furniture or such like. I can go to my local shop wearing tatty clothes, spotted with bleach stains, and everyone knows what household task I have been doing. They appreciate it because I am doing it myself. The local people have accepted us because we do not have money to throw at whatever needs fixing, we live very much as they do.

Portugal is many things to different people; it may not be for everyone, but for us it is a place called home.

✧෨✧ෆ✧

Phil and I met fifteen or so years ago, and we both had the same idea about leaving the UK some day. We considered running a B&B in the UK but everything we wanted, close to the sea, or rural, was always going to be far too expensive for our pockets. We travelled a lot together, both in and out of the UK, and had our favourite places. I wanted to move to Southern Italy, but Phil thought it might be difficult to do business there. He preferred the Languedoc region of France, but there was no way I ever wanted to see snow again, even from a distance.

When we seriously thought about it, Portugal was the ideal compromise and it was only a two-and-a-half hour flight from the UK. We discounted the north because of the wetter, colder weather, and began to explore the Algarve, away from the coast for budget reasons. During our travels we strayed into the Alentejo region, I think we actually drove past the house we now own on our first jaunt. We would book a cheap apartment in Alvor and use it as a base as we explored, often taking off for a couple of days and staying in the coastal town of Vila Nova de Milfontes, and fell in love with that area.

We started using an independent estate agent and found what we thought was our dream house. However, despite assurances from the owner that we could extend the house, we checked with the local Câmara and discovered the house had no permission in place to do so. It would have been improbable that our plans could be achieved. We also discovered that the nearby industrial estate, not visible due to the rise in the land, had the necessary permissions already in place to extend. That would have meant possibly widening the lane at the side of the property.

The entire conversation at the Câmara was conducted in Portuguese with a translator. The only time the man spoke English was when he said he could not guarantee that they would not widen the lane, nor that we would not lose land to it as the mains water pipe was on the other side. Sadly, we chose to walk away. In retrospect it was for the best, as the work involved would have been problematic and there was too much land for us to manage. Our other concern was noise from local vehicles close to what would have been our planned peaceful retreat.

We found a local estate agent, who I have to say had the patience of a saint. He drove us many kilometres to visit a range of properties which were too big, too small, or too remote, until eventually we found our little blue and white Alentejo home. It was the one I had previously seen online and rejected. We signed an agreement there and then with the estate agent, and completed our promissory note before flying home. Six weeks later, after a bit of a nail-biting wait, we owned a home in Portugal. Why nail biting? Well, in rural Portugal, once the owner agrees to an offer, if the land has previously been split from other parcels of land, they must offer it up to all the neighbours first. Luckily for us, there were no takers.

Six months after that, we made the move. We used an excellent company to move what we wanted to bring with us, they even stored our things for a few days so we could play catch-up as we drove all the way down ourselves. We made it a relatively leisurely trip, having an overnight stay in Elvas, a wonderful walled town. The hotel was built into the wall and though quite large, it was very quaint. In retrospect we shouldn't have brought so much with us, as many of the boxes are still in the garage just taking up space.

We had one strict rule when we moved, as we wanted to be free to explore our new country — no pets! In less than a year, a beautiful cat adopted us. At the most we have had seven, but now have three house cats and the old stray who just wants to stay nearby. The stray will eat anything, he prefers human food to cat food. He has stolen curry, chilli, literally anything, he also loves baked potatoes.

We do the odd overnight trip now. They are rarely just for fun though and usually involve a quick trip to Ikea or to pick up a delivery. For our yearly trip to visit family and friends, we either have house sitters or our neighbours step in to help. Of course the cats sulk when we return.

What can I say about our neighbours, they are just the best. They shower us with fruit, vegetables, and eggs, which of course we try to 'repay' by helping them. Phil is always on hand to offer electrical knowledge or we give them some sweet treats baked by me. Help is always there on both sides of the fence, which is a great comfort. We have watched one of our neighbour's oldest grow from a teenager to a hard-working young man with a son of his own, and the youngest from a child to a trainee chef. That boy can cook!

For around the first twelve months our neighbour, Luís, insisted on mowing the lawn for us until we got a lawn mower. This developed into tool sharing, since he lost his storage area when his house was remodelled. His tools now mostly live in our garage. On top of all his own garden work, he frequently helps out with the heavier jobs we struggle with from time to time due to our age or some injury or other.

After we arrived, we took the first six months off. We had friends over, we explored the local tracks, ate out far too often, and just enjoyed the sunshine before we began work in earnest. We started by getting the land ploughed and levelled. Levelling involved a rope tied to a weighted down ladder pulled by a donkey, or should I say, Phil. The garden work was tough, we had no proper equipment apart from hand tools but took lots of advice on what to plant. These days we are lucky if we make it to the beach, whether through being busy, too tired, or in winter, the weather being a little too chilly.

The land that came with the house had a barn, and this came in very useful for our business. We hired a builder to infill it with space for a toilet, two wet rooms, a corridor, and a kitchen. We kitted out the rest ourselves, which was a little tricky at times, as we are no spring chickens—closer to old boilers, if truth be told. The walls had been built with rough concrete blocks. I think we used close to sixty litres of paint. You put paint on—the wall slurps it up—and you repeat until the wall is full and you have a white finish. The builder also put up a garden wall for us which sadly fell over this year with us having rather more rain than usual.

Once we had achieved that, it was time to put the yurts up. We sourced the yurts from Mongolia; the ship carrying them sailed past us, passing the port at Lisbon forty minutes away and onto Antwerp, and we then had to transport them by lorry back to Portugal. They have been both an absolute delight and a bit of a nightmare to maintain, in that they are not entirely suited to the coastal winter climate, but that is when we are closed. Phil built the base and laid the floorboards, and then we put a shout out to friends for help in raising the first yurt. It was extremely funny as, with minimal instructions, we tried to raise it. It took ten people for stage one of erecting the structure, then four people helping to put up the covers as we knew we'd never manage it alone. Finally, our green yurt was in place.

We had to wait a further eight months to build the second yurt. We found a 'WWOOFer', a guy who travelled around working for bed and board; he was very useful for some things, but sadly teamwork wasn't his strong point. If you plan to take someone on like this, my advice would be maybe suggest a few days getting to know each other before committing to any length of time. We finished the blue yurt about five minutes before its first occupant arrived for the MEO Sudoeste music festival, a huge annual event.

After having a couple of friends play guinea pig for us by staying in the green yurt, we finally opened. Quintal Yurts was up and running. Originally, we were going to be called Monte da Estrada, the same name as our house, but we discovered the name had already been registered by a new *alojamento local* just down the road. We still retain the Facebook page of that name, and have a stack of unused business cards with a logo I designed that looks oddly similar to the one down the road that appeared sometime later.

So began a steady trickle of guests. Once both yurts were open, it became very full on. I think our worst mistake was a season where we opened for one-night stays. It nearly killed us, so now we have a firm rule of a two-night minimum stay. I have a greater appreciation of the work of hotel staff these days. I've always had respect for them, but now I understand everything they have to do. Our work has increased exponentially. I'll admit the last twelve months have been particularly difficult, with family problems and of course the dreadful Covid-19. We do, however, remain optimistic for the future, having learnt a lot from this past year.

Neither of us ever wants to leave Portugal. We have thought about having a 'Plan B' as we grow older, but going back to the UK is not for us. Perhaps somewhere smaller, less rural, with closer local shops and a bus service will become essential. Whilst living our dream we have to examine the practicalities of dealing with old age, and maybe not being able to drive anymore. What fits when you are in your fifties may not be good in your late sixties. Flexibility is everything.

I have to say we have learnt a lot as we have gone along, including the type of bedding to purchase, fitted sheets just aren't great for ironing, and rushing out to buy some things last minute. I discovered when someone books breakfast for 8 a.m. they might not turn up for it until 10 a.m. so we no longer offer that option. It wasn't until a week before we opened I realised we didn't own either an iron or an ironing board! If you are planning to do accommodation, buy a good iron or steam delivery system—the smaller or cheaper the iron, the more time you are going to spend ironing.

✿෨✿ఴ✿

My Portuguese language skills have improved, though we have not had the time to take advantage of the free local classes on offer because of our business. I watch English language TV with Portuguese subtitles which helps. I also use the Memrise app which offers European Portuguese. I advise people to avoid the Brazilian Portuguese apps as I found I was not being understood. You may also have to face the local dialect. I swear the locals round our way have a competition to see who can string out *boa tarde* (good afternoon) the longest, emphasising every letter. Friends and neighbours help too, and I often find I speak better after a glass of wine or two!

When we first moved here to live, we were a bit of a curiosity to the locals and they seemed to enjoy getting us as drunk as possible. Recently we went shopping to buy a new tap for our kitchen. They produced several, and we chose the one that suited us best both in price and quality. We always have a joke with Umberto in our local store, so when he asked would we like to see a cheaper tap, Phil said,

"No, this one is the mutt's nuts."

This was greeted with a quizzical look, so Phil said,

"The dog's bollocks?"

There was still no recognition of what we were saying, despite Umberto's excellent English. Then came my light bulb moment, something I had gained from TV subtitles, and I explained in Portuguese,

"*Os tomates do cão.*" The literal translation is "the tomatoes of the dog."

I haven't seen anyone laugh that hard in a long time.

Our favourite restaurant is O Martinho's in Zambujeira do Mar. It stands at the top of the cliffs offering a sea view, and the *camarão frito* (fried prawns) are to die for. Phil swears by the pork ribs. When we first moved, we ate there so often they adopted us. We are their English family. If you are adopted by a Portuguese family, please take it very seriously, they do not say these things lightly. To be invited into their home is a big deal. Our other favourite, which is open all year round, is the restaurant Alentejano, so in summer we eat at one and in winter at the other.

I couldn't pick a favourite beach in our area. They all have their own character and are fabulous. Our local beach is at Zambujeira do Mar, eight kilometres away. There are closer ones, but most are quite tricky to access. Think north Cornish coast, but with more sunshine.

The only things I miss from the UK are friends and family, and maybe the range of vegetables on offer, especially parsnips. One difference that surprised me here is that you pay the price for the weight of the whole fish in a restaurant or at the fish counter, even when they have removed all the bits. My advice is learn to adapt, where we are we have no Chinese restaurants, no Italian restaurants, and I have only recently been able to buy Asian spices locally. I have learnt so much more about cooking, Google is my friend, and cooking has become more of a passion for me. I find the local bread a little too chewy and packet bread too sweet, so I have a bread machine so I can make English-style bread. If you know you are going to have to live on a fairly tight budget, then have some ideas for cutting corners, and watch how the Portuguese do things, most of them are experts.

Some people's attitudes to animals infuriates me, although we have seen many improvements in the last seven years. I hate that bullfighting still takes place, though the nearest venue to us closed a few years ago. I try to come to terms with the fact that cats and dogs are not always treated as pets but as working animals, in a different way to how we would look after them in the UK.

If you are going to move to a rural area with few people or Brits around, make sure you are self-sufficient in each other's company, that you enjoy spending a lot of time together. Also, be prepared for the fact there is very little public transport in rural locations. There may only be one bus each day, if any at all, and the bus stop might be a kilometre away so you will need your own transport. Be prepared to pay a lot more for a second-hand car than you would in the UK — a lot more. If you have mechanical skills, buy an older car and order your parts from Germany, as parts are also very expensive here.

Portuguese bureaucracy can be slow and a little irritating, it also seems to vary from region to region. Everything will be done in triplicate and you can guarantee that on the first try you will be short of one document, but just sink into it. Think of all the good stuff. Don't get angry with the person behind the desk, mostly they are trying to get their heads around the rules themselves. It is quite common for a person to nip to the front of the queue to ask a simple question, try not to let it get under your skin, you're in a different country now.

Remember, things happen more slowly here. *Amanhã* (tomorrow) may actually mean *a próxima semana* (next week) or later. Don't worry about it, don't fight it, or you will just stress yourself out. At other times, the speed at which some things happen can be amazing.

We quickly discovered that nearly all the businesses local to us close for lunch. If you run out of nails at 12.55 p.m. you won't be buying nails until 3 p.m. and probably won't be continuing whatever you were doing until 4 p.m. unless you live in a city or are in the Algarve, which we are just outside of. Planning is everything.

Being a little humble and self-deprecating goes a long, long way. We have learnt to laugh at ourselves and smile, however frustrated we are. Keep using the Portuguese words you have learnt, it is appreciated and you will most likely find reciprocation in English from the person you are speaking to, that is, if they speak English.

After eight years, I never cease to be delighted at our luck of being able to live here. In some ways it is like stepping back in time, and in others it is amazingly modern. I don't think I could ever move back to the UK, it's too hectic, there are too many cars and people, too much need for the next best thing.

On our last visit to the UK we stayed in a hotel next to a roundabout, we saw more traffic pass by outside during breakfast than we see here at home in a year. We may even have gone a little feral here, and no one local cares. Today I gave a little boy a bag of unopened free toy give-aways from a supermarket, and he was so excited to receive them. A simple gesture goes a long way.

So if you make the leap, go with the flow, I'm not saying don't chase up the important things, but accept the differences, smile a lot, be humble, stumble through your Portuguese words, laugh as you do so, and you'll find peace, calm, and happiness. Oh, and enjoy the price of wine, some of the cheap ones are delicious.

To discover more about Quintal Yurts, including how to book a stay there, you are welcome to visit their Facebook page: www.facebook.com/quintalyurts

Discovering an Enchanted Land
SUSI ROGOL-GOODKIND

Think back. Can you remember the days before emails, when you used the post to communicate unless you—and the person you wanted to reach—had telex? You had a phone—fixed to the wall and with a coiled lead that never reached quite far enough to allow you to sit while you talked. Away from home there were telephone boxes with buttons A to connect and B to get your pennies back. And often a queue of people, coins in hand, waiting their turn. There were no mobile phones. And no internet, so no booking.com or lastminute.com, or any other dotcom. If you wanted to go on holiday, you went to see your friendly travel agent.

We had Benjy, our own Mr Know-it-all, who made the suggestions, sorted out the bookings, and handed over your flight tickets. He would also throw in some general advice about what to see and eat (gleaned from a recent trip designed to promote a particular area), and assure you that the hotel he'd chosen specially for you was top notch.

It was early summer 1979. It was hot, it was hectic, and husband Martin took himself off to see Benjy. An hour or so later he returned, wearing a big smile, and waving a fat envelope.

"We're going on holiday tomorrow, first thing in the morning," he announced. "To Portugal, to the Algarve, and we are staying in a five-star hotel, the Dona-something-or-other. And it's half price—Benjy's just had a cancellation."

So, just sixteen hours later, with two smallish children and three largish suitcases (one with the clothes that were due to be washed but weren't because of lack of time; one filled with foodstuffs that our youngest—allergic to everything—could just about tolerate; and one with all the things you think you might need when you have no idea where you are heading. And I for one didn't. To be honest, I knew little about Portugal, and even less about the Algarve. But hey, with a half-board, half-price deal, I was ready to discover!

At Faro airport, then just one runway and a small squat building that was the terminal, we awaited our luggage, which was passed out by one man through a hole in the wall. Conveyor belt? What's that?

Outside the terminal a couple of men squatted down on collapsible stools, pens behind ears, papers in hand. That's how you rented a car back then. We said yes to a yellow plastic Mehari with no top, no sides, no back, but enough space to hold the suitcases. Our own holiday convertible.

The road from the airport was cobbled and slow going, (just as well, our Mehari never topped fifty kilometres per hour). And the N125, heading west, was more like a country road than the key route across the Algarve. One lane each way, and more bicycles and donkey carts than cars.

It took an hour to get to Vale do Lobo, the first resort in the Algarve, founded in 1962, and looking to attract an upmarket audience. A luxury settlement emerged with pukka properties and a Henry Cotton golf course and, in 1968, our cut-price bargain hotel.

Speechless comes to mind as the adjective to describe our first reaction. That stretch of golden beach in front of us, the wide blue sea, those red cliffs, and that big, big sky, bright blue and cloudless. Bougainvillea-clad walls, the pinks and whites and reds of the oleander bushes lining the road to the beach. Even the kids were in awe.

Our adjoining hotel rooms were not home from home; they were home to palace. I called the front desk and explained that we had a suitcase of edibles and why. A porter arrived to carry it off, followed by the housekeeper who removed the unwashed laundry and promised to return it within the day. The manager then appeared to say that he would ensure that smaller child was not offered any food that might tempt him and result in a rash. He asked for a list of no-no's, and said that any special requirements would be sent down from Lisbon. I was already smitten.

Now we were two townies — growing up and living in the centre of London. Holidays meant investigating major cities, visiting special places of interest, writing about the experiences. Beaches didn't figure in our time-out plans. And golf was not on the agenda. So, once we had settled in, and the concierge had answered our list of questions, we were back in the yellow box and off.

Where did we go? The man at the desk dismissed Olhão as "a little uninteresting fishing village". So that was settled. First stop Olhão, and it took forever.

No apartment buildings lining the roads, no fancy roundabouts, no shops selling far-eastern imports. But lots of tiny winding streets, rows of cubist houses, and a handful of bakeries with trays of still-warm pastries. There were small bars, and the odd café, and cottages with peeling paint, wonderful doors and ornate plasterwork. Flowers were everywhere.

Heading to the waterfront, where the market buildings stood and the fishing boats pitched up, we turned down a street barely wide enough to take the car. A woman ran out of her house, flagged us down, and gesticulated wildly, pointing to her mouth and rubbing her aproned tummy. She took us into her kitchen for dinner, the car resting exactly where we had stopped, blocking the road.

She served us a huge dish of squid, still bathed in its ink, and warm bread, and a casserole of lamb with toasted bread in its juices. Number one child ate everything. Number two did the same. We had baked apples for dessert. No one had hooted outside to get the car moved. Our hostess refused the offer of help to clear the dishes, had to be forced to take our escudos notes, and kissed the kids first, then us. That was me, smitten twice in the same day.

Over the following couple of weeks we walked along the beach, we swam in the sea, and we used our half-board allowance to have the buffet lunch by the hotel pool. That was a grand affair with a huge whole sea bass dressed with garlic mayonnaise, dishes of giant-sized prawns, and copious amounts of ice cold *vinho verde* wine. And number two kid didn't itch or scratch once.

One particular evening, we ate chicken from a little barbecue on the beach at a table surrounded by tree stumps (first come, first claim a stump to sit on). That was Julia's. If you wanted clams, one of her sons would run down to the sea, and pull out a kiddy's bucket full of them. With a squirt of lemon, a knob of butter, and a glass of white wine, there was heaven on a plate.

We dodged the horse-riders crossing the sand, climbed into the Mehari and went back to the hotel. I was barefoot. Number two child was sitting on my hip, head on my shoulder, fast asleep, clutching the remains of a chicken leg in his hand. I got into the lift, as did an elderly gentleman in an elegant suit (dinner at the Dona

Filipa hotel meant formal attire). He looked me up and down, from sandy feet to see-through sarong, to sleeping child, and smiled.

"Madame," he said, "you have obviously had a far better evening than I."

That comment only added to the experience!

We went to Vilamoura, which was then just a single parade with a few restaurants. We rented a boat that took us out to a cove in the west to swim and eat lunch and gaze in awe at the astounding rock formations that form the basis of many a postcard. We found the little old lady with the key to the church in São Lourenço, and stood in amazement within this small but perfectly formed architectural masterpiece. We went to the castle in Loulé, climbed the steps to the vast park behind the monument, and took photographs in the old town in Faro.

We travelled inland to tiny villages untouched by time and the mod-cons that usually mean progress. Women dressed in black standing outside their houses, or gathering wild herbs from the roadside, would stop and smile and wave. Often, we would not see another car or hear another English accent all day. We danced in the sand and ate sardines grilled by one old man on his hibachi-style barbecue at the side of the road. We had a huge *cataplana* (fish stew) in a backstreet restaurant in Faro, with a bottle of local wine. And when we finished, we ordered the same thing all over again. The owner beamed; the other diners applauded.

We were living the picture-postcard holiday, each sun-filled day confirming that thanks to Benjy we had discovered paradise. Two weeks flew by.

✧ཉ✧ଔ✧

They say that all good things must come to an end. That's nonsense. All you have to do is vow to relive them. And keep that promise to yourself. Which is what we did.

We returned the following year. And the year after, and the next few years after that, each time finding things that were new — new to the Algarve or just new to us. And with every discovery came a thrill that washed over us, like the sea that washed over our toes as we walked along the beach.

We rented cottages, apartments, even the odd villa, and occasionally stayed in a wonderful hotel. And each year we drew up our Big Plan to see more. We included at least two adventuring side trips every visit.

We went to the opera in Lisbon and walked the streets of this dazzling city that remains our first choice of European capitals. We listened to real Fado right where it was born, ate traditional food with the locals, and praised the children for their ability to stay up late. We read everything we could find about Portugal. We discovered Braga and Beja, Guimarães, and Coimbra, Aveiro, Arraiolos, and Évora, and, closer to home so to speak, the length and breadth of the Algarve from Cape St Vincent to Vila Real de Santo António. We marvelled at what we saw, delighted in learning the history of ancient places, kept copious notes, and took hundreds of photographs.

We journalists are used to travelling. But can you imagine the sheer delight when you are approached by a tourist board to visit and write about… Porto? Never was a press trip so appreciated. Our allocated guide got us up at the crack of dawn and made us do all the tourist sights first. Then she changed gear, stuffed the 'list' in her bag, and took us to the places we'd never have known about, let alone found by ourselves. Our passion for Portugal was confirmed. And with the children tucked up in bed in London under grandma's watchful eye, it was something of a second honeymoon.

We fell in love with the people wherever we went. The gentleness, the kindness, helping you understand the language and listening patiently while you struggled with pronunciation, and correcting you without ever criticising. The soft smiles, the hugs and kisses for children. And in the little local restaurants where, on asking what a particular dish was, being taken into the kitchen to see the ingredients and watch the cooking in progress.

Let's fast forward now to 1987. We had been holidaying here with our daughter, her friend, and our no-longer-allergic son, having taken a month off. It was August. We went up to Loulé to shop at the municipal market. Bags filled to capacity with the freshest of fruits and warm *pasteis de nata* pastries, we sauntered down the road for a coffee, pausing outside a little estate agent, as one does. We were stunned to see that chunks of land in the countryside were for sale and at what, to Islington homeowners, was a crazy price.

It rained the next day. What shall we do? We had an idea—let's just go look at what you could buy, if you were interested, that is, in the hills and, of course, if you had the required funds, which we didn't.

"Follow me," said the estate agent. And we did.

Three plots of land later, we were talking money. And Napoleonic Law, which means all the children have to agree to a sale of the family estate. The rules were different back then. You could build on agricultural land; the presence of a ruin was not a requirement.

"This one," pronounced daughter and her friend who wanted to get back to the beach. It was 4,000 square metres, sprawling in every direction, and with a view of the rooftops of Loulé. We made an offer. It was accepted.

We were leaving for the UK the following evening. So that night we went to celebrate our madness at a hippy haven on the beach where food and music were on the menu. We were due to meet the estate agent there. By then, I had already designed our dream home —one that looked like it had been there for a hundred years, with shuttered windows, plaster detailing, tiled floors, archways, and complete with muslin curtains floating in the early evening breeze. The agent arrived. You can sense instinctively when all is not well. He looked glum, ordered a drink, and proceeded to tell us that because we had not formally paid a deposit, the owner had the right to change their mind, and had done so because another 'wanna-live-here' had arrived, said yes please, and written out a cheque.

I was devastated. Crazy, I know, when twenty-four hours earlier there had been no thought of being a land possessor or house builder or second-home owner. That evening, as I packed for the following day's departure, tears flowed. It was a dream that had come from nowhere and been snatched away.

The next morning, Martin went out early, supposedly to the Dona Filipa, the only place you could buy an English newspaper. He came back, accompanied by another agent, to whom he had given a two-hour slot to find an acre of land in the middle-ish of nowhere. She did. And she had power of attorney over the family's siblings, and yes, she'd take our cheque for the equivalent of one thousand pounds.

There it was. A bit more than an acre, atop a hill and spilling down to a rough track, with a 360-degree view of the hills—bands of green and grey and mauve and purple. Olive trees, fig trees, ancient carobs, wild oleander, pepper trees—and that was all on our patch. It made the previous find, well, so yesterday. More tears … this time of sheer joy.

En route to the airport, we signed papers at the notary's office. The agent explained it could take many months for the Bank of Portugal to give permission for the sale to go ahead—a requirement then, as they wanted to ensure the right price was being paid. It did take months—up to Christmas in fact. And then there was the not inconsiderable concern about where the money would come from. That aside, we agreed no television, and no eating out. Every night was spent drawing floor plans and wall plans and everywhere-else plans for that dream bolt hole in the sun—if it could ever be realised.

We had a PR company with some pretty good and well-paying clients. We had an agency that represented top photographers and hair and makeup artists, and owned a studio complex in Islington. And we both wrote. I was a consultant to a magazine publishing company, developing new titles for them. They were bought out by Maxwell (yes, that Maxwell), and they offered me the full-time role of editorial and design director of their international contact publishing division. As part of the deal, they bought our PR interests, and our partner in the agency and photographic studios took over my share.

Manna from heaven. You've never seen two people get on a plane so fast, drawings in a folder, waving a cheque for the agent.

It was February, the most beautiful time of the year here. Almond blossom was everywhere, the mimosa was just coming into bloom, and there were carpets of wild flowers.

We went to see three builders. The first said,

"Where? What's wrong with the coast?"

The second declared,

"Yes, we can offer you one of three styles…"

The third one said,

"Fine, and we accept staged payments."

How often in life can you say this is meant to be? Just once, and then it is a miracle.

Building work started in May and took a year. It was the days of cheap flights and we were out once a month for a few days at a time, staying at a cheap and cheerful hostel in Loulé. We spent the time walking our land in wonderment and asking for permission to lay a stone here or fix a tile there. The builders put up a shack that they lived in for the duration, a tin bucket with holes drilled in the base serving as their outdoor shower. Our only neighbours, a tribe of goats, visited daily with their master whose home was a rough stone shelter farther down the track.

The months went by. And suddenly there was a house. A house on the hill, with windows and shutters, doors and balustraded balconies, and two huge olive trees on the terrace, left where they had always been to provide shade from the hot afternoon sun.

We were nervous about what the locals might think, after all, they had been there for generations, raising their children and working their fields. We asked Jamie the electrician for his opinion. He spoke a bit of English, gleaned from when he'd worked on the Christmas street decorations in London. He waved us into his truck, took off along the dusty track that led across open fields, and suddenly jammed on the brakes and did a U-turn. From there you could see our house, standing proud and gleaming white, surrounded by a world of green—every shape and shade and texture and height. Jamie pointed to the house and said,

"She looks like she has been there for always."

Months followed, filled with little shopping sprees, here in the

Algarve and back in London. In fact, wherever we were. We looked at what could be re-loved (even in those days); at things with a design quirkiness, at items that made us smile. There were few home furnishing options on the Algarve then, and those that existed were top dollar. But slowly and surely we got there. Hand-painted headboards from the Alentejo, and carved cupboards we could breathe new life into with a tin of antique wax and some strenuous polishing.

We found a stone and marble cutting workshop on the road to São Brás de Alportel where, for the princely sum of around eighty pounds, they made us a huge dining table, console tables, and shelves. Nights were spent sewing curtains, cushions, and bedspreads; grandma was put in charge of knitting throws.

We went to little local auctions and cut-price sales, and renamed a bedroom of our London house 'Ready to go'.

In Portugal we found old painted plates, metal figurines, and mirrors in need of love. And we bought a bed. That in itself was an experience. The mattress shop was on the corner of the Avenida and the road to the monument. Right on the roundabout. The mattresses were plastic-wrapped and stood on their sides, roped to the walls. Want to see which one is right for you? The ropes come down; the mattress is carried onto the pavement, and you lie down. You twist and turn and stretch and curl while pedestrians, quite unfazed, walk round you. You make your decision and leave with a great mattress, and a story to repeat over the years.

By summer, we were as good as ready to move into our amazing holiday home. We called an insurance man to come and look and give us a quote. He climbed up the land—we had no boundaries, walls, or fences or gates—sat on the grass bank, looked at the view all around, and made his pronouncement,

"You have bought yourselves ten more years of life," he said.

Grandparents came to visit and for once were rendered speechless. Friends came—some amazed we had picked the wilds of the countryside rather than the glitz of the Golden Triangle as the main tourist area was known, others delighted and demanding a further invitation. Daughter brought her friends, who arrived with their backpacks stuffed with schoolwork (they were the first batch of students taking their 'GCSE' exams).

Newly planted trees bore fruit, vegetable beds were dug and were soon spilling over with herbs and onions, tomatoes and strawberries. The locals left baskets of lemons, oranges, apples, and avocados from their own trees on our doorstep, and brought cuttings to fill borders in the garden. In London—fast-moving London—we barely knew our neighbours. There our house was locked, bolted, and alarmed when we went out. Here we felt a sense of safety, and of being protected.

We didn't have a phone. But the tiny bar halfway up the hill where they sold home-made bread, chunks of cheese, cabbages, and wine in dusty bottles, and where the old men, waistcoated and behatted, played cards for peanuts … they had a phone. And a stool, and a half curtain in case you wanted privacy. When the owner, Leita, spotted a telecommunications company van by the market in Loulé, she sent them to us, insisting we had a phone of our own.

We were there every opportunity we could take—school holidays, long weekends when grandparents took over; give us an excuse and we were on the plane. No luggage needed.

Once, Martin parked the car opposite the municipal market in Loulé. He did whatever he needed to, returned to the car, and found it clamped. Yes, clamped. He went to the Câmara, was fined, and told to look for the man with the green armband, the holder of the clamp key. He found him in a bar in the Avenida. Back at the car, Martin noticed there was still time on the newly installed parking meter, and challenged the key-holder, who took out his notebook, flicked through the pages and said:

"Senhor, we have one clamp only for Loulé. Yesterday you stayed too long, but it was not my turn to have the clamp. Today it is. So this is for yesterday."

You have to smile. And enjoy.

Slowly, we started to have neighbours, expats from Holland, Germany, France, and the UK. Just a scattering over the big expanse of Vale Telheiro. We are still, decades later, close to them all, and feel lucky to have been blessed.

We were travelling too, for work. To Hong Kong, to China, to the US, to Australia, to Iceland, to Borneo.

Maxwell died, the magazine group went into administration, new owners emerged, and I got a three-month sabbatical and full use of a 4x4 vehicle. Decision time. Well, that was an easy one. We drove with son Jonathan the length of Spain, stopping in cities that were new to us, then crossing the bridge into Portugal … and heading home.

I think it was then, in those glorious three months, that we both considered, for the first time that maybe one day…

✿✎✿✐✿

Some sixteen years ago, we had our daughter's wedding in August on the terrace where those two proud olive trees gave their shade for some 150 guests. The couple did the official bit in the UK on the way to the airport so we had a faux ceremony, with the newlyweds and five bridesmaids standing beneath the old pergola which we'd dressed in yards and yards of the floaty muslin I'd once wanted for curtains. A precious friend conducted the event, with a mixture of Bob Dylan and Native American quotes. Guests were presented with flip-flops and paper brollies. Fairy lights sparkled everywhere. The barbecue was wonderful, but the wedding cake was a bit of a disaster; the icing had 'slipped' off the three layers which sat in the spare bedroom in a puddle of pink, white, and mauve. While guests were still arriving, I was busy clipping bougainvillea from around the balcony and showered the cake with it, ready for cutting. Daughter raised her eyebrows, mouthed "What happened?" and then had the largest slice ever. It was a joyous occasion, shared with family and people we loved. But a few days later, we were heading back to London, sad to be leaving the celebrations, our friends, our home.

I suppose it was the advent of email and mobile phones, and iPads, laptops, Mac technicians, and communications made easy, that brought home the realisation that as a journalist/editor one could work anywhere. Literally anywhere, so long as you had the connections that didn't exist when we first visited Portugal all those years ago. Extended holidays became viable.

So much had changed. Apolónia, once a tiny shop with a single cash till had become a large supermarket; there were motorways and fast roads and estate agents by the dozens, and Michelin-starred restaurants, Porsches, Mercedes, and Jaguars at every turn. Progress indeed, and good for the economy, but up in the hills, life has continued at its laid-back pace.

Eleven years ago, finding ourselves parentless, we saw the opportunity for the next chapter of our lives opening. I talked to my various publishers — I was producing a big glossy business-to-business bi-monthly for the wedding industry; a quarterly magazine for retired Metropolitan police officers, and titles for a Dutch publisher with interests in Germany and Italy. And feature writing for others. How would you feel, I asked, if I worked out of my home in Portugal instead of my home in Hampstead? Makes no difference, they all said, so long as you deliver.

We put our possessions in storage. Our daughter, with husband and baby, took over as guardians of our flat. And we made the move on Good Friday with our son. The three of us, driving two cars from Santander to Loulé, ready to dive into a new tomorrow.

In those eleven years since that day, our lives have changed in so many ways, and in others remain unaltered. The husband who said he could only ever live in a major European city, is now a confirmed countryphile. He joined a rock choir and a photographic group. The son who struggled has blossomed against all odds. My monthly to-ing and fro-ing from London has come to an end — not only and obviously as a result of the pandemic, but simply because it wasn't necessary, thanks to communication possibilities.

In 2020 we launched a new magazine, *AlgarvePLUS*, pouring heads and hearts and an enormous amount of passion into a publication that we believe stands out from others available. We didn't want it to be a directory. We didn't want to produce an also-ran. We wanted a stand-alone title that portrayed the very best of our adopted home territory, that promoted young talents, fresh attitudes, and new ways of life. Quality and originality were top priorities. And I think we have achieved that. It is a joy, at the start of each month, when the latest issue goes into distribution and copies race into hands from Tavira to Guia and up into the hills from São Brás and St Barbara to Boliquieme and Paderne. Readers have been fast to come back to us with praise, and advertisers with thanks.

Martin has learnt Portuguese and although he says not, he is mastering it. Mine is rubbish, but with a good supply of nouns and lots of hand-waving, I can make myself understood. When we are able, we keep busy with friends, entertaining, eating out, going adventuring, getting involved. I do a lot of baking. Daily, in fact. But coming from a Viennese mother, it was to be expected. I am hoping for an outdoor bread oven as my next anniversary present; who needs jewellery?!

Here there are people who work together, share problems, tackle issues, look to put back into the community what they have been lucky enough to take out—things like kindness for a start, and a willingness to help. And there are so many journeys of discovery ahead.

So this is our life now. In an enchanted land that we discovered for ourselves over forty years ago, in a home that has made us feel blessed every day, with a full workload that never fails to delight and excite. Do we miss the pace of London? Not at all. If we want a bit of city, we have Lisbon just a couple of hours away. The world is our oyster, no question, and we have chosen the oyster that is the Algarve.

When the climate improves and Covid-19 is no longer prevalent, which it will if we respect the necessary lifestyle adjustments, we will appreciate even more what surrounds us. And get to see daughter and husband and her family of now three boys…

✿ೞ✿ಚ✿

You can read every issue of the *AlgarvePLUS* magazine free online: www.algarveplusmagazine.com

A Walker's Paradise
JOHANNA BRADLEY

I'm fondly known as Restlessjo, perhaps not always so fondly, as my husband, Michael, will testify. He's a bit of a homebird, so there is sometimes a conflict of interests. He was born and brought up in the north-east of England, on a coastline that, though beautiful, is not renowned for its warmth. We met one bleak Christmas. I on one side of the dance floor, he on the other, while our mutual friends gyrated. He was a shy version of Barry Gibb of the Bee Gees, complete with curly perm, tank top, and platform shoes. How could it not become a lifelong partnership? Though I'm not entirely sure how it did!

Many years down the line, we married and started life together in our hometown of Hartlepool. A place with a strong maritime heritage, it had been dealt a few cruel blows by World War II, and thereafter. The docklands from which it made a living fell into decline, but the town gained a much-needed new lease of life when a new marina was proposed in the 1990s.

They utilised old shipbuilding skills to restore a beautiful tall ship, HMS Trincomalee, to become the centrepiece of a museum where I worked as a volunteer for a while. I had always loved being close to the sea, and yet I spent the greater part of my working life confined to an office.

My mam was a north-easterner too, but my dad was Polish. They met after the war, when dad was a displaced person, his family and friends left behind in his homeland. The story of how he was reunited with them, after sixty-four years in the UK, is a defining moment in my life.

I've long thought that my restless nature came from my dad. He and mam separated when I was small, and I was brought up by my maternal grandmother. I couldn't wait to escape from my small town to the big city, and secured a job as a trainee fashion buyer with the Peter Robinson department store in London's bustling Oxford Street. What a wide-eyed youngster I was then! It wasn't too long before my dreams had crumpled around my ankles though, and I was back in the North East, where, of course, things looked up when I met Michael.

One thing that we had in common was a love of sunshine. After our first few tentative trips together, and a memorable extended lunch spent in a rainy Bury St Edmunds pub, we always took our holidays abroad. The Greek Islands, with their blue skies and even bluer waters, seemed like paradise to us.

Our daughter loved Italian style, and developed an enduring love affair with Venice. So much so that she eventually honeymooned there, timing the wedding to coincide with Carnaval. It's a lasting source of pride that the wedding outfits she made (and that included the groom's hand-embroidered topcoat, her own sumptuous gown and all accessories) graced the ballrooms of Venice, surviving the Acqua Alta with ease. A true belle of the ball!

Nineteen years her junior, our small son was happy at first just to toddle on the beaches, then to play king-size chess and table-top games. Guitars were to become the love of his life, but he too was impressed with Italy. Ferraris were very much his style. Italy supplied the warmth that we all craved, and pasta, pizza, and ice cream seemed to become our staple diet. Then the Canary Islands gave us back our connection to the sea, before a special birthday was celebrated on the island of Madeira.

This was our first introduction to Portugal, though our motivation had been purely to find somewhere that was still warm in November. Rain scarcely detracted from the sheer beauty of the place. Flowers cascaded freely, and after the rain there was always a rainbow. I didn't know it then, but perhaps our love affair with Portugal had begun.

Our son was already a teenager, bored with being dragged around the world. He had no idea how lucky he was! For many years I had watched the TV programme *A Place in the Sun* with a wistful eye, never sure that I could make this dream a reality. When Michael's mother died, the sale of her bungalow and our combined resources gave us enough to hope. But where to look? We had never been to mainland Portugal and, on a whim, I booked a week's holiday in the Algarve, in the October half-term of 2003. Vilamoura seemed a good base, and the fancy yachts and sports cars certainly impressed our son, but Michael and I lost our hearts to Tavira.

I had done a little research, and booked half-a-dozen house

viewings along the coast of the eastern Algarve, and over into neighbouring Spain. Tavira's turn came on a rainy day, but as we wandered through the town, pale sunshine reflected on the puddles, and we were smitten by its charm. Beauty is completely in the eye of the beholder, for our son couldn't believe we preferred the stately old houses with their tile-clad fronts to the sleek modern builds of a resort. Many of the streets shared ramshackle ruins with their grander neighbours. We found it charming and held firm in our resolve. Tavira was the place for us.

Of course, there was angst! Were we doing the right thing? Was the new-build estate house on the edge of town the right one for us? But by the end of that week we had made up our minds, and we flew back to sign the contracts the following February, over a few crazy days. We had three days in which to buy basic furnishings, which included a boiler and all the necessary light fittings. Much to our dismay, we discovered that wires dangle from the ceiling of a new property in Portugal. But we did it all with mounting excitement.

Although we were still working, the dream of actually living abroad had become a possibility. And in the meantime, how many wonderful holidays we could have. And our doubting son? Well, he brought first his mates, then a girlfriend, and finally a prospective wife and charming little boy to visit.

✿❦✧᳇✿

But life is never without its complications, is it? Good ones and bad. I mentioned my dad had found his lost family, or rather that they had found him. Suddenly my life was divided between my home in the North East, the dream of a life in Portugal, and an amazing new reality for me. I had a Polish family who wanted to know me. That thought had simply never occurred to me before. From being an only daughter, in my late fifties, rarely even considering myself half-Polish, I had become one member of a huge and loving family. I had two new aunts and two new uncles, and a whole raft of twenty-six cousins with their partners and children.

Holidays now included visits to Poland, and didn't we have good times? They embraced us with open hearts. But occasionally it was bewildering, especially for my husband, an only child. And I couldn't speak Polish, though I tried, and I tried.

Throughout all of this time, I had been nursing dreams of being a writer. Travel fired my imagination, and I would spend many an evening writing travel articles and being ridiculously pleased if I could get one into print. I always kept a diary when I was young. Later, on holiday, I would collect postcards and write my diary on the reverse side. I loved them for their beauty, but they were also a fallback in case our holiday photos were a disaster. My husband took most of the shots back then, and I stuck to scribbling.

I'm not good with mechanical things, and even worse when it comes to technology. Not knowing exactly what it involved, I liked the idea of blogging, but had no idea how to set one up. An American organisation, Wordpress, seemed to provide help and guidance and to be 'user-friendly'. Eventually I fumbled my way in and *Restlessjo* was born. My friends chuckled when I told them, finding the name highly appropriate. I'd done my share of travelling but, wherever I found myself, I always wanted to see what was round the next corner. To the exasperation of my husband, and later, our son. It never mattered whether I was roaming the Yorkshire Moors, in Malaga, trudging up a hill in the melting heat for the view from the castle, in Bristol or in Birmingham, skipping along the towpaths, or here in my beloved Algarve. I always needed that extra step.

I started *Restlessjo* with what I knew and loved, my north-east coast and moorlands, telling my stories and hoping people would like them. I found it easy to establish a rapport and respond to comments. Building a relationship with your readers is an essential element of blogging, and one that I very much enjoy. Initially, I was sparing with my photos, but there was no doubt they enhanced the stories. I bought a small digital camera, a Canon Ixus 185, which took great shots, with very little help from me. I soon found that I went very few places without it.

I had plenty of material, and set about organising it, dividing the blog into four pages. Home and Abroad—now rather dated, with stories from life before Portugal; an A-Z page devoted to the Algarve; another A-Z for the Polish saga, and one for 'Six Word Saturday'—a fun weekly challenge I adopted almost from week one. I had already discovered *Algarve Blog* online, and the lovely Alyson was happy to provide me with advice and her technical expertise.

My readers were often avid travellers, with whom I could exchange experiences, but the blogging community is diverse and gradually my readership widened. Within my circle I have superb and skilful photographers, talented artists, wonderful writers, great cooks, keen gardeners, and people who are good at crafts. Many of them wear more than one hat.

✿ॐ✿ॐ

In England we were members of a walking group, a pastime that gave us hours of pleasure and companionship, and helped keep us fit. Looking for direction and focus for the blog, I started a weekly feature called 'Jo's Monday Walk'. I would focus on a walk I had done and then showcase the walks of any readers with a story to share. Wordpress has a worldwide readership, and soon I had friends across the globe. I loved it!

Vistas opened up in my imagination, and the warmth of the community I was writing for astounded me. I encountered several people who I now consider close friends, and over time I have met many of them in person. I cannot explain how extraordinary this feels, for I am, despite the bold front I wear, quite reserved.

Walking is a whole subject in itself and has become a large part of our life here in the Algarve. Preparatory to making the 'big move' we wanted to find a community with which we felt at ease. And we were so lucky! When we first came here, a fellow north-easterner led a regular weekly walk for the princely sum of five euros. And that included a lunch! It was his way of supplementing his income, built on house-sitting and dog walking. We had no idea that was even possible. Over time, much to everyone's distress, he made enough income from the other occupations to drop the walks.

Fortunately, a couple of good folk stepped forward to take the reins, and we split our growing numbers into Strollers and Striders. Needless to say, the Strollers liked a cup of coffee and a bit of cake en route, over level easy terrain. The Striders enjoyed hills! Or at least, some of them did. Most of them loved cake too, but they were usually prepared to wait for the end of the walk and a three-course meal with wine. The Strollers also liked a three-course meal with wine, and all of them were fond of a bargain.

The groups were almost exclusively expats, though there weren't any restrictions. Some people were members of both groups. The mix of people was interesting, and a good way to make new friends. The Portuguese are not generally walkers, often working long hours. Most would rather go to the beach or spend their free time with their families. But walking has increased in popularity as a healthy outdoor pursuit for us oldies.

We were often asked if we knew of a group that newcomers could join. Both the Strollers and Striders had hit maximum capacity, and neither wanted the responsibility of new members. The leaders ran the groups voluntarily, and we walked at our own risk. Additional groups formed, including one for the locals, called 'Todos a Caminhar' (Let's all walk). Led by young fitness instructors on Sunday mornings, it felt like a good opportunity to practise our Portuguese. It was not entirely successful in that respect, but we enjoyed the easy camaraderie.

Walking could become a full-time pursuit here if you let it! Overall, we thoroughly enjoy our walking. We are spoilt for choice, with level walks through the salt pans, or along the beach, and a wide range of countryside and hill walks with beautiful vistas.

But then dad died suddenly in October 2017. Worse still, I was in the Algarve at the time. I had been at his home to do my usual bit of cleaning and share a meal with him just days before, and all seemed normal. A text message alerted me that he had been taken into hospital, but said I was not to worry. Before I had time to do much worrying, a phone call told me he was already dead. My only consolation was he was not alone, but with my stepbrother and his family.

My dad was a man with a big heart, who loved being in the bosom of his family, whether in England or Poland. Throughout my life he was there for me, and we shared some amazing times, dancing at five Polish weddings and a Silver Wedding in Zakopany. Representatives from the Polish family gathered with our English family, and friends who had known him since I was small were at his funeral. Such an emotional day!

My mam had died many years earlier, claimed by cancer aged just sixty-five. Dad's second wife died tragically on his seventieth birthday, never living to see the reunion with the Polish family that she would have so loved. They were sad times. Michael was now nearing retirement age, and our 'youngsters' had grown up and were settled with their chosen partners. Suddenly there was no reason not to pursue our dream. I made one more visit to Poland, solo, to say my farewells and to kiss and hug all those that dad no longer could. And then it was time to get on with the business of selling our home of thirty-five years, to start a new life in the sun. We finally made the move in November 2018, a year after dad's death.

※※✧◎※

Much of the above made its way into the blog. People were interested to hear about our decision to move abroad, and I provided three-monthly updates on the trials and tribulations of 'living the dream'. One of the greatest obstacles was my lack of Portuguese language, another huge subject. Once we obtained residency here, we felt we needed to speak the language. It's common courtesy, isn't it? Yet a lot of expats don't bother, or feel the need. Here in the Algarve many of the restaurants and shops have English speakers, who rapidly identify our hesitancy and respond in English.

Portuguese isn't an easy language to get your tongue around. Written down, it looks like Spanish, but the sound is very different. I found I could get to grips with it in a textbook, but for me, understanding or speaking Portuguese was a problem. My husband doesn't like book-based learning, preferring to tackle the language head on in a practical way. We enrolled in a class with an excellent teacher, Ana do Carmo, who ran her own language school. At first this was an adventure, for we took the train to Olhão, forty minutes away, and made our way to a beautiful old building, which was a former merchant's house. About twenty people enrolled on the course, and Ana split the class into two, to give people plenty of opportunity to practise spoken Portuguese.

You had to concentrate so hard that the forty-five minute lesson was exhausting. We would make straight for the tiny bar afterwards, theoretically to practise a little with the young Hungarian barman. With a Portuguese partner and a small child, he was happy in either language, unlike us. At the end of the first term we were offered an intensive two-week course, but this coincided with a holiday in the Azores that I had promised myself for many a year. We told ourselves that we could practise our Portuguese there, and sadly never went back to Ana.

We opted instead to join a Seniors Club in Tavira, which offered social opportunities and language lessons all on our doorstep. In retrospect, this was a very bad choice. Over sixty people turned up for the first class! To say it was chaotic is an understatement, but we persevered for the first term. Our teacher was a charismatic lady who did her very best against unfair odds.

Covid-19 finally put paid to the class, but we had already decided it didn't work for us. Michael continues to use the translator on his phone and proceeds as best he can. Sometimes the ensuing misunderstandings are hilarious! We recently arranged for someone to come and clean our three-piece suite. As I usually do, I kept a low profile as the bumps and bangs drifted up our stairs. Five minutes later, my husband, speechless with laughter, staggered upstairs to tell me they'd taken the suite away! We'd carefully removed any obstacles so they could work in our living room, but they lugged it out of the front door. If my husband's understanding was correct, they would return it in four days. After we'd finished giggling, and then worrying that we might never see the suite again, we brought the patio chairs in to sit on in an echoing empty room. We shouldn't have doubted, because this is Portugal, with its own way of doing things. Two days later, we had a phone call to say they would return our furniture within the hour. It arrived, immaculate, and impressively cellophane-wrapped for protection.

Recently I started lessons with a local Portuguese lady. There are just three of us in the class in her home—so there is no place to hide. I can't say that it's going well, but it's going. You have to find what works for you.

✿෨✿ଔ✿

There was never any question that our new home had to be beside the sea. In the UK our house was on the north-east coast, with fine beaches of its own, but a popular trip out for us was the city of Durham, just twenty minutes away. Situated on a river, with a majestic castle and cathedral overlooking the water, in some ways we found Tavira very reminiscent of Durham. As you drive into town, the Santa Maria church dominates the skyline, along with a large water tower which houses a camera obscura. On a sunny day this makes a fascinating experience, for you learn a little of the town's history while gazing at the antics of people in the town below.

Beside the church is a lovely old garden, enclosed within part of the original town walls. In summer you'll often find musicians there; the walls are clad in bougainvillea, and hibiscus plants flourish everywhere. Descending the hill you have the Galeria Palace, a wonderful building with fine timbered ceilings and the excavated ruins of the former town visible through glass panels in the floor. Further down the hill, the Igreja da Misericórdia has some of the finest *azulejo* tiled panels you will find in all of Portugal.

And then you reach water level. The tidal Gilão river is spanned by the graceful arches of the Ponte Romana (Roman bridge), and a contrasting new bridge with sleek modern lines. The riverside gardens provide gentle shade and a place to linger with an ice cream, or in the winter a bag of roast chestnuts. It's a town that repays wandering and poking around in the many side streets and squares, until you find your own favourite spots. Count the number of churches you pass along the way. There are said to be in excess of twenty, some of them very beautifully restored, others patiently awaiting their turn.

Something I love to do is catch the town ferry from the quayside, out to Tavira Island with its golden sands. The ferry meanders out through the salt marshes, and from the top deck you can almost always spot flamingos, as well as a variety of other bird life. The ferry stops at Quatro Águas, at the river mouth, to pick up and drop off passengers, the winter schedule only operating from this point. In summer, your choices are much wider. The ferry from pretty little Santa Luzia crosses to Terra Estreita beach on the island. Just around the bay you have the unlikelihood of a steam train at Barril. It's popular with old and young alike and will take you painlessly out to the beach, a highlight of which is the Anchor Graveyard. With a bit more energy to spare, you can walk back across the causeway and bridge, or even walk along the beach to catch a ferry back into town.

Ferries are a necessity in this part of the world. From the seaside resort of Cabanas, a small boat will whisk you across to the next barrier islands, with equally beautiful endless beaches. Edging east towards the Spanish border, Cacela Velha is one of the Algarve's true beauty spots and one I often wish I could keep to myself. A tiny ferry will scoot you out to an immaculate beach. At low tide you can even walk across yourself, but do keep an eye on the fast-turning tide.

This is a watery world, and the eastern Algarve is brimming with opportunities to be on the water. I must just mention two other islands you can access from nearby Olhão or Faro. Armona, with its colourful rows of beach houses, is my personal favourite, but Culatra is beloved of local fishermen. The iconic lighthouse at Farol is a beacon across these seas.

So how does being here full time differ from having a holiday home? To be honest, it required more of an adjustment than I had expected. I loved the Algarve from our very first visit, but living here I began to question how good a fit I was with my chosen country.

My lack of language became a total frustration. I would sit on a bus or train and try to follow the conversations around me. At best, I could pick out a few words. It's hard to feel you belong if you can't communicate properly. At school I had felt an affinity with languages, and 'A' level French was no problem. How was it that this facility had deserted me, first with Polish, and now with Portuguese? My head was a constant muddle of words — never the right one for the occasion.

I began to find fault with things that hadn't bothered me before. We had taken up residence in the winter and, while the climate here is undoubtedly warmer than the UK, our house wasn't. Out and about in the daytime sunshine I was a happy soul, but I would turn grumpy back indoors when I had to don additional clothing and still not really feel warm. The joys of central heating and fitted carpets are almost unknown here, where the priority is to keep out the intense heat of summer.

Living here, you can't go out to eat every night, as you would on holiday, and the evenings sometimes felt long. I had plenty to do, but often lacked the motivation to do it. Boxes from 'home' remained under the bed or in the second bedroom where I didn't have to think about them, and I stayed in the living room, close to the plug-in heater. Fortunately, I had understanding friends, who assured me that the first year was a period of adjustment and tried to find practical solutions to my problems. Sometimes I found myself wearing a fake smile and reassuring people that all was great. How could I not be happy here in paradise? Or admit that I wasn't? I felt the fault must be mine, especially since my husband seemed to have no such difficulties, and appeared to have adjusted easily.

The hardest part of the move abroad is the separation from our children, which has, of course, been made much worse by the advent of Covid-19 into all our lives. I have to admit that the virus has caused me to regret our decision to live abroad. We have a great life here, far better than in the UK, and wonderful neighbours. A mix of races, they are mostly Portuguese, and very kind. But nothing can replace hugging your children when you need to.

And so we come back to the question, why did we choose the

Algarve? For us, it provides so many of the things in life that make us happy. Primarily the warm climate and endless beautiful beaches. Life is often absurd, and while I love proximity to water, I'm not very good at being in it. I'm much better at swimming when my feet can touch the bottom, and I'm very squeamish about jellyfish and other creatures that might share the ocean with me. The eastern Algarve is a pure paradise from that point of view. I can hop on a ferry and bob across to the offshore barrier islands that protect our coastline, any day of the week.

And if I want a hike in the hills, that's no problem either. I can walk from our estate into varied and lovely scenery, with oxalis plants dotting the fields with their vibrant yellow colour from January onwards. Spring arrives early here and in the winter I am already thinking ahead to enjoying almond blossom days, closely followed by radiant red poppies twirling their flamenco petals in the breeze.

I've met some great people here. I looked for, and eventually found, a tai chi group to continue a pastime I enjoyed for many years in the UK. The style was completely different, but that challenged me to adjust my thinking. No bad thing for an ageing brain. And there are many opportunities to try new things. Much to the amusement of my husband and friends, I have recently taken up croquet. It's great fun, highly competitive, and a chance to meet a different circle of people.

The social life here is better than I could have ever expected. People want to enjoy life and realise what a God-given opportunity they have. It's such an outdoors and friendly life that my writing has to fit into the early morning, or evenings when we are home.

Of course, Covid-19 had devastating consequences for meeting in groups. But we continue to walk, in twos and fours, our knowledge of available routes standing us in good stead. We use signposted PR (*pequena rota* – short route) trails for variety, taking care not to flout the restrictions imposed by the Portuguese government.

Have I tempted you yet? You will find lots more reasons, and favourite places on my blog, which I like to think of as a kaleidoscope of Portugal's countless treasures. Come and say hello!

I'm sure we can share some cake. That's a magic word in our house, and a favourite indulgence. The culmination of many a fine walk.

※☙☼❧※

You can find out about Johanna and her love of Portugal and the Algarve, together with more about her Polish family and story, on her blog, *Restless Jo*:
www.restlessjo.me

8

The Art of Wine – Quinta dos Vales
KARL HEINZ STOCK

The beginning of my life's journey started in a small village in Germany called Kleinostheim, which was my home up until my late teenage years. It is a beautiful town, but even the name itself entails the word 'small' when translated from German. Even back then I knew I wanted to see the world, to know what else was out there, and so I worked towards this goal.

While school wasn't always my forte, university was where I realised that if I truly put my mind to something I could achieve it, and so after trying out various areas, I completed my bachelor's degree and master's in business administration.

After this, I immediately started my work life in banking at the Grundkreditbank Berlin, where I was employed from 1983 until 1986, working as Personal Assistant to the CEO. I then became the branch manager at Commerzbank Berlin, which was my stairway to entering the Russian business life.

In December 1988 I visited Moscow with clients and immediately fell in love with the country and my future wife, to whom I have now been married for almost thirty-two years. In a rather short time span I proposed to my wife, quit my job in Berlin, and became self-employed, all the while establishing work-related contacts in Moscow. I experienced the fall of the Berlin Wall, which came just a year later. It left my family without a source of income for two whole years, except for my just born son's child allowance.

Things took a turn for the better when I received two extremely generous offers almost simultaneously. The first was from my previous employer, which would have put me in charge of a high-profile branch of the company, and the other was from Moscow in the field of consultation. Even though it meant flying back and forth between my family in Berlin and my work in Moscow, I decided to start a company jointly with a Russian partner, because it was an offer I couldn't resist.

My partner's tasks entailed establishing contacts in politics, economics, and construction. I took care of the management aspect, as well as the acquisitions of international customers, financing, and take-overs of buildings ready for demolition, which were in the ownership of the Moscow City Government. Our work mainly involved the financing, demolition, conversion, new construction, and leasing of buildings to exclusively western AAA-rated companies and institutions, some of these being IMF (International Monetary Fund) organisations, various oil and pharmaceutical companies, and banks. All this working in joint venture with the Government of Moscow as this was the only way to acquire the buildings and the licences.

Financing through banks was practically impossible, so we established strong bonds with our western clients. After the first successfully delivered building, we financed one hundred percent of the constructions through rental pre-payments. To safeguard these investments, which were in some cases substantial eight figure numbers, guarantees were necessary—guarantees which we could not provide as we were just a start-up with a lot of spirit but no funds. Mortgage structures were also required, but Russian law at that time did not allow for private ownership of either land or buildings.

As always when alternatives are missing, the impossible becomes possible. We designed the first transition laws from state ownership into private ownership, created the first private law firm in Russia with the best law talents from Moscow University, and managed to initiate new legislation which allowed the transition of real estate ownership from the state to private entities. (As a side-note, I was later offered an honorary doctorate for this initiative).

In the midst of all this, in 1996, my family and I moved to the sun-kissed Algarve rather spontaneously to escape the cold, and to enjoy a calm lifestyle to balance out the non-stop mindset in my working life. Shortly after, in 1999, our family grew and our daughter was born, which was one of the reasons I was spending increasingly more time at home than before.

My partner and I then founded the first foreign gas station chain in Moscow together with BP. In addition to this, we worked on various major construction projects with the English star-architect Norman Foster, and soon we became one of the largest building developers in Russia. Another milestone in our business life was the takeover of a Russian oil company, of which we then owned more than sixty percent. This became the biggest private oil company in Russia, listed on the Alternative Investment Market on the London Stock Exchange.

Even though workwise everything was going smoothly, I felt I wasn't spending enough time with my family and so in 2004 I resigned as director of most of the companies. Between that time and 2009, I also sold most of my shares in the oil business. I tried to retire and took up tennis, and sculpturing which has been a hobby of mine since the mid-1980s, amongst other activities, before realising that not working wasn't and never would be for me.

Luckily I then found a new project which immediately spoke to me, the wine farm now known as Quinta dos Vales. A lot of hard work flowed into it, but in 2007 we founded the farm which was a combination of wine, art, and accommodation, to give people the chance to experience the life my family and I were now living.

While I will always cherish the time I had in banking, real estate development, and oil exploration and processing, I can honestly say that I am most proud of what Quinta dos Vales has become. It is far more than a wine farm, it is an ever-growing project, bringing everybody a little closer to sharing my dream of living the life of a winemaker.

✿ఠ✿ଓ✿

'Why Portugal?' is a question I am often asked. This does not surprise me, because how did it come to be that my family and I now live in a place where others go on holiday?

For us, too, it started with a holiday to get away from the cold in Berlin and Moscow, which was why we chose to stay in a small house in Guia, in the Algarve. I immediately fell in love with the country—the warm weather, the relaxed and kind people, and the calm atmosphere, which was such a stark contrast to our busy and rushed life in Russia.

It wasn't long before we decided to purchase the house as a holiday home, so that we could always return to Portugal whenever we pleased. This then led to the thought of moving permanently to

Portugal. Since I had to fly back and forth between Germany and Russia for work regardless of where we lived, the decision was quickly made that Portugal would now be where I would fly back to, and so in 1996 we made the jump.

Portugal quickly became home when our first child started school and our second child was born here.

In 2007 my wish of planting an olive tree became so much more when I made a dream of mine come true by opening Quinta dos Vales, complete with all kinds of trees and animals. It also combined two of my passions—wine and art. At the time I didn't know much about wine, except that I enjoyed drinking it occasionally; and art, more specifically sculpting, was simply a hobby I pursued.

Quinta dos Vales, which means the Farm of the Valleys, is located on gently undulating hills near Estômbar, in the Algarve. The estate is steeped in history, harbouring many tangible reminders of bygone days. One of the most intriguing is a deep ancient well accessible by a staircase hand-carved by our ancestors through solid soil and stone. The eighty steps descend forty metres to a water level which, according to local legend, was discovered by the Moors. In the old machine room are pumps built at the beginning of the last century; before that time, the water had to be pumped manually, which was tiring work under the Algarvian sun.

Nearby is another deep well, which is the subject of many stories and legends. Estômbar dates back to an era long before the Moorish occupation, and in the 11th century it was the home of the famous Arab poet, Ibn Ammar. It is said that from this well, along with other places in Estômbar, deep subterranean tunnels, up to twelve kilometres long, lead to the ancient Moorish capital of Silves.

The previous owner had several clothing factories in the north of Portugal and only used the farm privately, distributing his wine mainly for friends and employees. When I took over, I planted new vines, grafting them with different varieties. I moved the winery from the basement to the ground floor and renewed all the equipment. The farm had dirt roads, which were all replaced with cobblestones, and the infrastructure and buildings required intense renovation.

Today, the vineyards cover more than 200,000 square metres. We grow grapes unique to Portugal, such as Touriga Nacional, along with international varieties, including Syrah, Cabernet Sauvignon, Aragonez, and Viognier, which have adjusted to the unique climate and soil of the region.

Two top oenologists, Dorina Lindemann and Paulo Laureano, supervise the selection and development of the wines. They collaborate with me and my wine consultant engineers throughout the entire production process.

After the hand-picking and selection of the grapes, we use the latest machinery to make the wine. We press the grapes gently, which are then fermented in temperature-controlled stainless steel tanks, and then stored in French oak barrels. We produce white, rosé, and red wines which have won a plethora of medals and awards.

We also have a beautifully decorated wine-tasting room. It is spacious and bright with a comfortable and traditional atmosphere, and the entrance displays an antique statue of Bacchus, the god of wine.

The grounds of the estate are filled with many sculptures in different materials, sizes, and styles. These include a giant tortoise, a wooden dolphin, three-metre-high kissing hippos, painted bears, mosaic-covered elephants and bulls, and big ballerinas. This is probably the most intriguing sculpture park in the Algarve.

A farm on site provides a home for animals, and Quinta dos Vales even has its own zoo. The selection of species goes far beyond the traditional Algarvian goats, deer, horses, and sheep. Exotic animals such as llamas, kangaroos, and Vietnamese pigs live here and proudly present their newborn offspring to visitors.

One of the visitors on the opening day eloquently summed up Quinta dos Vales' ambience as follows,

"The estate has experienced a magical change," she said. "When walking through it you feel free as a bird, your mind can drift, the art and artists inspiring your thoughts. Wherever you go you find joyfulness, natural beauty, and little oases of serenity which invite you to forget the pace of everyday life."

Not surprisingly, Quinta dos Vales has developed into a venue where people like to celebrate their parties and weddings, where schools have their annual trips, writers talk about and read their latest books, artists exhibit, and musicians perform. It is a place full of surprises, which offers a unique experience based on the symbiosis of art and wine.

Nowadays, one should not become a winemaker to make big money. My goal was very simple. I liked the challenge of converting myself from a passive fan of Portuguese wine into an active one as a winemaker. I didn't realise at the time that it was going to be a round-the-clock task, but I am not complaining because success is a good reward. I am also very relieved that my assumption that the Algarve has ideal conditions for producing high-quality wines proved to be right!

Today Quinta dos Vales is widely recognised as the leading wine producer of the Algarve, which is underlined by more than one hundred international medals and awards for our wines. We produce about 150,000 bottles a year (which is a lot for the Algarve, but only a fraction of what industrial producers put into the market each year). Distribution is eighty percent to Portugal — mainly the Algarve, with twenty percent going to Northern Europe.

My recipe for success stems from my past work in the oil corporation industry. We were newcomers back then with limited finances and nothing other than brains and guts. We converted what was a bankrupt company into a vertically integrated oil firm, which controlled the whole business from exploration through refining and finally distribution through its gas stations. Critical situations in one sector could be secured through the other sectors. In other words, it was built on several legs that were linked together to support the aim for quality.

What I did with Quinta dos Vales was the same. I converted a low-profile agricultural unit into a modern wine farm with the newest technology, aided by motivated and skilled engineers, and transformed the vineyards with the help of top consultants into a tailor-made production unit. Even a star cook cannot succeed if they do not have the right ingredients, the correct technology, dedicated assistants, and if they do not fight for the best. Keep it simple and ask only one thing from yourself, your team, and your product: quality.

Because of the supports of our 'other legs', we can always go one step further. It is at a cost, but a cost that doesn't translate into extra financing, but simply hard work and creativity. This is where the concept of 'full integration' of wine, art, rural tourism, and event management comes into action. Cash flow needs in one sector are secured by the other sectors. And this is not theory anymore, it's reality. Our farm tourism, in particular, is currently funding extra financial requirements in our wine business. The sculptures, which were formerly more of a private passion for me and therefore in need of cash flow, started to generate an income after we started selling them in a shop in the nearby town of Porches.

Through our travelling exhibitions and other art activities, we have also seen a much stronger demand for our luxury accommodation, and the wine tastings and tours around the farm. This, along with monthly cultural events, incentive meetings, weddings, and medium-sized board meetings, as well as larger enterprises that enjoy our conference and accommodation facilities, all produce funds. We can then invest back into our core interest: the production of the quality wine I want to create in an environment that is as local as necessary and as international as possible.

I am always searching for new directions, ideas, and partnerships in both sculptural art and wine, as long as no compromise in quality has to be made. I have many more projects planned, which all have one thing in common: I want to share my positive experiences and discoveries with others.

○೫ಲ೦ಐ೦

The sculptures that grace the Quinta dos Vales estate are designed by me and produced with the help of a team of craftsmen in my large workshop. Apart from enhancing the ambience of the farm, the sculptures also go on tour, exhibited in different parts of Portugal.

The sculptures come in a mixture of subjects, styles, and materials. Some are classical, others are designed with a touch of whimsicality and humour. There are dancing cows, kissing hippos, voluptuous nudes, giant smiling frogs, near life-size bears, and graceful human figures. Many are made in brightly painted fibreglass; others are crafted in local stone or marble from the Alentejo, or cast in ceramic or bronze. Most of the stone used for the sculptures comes from the fields around the estate. It is a partly metamorphic material composed of compressed sand and fossilised remains, and is notoriously difficult to craft by hand. Abstract and representational works cut from pieces of this stone can weigh up to twenty tonnes.

As a starting point, I construct a wooden base surmounted by a metal armature, and then make a maquette in clay or plaster. This early study is then handed over to a studio assistant, who crafts a replica from large blocks of polystyrene, often on a larger scale. Once I have supervised or carried out the finishing touches to the polystyrene model, it is covered with layers of resin and fibreglass. When this is dry, any small defects are repaired with car body filler, and the figure is burnished and polished to create a perfectly smooth surface. This exacting task can take up to six weeks.

The finished sculpture can then be painted, or sometimes decorated with ceramic appliqué in co-operation with other artists, like the Swiss artist Ivan Ulmann, and left as a unique piece. We also create smaller sculptures, including versions of my 'Graces' series and other animals. This makes them more accessible in terms of price and more appealing to those art collectors with less space to exhibit works at home. These are made in ceramic using a silicon rubber mould, reinforced with a plaster casing to prevent distortion in order to cast a limited number of copies. After the liquid ceramic is poured into the mould and hardens, it leaves a beautiful smooth surface to the finished sculpture.

I have introduced bronze powder to the painting of some of the smaller pieces, which endows them with an attractive metallic finish. I am also experimenting with the colouration of the patinas of the bronzes, which are cast by a special wax technique in a foundry in the Alentejo.

One of my most imaginative projects was 'The Dance of the

Bears'. From my own design, we produced sixty-two fibreglass sculptures of near life-size bears. More than thirty artists of different nationalities throughout Portugal were invited to design and paint their interpretation of the theme of 'evolution' on each bear.

The working title of the project was based on a proverb by the ancient philosopher Lao Tse,

"A journey of 10,000 miles begins with the first step."

I see this as an apt representation of man's ability to develop and overcome all obstacles. I consider this concept to be the driving force behind positive changes for mankind.

Fibreglass is extremely tough, resilient, and very light, so large works can be easily transported. This enabled the bears, painted with diverse images and patterns, together with other sculptures like the elephant tree and bull parade, to go on tour. They are exhibited at numerous events and locations in Portugal, thereby bringing the spirit of art, wine, and nature to the minds of the public.

As a follow-up to the success of 'The Dance of the Bears', we created the 'Passion' and the 'Multifaceted Globes' projects, both with a similar approach of making art a communal thing. Most of these sculptures, between thirty centimetres and seven metres high, can now be viewed as a huge open-air permanent exhibition in the gardens of Quinta dos Vales.

The ideas behind the sculptures we produce are the same concepts that drive the evolution of wine. Both are linked to the aesthetic of man's urge to create. True appreciation of good wine goes hand in hand with the finer things in life. My main aim is to bring the chance to experience art alongside good wine to both wine connoisseurs and art lovers everywhere. My art pieces have already made their way to Germany, Austria, Switzerland, Slovakia, and even Russia. One day my wine will reach these countries as well!

☼ↀ☼ↂ☼

Quinta dos Vales might have started off as a simple project, but over the years, it has become one of the most important pillars in my life. Whilst I already knew in 2007 that when choosing quality over quantity in the wine and art production we would need to branch out into other areas to support ourselves, I never dreamt it would become the business that it has.

Another milestone was the introduction of the 'Open Door in the Algarve' project. This is an event we organise annually when we invite small local businesses such as bakeries, chocolate makers, and artists, among many others, to present their goods and services while we do the same with wine tastings, music, and tours of the estate. It is one of my favourite events of the year, because it gives people the opportunity to come together, and the smaller businesses that often go under nowadays, a chance to really be appreciated.

After years of focusing on the wine and art aspects, I decided to branch out and let others participate in my own experience as a wine-lover turned winemaker. In 2015 my son, Michael Stock, joined me at Quinta dos Vales, becoming the Real Estate Director, making us a family business. With him now by my side, this allowed me to dream bigger.

We created The Winemaker Experience, which aims to turn wine lovers into genuine winemakers, each with their own privately owned vineyard. We guide participants through the full wine-production process, offering them our winery and consultancy, but encouraging them to make their very own wine, to their own preferences.

Each private winemaker has the option to purchase or rent their own parcel of vineyard, which is where their grapes grow. The participant makes every decision, from the harvesting date to the origin of the oak used for ageing, just like a real winemaker. Our team is there only for support and guidance, and the result is an annual production of around three hundred bottles of wine, that the wine lover can authentically claim they made themselves.

My vision for this project was always to combine The Winemaker Experience with our own accommodation, called The Vines. We built sixteen villas, which are located on the estate and are completely surrounded by vineyards. This creates a truly tranquil and peaceful atmosphere for holidays or second home-owners, and all the residents have access to a pool and restaurant. I created it to be my perfect holiday home, and I hope others will enjoy it just as much.

※※※※※

When I first arrived in Portugal, learning the language was honestly not one of my priorities, because by knowing English you can manage very well nowadays. Of course you pick up certain words and phrases just by living in a country, but truly learning a language requires dedication, and for me my energy was flowing into the start of my new business.

After living here for many years and realising that this is and will, most probably, be my home forever, I started learning the Portuguese language not just for myself, but also for the people in my day-to-day life. Running a business here makes for a lot of interaction with people who would prefer to or can only speak their mother tongue, which is why I decided it was time to make learning the language a priority for me.

My wife was previously a language teacher back in a university in Moscow, so she tried to take me down the route of Portuguese courses, which worked out well for her. However, I quickly realised that I learn better by myself through trial and error. So I started learning the vocabulary and began to speak and write in Portuguese, knowing the sentences were often grammatically incorrect. In this context I live by the quote,

"If they want to understand me, they will."

My Portuguese language skills are far from fluent, but I can now communicate both in the written and spoken word and have really felt the difference in getting to know the language of my adopted country better. Not being fluent, though, can lead to a lot of funny mix-ups when talking to people, of which I have witnessed and even caused various myself.

I recall a conversation I had with a taxi driver in our early days in Portugal, who was telling us a story about his wife who was currently in Monte Gordo. I was rather confused and asked my wife later on why was it that the man told us that his wife was fat. She explained to me that he didn't say she was *gorda* (fat), only that she was in the little Algarvian town called Monte Gordo. That was honestly a mix-up just waiting to happen if you ask me.

Another story that keeps repeating itself is that my wife has to hold her nose at the cheese counter, not because she doesn't like the smell of it, but because the cashiers don't understand her when she says the word for one hundred in Portuguese. The Portuguese language can be rather nasal and so to facilitate it for both parties she started holding her nose while saying *"cem"* even before they asked her.

✧ℓ✧ჴ✧

While we as residents here will often tell people the Algarve has much more to offer than just picturesque beaches, high-quality restaurants, and delicious wine, these are some of the luxuries that make living here so special. After being here for over twenty years, I have a list of favourites.

First up is one of my newfound favourite spots, Fábrica, a small waterside town close to Tavira. It has remained mostly traditional and gives you a feel of how the Algarve used to be, before becoming one of the main tourist spots in Europe. Here you can take tours through the salt mines, which are typical for the area, as well as exploring the nearby small fishing towns and the nature reserve, the Ria Formosa. This is a long stretched lagoon by the ocean, which changes like night and day depending on the tide.

Another beach I often visit, mostly at the end of a hike to meet my wife for a *bica* (espresso), is the Praia de Nossa Senhora da Rocha. It is divided in the middle by a cliff on which sits a small chapel where we have witnessed many weddings. While one side is filled with fishing huts and boats, the other is completely bare, and if you are willing to descend the numerous steep stairs, turquoise (still freezing) water awaits you.

As previously mentioned, the culinary variety is vast here and so naming just one restaurant as my top pick would be difficult. All I will say is that one should make the most of living in the Algarve by trying out the restaurants by the beach, on the south, along with the west coast. Fresh fish is one of the perks of being in Portugal, so learning more about it was a game changer for us. For example, we found one of our preferred fishes is named after the pig (*Peixe Porco*).

One of the culinary adventures I enjoy is visiting a *marisqueria* where you will be served seafood that at first sight you wouldn't think to be edible, but is delicious once you let yourself in on the experience.

Travelling throughout Portugal is a delight, because even though it is one of the smallest countries in Europe, there is such variation both in lifestyle and nature from the north to the south. Last year we drove to Douro, one of the main wine valleys in Portugal, named after the Douro river which flows through it, and it felt like we were in a completely different country. The hike along the river had a wild forest feel to it—because of the colder climate, the nature is much more lush, and the sparse population in this area gives it a very secluded feel.

Last but definitely not least, I recommend exploring the Algarve's nature, because it has so much more to offer than its beautiful beaches. In the last couple of years, I have increasingly enjoyed biking and walking tours. These have taken me from the mountain slopes of Monchique covered in the typical cork trees, to the cliffs by the ocean that stretch from the middle of the Algarve to the west coast. Even in the height of summer, when most little towns are overflowing with tourists, you will find some peace and quiet in the various nature spots.

My relationship with this country is ever growing, and I have many more plans for the future.

✥ⓢ✥ⓒ✥

Discover more about the Quinta dos Vales wine estate on their website:
www.quintadosvales.pt

9

Ayurveda in Aljezur
IRINA ADRIAENSEN

I grew up in Antwerp, the second biggest city in Belgium. A born city girl, I used to love all the clubs, the cinema, museums, and shops, and there was always a new restaurant or café to discover. I even lived in London for three years and had the time of my life. My stint in London ended with the 2008 financial crisis; I was laid off together with half of my team and decided to go travelling to Central America for a few months. I came back to Belgium when my brother had his first baby and I wanted to spend more time with them.

I found a new job; worked hard, bought an apartment, and climbed the corporate ladder. I was leading a very cushy life. And yet… I had a niggling feeling that something wasn't right. I wasn't enjoying my job, spent way too many hours working cooped up in an office, never seeing daylight in winter, and I was constantly tired. I was burnt out. OK, I thought, change jobs, it will get better.

Things did improve for a little while, but I soon found myself on the same path. I was working too much and exhausted every day. At a time when I was struggling a lot in my job, I went on a yoga retreat in Italy. It was so good to be in the sun, practise yoga every day, eat gorgeous food, and have the space to think. By the end of that retreat, I decided that organising yoga retreats would be my dream job … but I just didn't think it was possible. I figured I had missed the boat and I should just stick to the career I had. I parked the idea, and it wasn't until years later that I picked it up again.

I put my head down and went back to work. Of course, this couldn't go on. I was working myself into being ill once again. I could no longer close my eyes to the things that were happening at the company I worked for, things that went completely against my values. I didn't recognise myself anymore, becoming someone I didn't even like because of the amount of stress I was under every single day.

I was doing everything I could to find balance—eating healthily, practising yoga, cycling one-and-a-half hours to work and back, training for running the 'Ten Miles' race in Antwerp, or walking daily to get some vitamin D and blow off steam. But I knew at some point I had to face it—I was burnt out—again. I was thirty-three and really disappointed in myself and life, and thought, this can't be it?

On a magical winter holiday with a friend in Norway—I'd always wanted to see the Northern lights—we started talking about going travelling together. Not long after that, I put in a request for a six-month sabbatical from work. I planned to travel for three months with two friends and then continue by myself for a further three months.

After whizzing through Australia and Bali with my friends, I found myself alone on another Indonesian island, Lombok. There I was, in a nice homestay, doing yoga and going surfing every day. And then I completely crashed. Literally and figuratively.

During a surf session, a surfboard hit my head, and I needed five stitches. I wasn't allowed to go surfing or to travel, and all my plans fell into the water. I wanted to continue to explore South-East Asia, but I couldn't. It forced me to rest and finally feel how exhausted I really was. My body simply said no.

So I stayed there. One month passed, then another. I was actually enjoying myself, living in a tropical paradise, in a little hut close by the sea, doing the things I loved, and eating avocados and mangoes aplenty.

But at the same time, I was also getting nervous. I was five months into my six-month trip, and I *still* hadn't figured out what I wanted to do with my life. I was fearful that I would have to return to my old job, onto the same old hamster wheel, but I didn't know what else I could do.

One thing the travelling did for me was help me see lots of people living their lives in different, non-traditional ways. The banker who became a dive instructor. The women who worked in marketing and then opened their own hostel or yoga studio. I met so many digital nomads, people working from their laptops who were free to travel anywhere.

Then one day, I had an 'aha moment' while I was relaxing in my hammock. I realised I was putting way too much pressure on myself to figure out *what* I wanted to do with my life. Maybe I just needed to decide *how* to live it, and the rest would follow. Travelling for six months with only what fitted into a backpack, I knew I didn't need so much stuff. I was spending my time outside every day, doing yoga and surfing, and I knew there was the key.

I decided to do a yoga teacher training course, to deepen my own practice, intending to start organising yoga retreats while travelling the world. Picking up that old dream of mine again. I wasn't really planning on teaching yoga myself, but then life doesn't always happen according to plan…

When I told my dad I was going to India to do yoga teacher training, he didn't speak for at least a minute, then he said to me,

"You're going to INDIA… ALONE?!"

I did some research online and found a Hatha yoga course in Rishikesh, at the foothills of the Himalayas. The Beatles had been there in the seventies—surely I could go there too.

Yoga teacher training courses are intense. In the space of one month, starting at 6 a.m. and often only finishing at 9 p.m. you do a few hours of yoga daily. The rest of the day is filled with theory classes, with mantra chanting or meditation in between. There is a lot of information to take in. Yoga philosophy, Sanskrit, anatomy, learning all the postures and their benefits and contra-indications, and also how to be a teacher and teach in front of a class.

The very first yoga teacher training I did included a module about an introduction to Ayurveda, the sister science of yoga. Ayurveda teaches all about nutrition and lifestyle to support your dharma, your purpose in life. When we feel balanced, we have the energy to live in alignment with our deeper purpose, and the key to balance is in what we put into our bodies and how we decide to spend our days.

It just clicked for me. I had always been interested in the link between food and health, particularly mental health, and deep down I knew I couldn't spend my days anymore working for something I didn't believe in. My body had given me plenty of signals through the years, with symptoms getting worse the longer I ignored them. I had disregarded them all, thinking this was the only way. I realised if I didn't want to end up burnt out again; I had to change.

I wanted to learn more about Ayurveda, and did a practitioner course in India, that covered Ayurvedic nutrition, lifestyle, massages, and detoxing. I wasn't quite sure how I would use all this new knowledge, but I realised I had to make a few decisions. I knew I wanted to live somewhere warm, where my body wouldn't hurt so much. I wanted to be where I could be more outside, in nature. I had very much enjoyed living in Indonesia, Australia, and India, but I also didn't want to be too far away from family and friends. I wanted to be able to surf. And that's how I ended up in Portugal.

✧✌✧✍✧

When I told my dad I was moving to Portugal, I could tell he was relieved. Not *too* far away, then. And no more India ... for now. I had visited Porto and Lisbon on city trips, but when I came to Portugal this time, it was to explore the Algarve. Would this be a good place for me to live? I knew nothing about the Algarve before I came. I was simply going on a hunch.

I joined Workaway, a website that connects volunteers with hosts. The hosts offer food and a place to live, and the volunteer works for four or five hours a day on various projects. On the Workaway site I found an eco-permaculture project in Budens, where I stayed for two months. I lived in a dome tent and learnt so much about regenerating arid land, harvesting water, starting a vegetable garden, and best of all, building with mud. Very few things are more satisfying to the soul than mixing sand with straw and water and then throwing it against stone walls. The couple I worked with became good friends, and in the future we would even organise retreats together.

I decided yes—this was a good place for me. I loved the nature, the mix of people, the weather, and being close to the ocean. Finding a house to live in was really difficult, as long-term rentals are hard to come by in a touristy area like this. There are more Airbnbs than houses for long-term rent! And sadly, a lot of these Airbnbs remain empty in the winter just so they can be rented as holiday homes in the summer.

I lived in a hostel in Lagos for a while where I taught yoga on the rooftop, worked on my blog, and went to the beach every day. Then

I finally moved to Aljezur, a little town in the south-west of Portugal where I found a place through a friend of a friend. I had visited this town before, and I always liked the name. Maybe it was a gut feeling I had then that this would be the place I'd call home.

There I was, the city girl, a city girl no more. I was living close to the Atlantic, near to a beautiful national park, in a pretty faraway place in a scarcely populated valley, but I was enjoying it. I didn't know many people, but I started feeling like myself again. Being so close to nature was really soothing to my senses. I have always been highly sensitive and had developed many unhealthy coping mechanisms during my days in the corporate world. Here I could let go of them one by one.

My neighbours were old Portuguese farmers. Starting my own little veggie patch with some applied permaculture soil-regenerating principles raised some eyebrows, but they were very sweet. When it was time to till the soil, the eighty-seven-year-old farmer came to help me with his *enxada* or hoe, showing me how it's done. I didn't even last five minutes, and he just kept going.

My first winter here was not what I expected, though. The days were nice enough—but I hadn't anticipated the freezing temperatures at night. The houses are built to withstand the heat in summer, but they get very cold and damp in winter, and central heating is practically non-existent. I was still used to the tropical conditions of Bali and India, and I walked about the house with a woolly hat on my head and a hot-water bottle permanently attached to my back. Suddenly, I wasn't so sure about living here anymore...

Time went by, as it always does, and I made new friends. Summer came again, and I didn't want to leave. I started my business as a yoga and Ayurveda teacher. I was busy going through all the paperwork, finding an accountant, buying supplies, bringing over my massage table and other possessions from Belgium.

In the beginning I was commuting a lot to Lagos, about thirty-minutes' drive from where I lived, teaching yoga in different places. I then started offering a mobile massage service in Aljezur with Ayurvedic massages and also began working with some local hotels and guest houses.

There is one Ayurvedic massage I do with my feet that's really unique. The client lies on a mattress on the floor and I use the soles of my feet, toes, and heels to do the massage, sometimes using only light pressure, sometimes using my whole body weight. It sounds scary, but it's not! The massage works on the deep tissues, releasing blocked muscles, yet it's extremely and strangely relaxing. It's not at all like Shiatsu or Thai massage. I call it the 'hurts sooo good walking massage' and it's definitely the most popular treatment of the ones I offer.

I also started teaching yoga in a small nearby village called Bordeira, mainly to Portuguese clients. Admittedly, in the beginning I probably taught in an embarrassing mix of Spanish, French, and Portuguese, mixed with some English, but practice makes perfect! I watched Portuguese yoga and meditation videos on YouTube to learn the language, and while I'm not as fluent in Portuguese as I am in English, I started getting better and better with time.

Then came the opportunity to open my own yoga studio in the countryside where I lived, teaching in a converted donkey barn. I didn't hesitate. Now I had the studio, I was staying in one location and not travelling so much to faraway places, which allowed me to create more of a routine. It was doing me good. I no longer had to drive all over the place to teach classes, and it was bringing my community together.

꘍꙳꘍ଓ꘍

One of the first things I did after moving to Aljezur was join the local dog shelter as a volunteer to walk the dogs. The idea behind it is that the dogs get much needed exercise and can be socialised. Every week I would go dog walking. I started thinking that since I had more free time and stability in my life now, and living in the countryside, I could probably take care of two of the poor creatures and give them a better life. So that's how I adopted two rescue dogs.

I didn't fall in love with them at first sight. Well, actually I did, just as I do with all the dogs in the shelter. I explained to Kerry, who manages the shelter, that I wanted two dogs, so they would have each other for company when I was working or travelling. I preferred friendly dogs that were already house-trained, that I could take for long walks. Cute as they are, no puppies for this inexperienced dog mum! And I figured puppies get adopted more easily, anyway. I always had a soft spot for the ones that were unchosen and unwanted.

She said she had just the ones for me. They were black, a brother and sister, four years old, and they had been in the shelter for over two months. They had been languishing there as many people don't want black dogs as they believe they bring bad luck (I thought that superstition was only about black cats!). The shelter also wanted the dogs to stay together because they were quite anxious, and few people were in the market for two dogs.

We were introduced and went for a few walks together on volunteer walking days. And then the big day came, I signed the adoption papers, and they were in my care. I took them for a walk around my neighbourhood, and for the next five days they stayed under my bed, shaking with fear at every unfamiliar noise and movement.

They were abandoned by their previous family and never properly socialised, so there I was, suddenly caring for two traumatised dogs. They were scared of people, cars, motorbikes, bicycles, wheelbarrows, and prams, as I would soon discover.

With endless love and patience, it started to get better. Paula Vieira, a local dog trainer, had some great advice for me as we met up a few times for dog coaching. She told me everything was new to them; they were like babies discovering the world. The fear they had was by now probably ingrained into their nervous system.

Their standard reaction to a trigger is shaking and trembling. And maybe this will never change. But she advised me I could work on making new experiences more common and comfortable by taking them everywhere with me. Now I know if they eat a treat while shaking, they are scared but they are learning and adapting. If they don't accept any treats, the perceived threat is too big for them and I have learnt it is better to remove them from that situation to avoid further trauma.

I often get comments and questions when I take them for a coffee sat outside at a café: "Are they cold?", "What happened to them?", but now it only takes about fifteen minutes for them to calm down and stop trembling. They are not completely at ease, just taking it all in. And each time it gets a little easier.

They desperately needed routine and walking every day. The first two weeks I did the exact same walk each day. Then I started changing it up a bit, so they would have new stimuli and continue learning. It's probably what helped them the most, allowing them to discover the world at their own pace.

It helped me in a big way too, being outside regardless of the weather, exercising gently every day. My body was still recovering from what I'd put it through previously, and there were days where I would not have got out of bed if it wasn't for the dogs.

It's a terrible thing, not to have any energy to do what you used to be able to do, what you should be able to do, as a thirty-something-year-old. To do what you want to do, when you want to, without thinking about the consequences for the next day. Living a stress-filled life in my twenties and thirties had really wrecked my hormones and my body, and some days I felt like an eighty-year-old.

Ayurveda really helped me understand my body better, what it needed to heal and to function properly. I realised that the things I had considered normal: the ongoing stress for years, the sugar and coffee cravings, my troublesome period cycle, feeling exhausted all the time, not being able to get out of bed in the morning, and not being able to sleep at night; are not normal. It was a consequence of the choices I had made up to that point.

I knew that was not a good way to live. It's a way to die without living life to the fullest, without purpose. I realised if I walked down that same street ever again where I would end up. And I was very much done with that.

ଓ ഇ ✪ ଊ ଓ

When I went on my sabbatical, I had started a blog called *ForeverSunday* as a creative outlet and a way to keep friends and family updated of my travels. But as my life increasingly changed, I started writing more about yoga, Ayurveda, and meditation, and suddenly this thing was taking off. The articles about Ayurveda were especially popular, so I focused mainly on writing about that. Ayurveda is still where yoga was in the seventies of the last century, but it's getting better, and I am happy that I can contribute to that as Ayurveda helped me so much in my healing process.

Funnily enough, running my business, I am also using skills retained from my corporate life, so I feel it must all have been for a reason. I learnt so many new things about starting up an online business, and it's been a real rollercoaster. Never could I have imagined living this life. No two days are ever the same.

I now teach yoga and meditation online, have several online courses on Ayurveda, organise yoga weekends and retreats in Belgium and Portugal, and do Ayurvedic massages. I also do one-on-one Ayurvedic coaching, working with women who are struggling with burnout, chronic fatigue, and other illnesses that modern medicine considers vague and mostly 'in your head'. And I am also teaching other yoga teachers and 'wellnesspreneurs' how to build their online businesses.

I work a lot, but I also truly enjoy what I do, I feel joy and purpose, and am more careful of my limits. I usually work on a bigger project in the morning, which is the time I can focus best. In the afternoon I might have a coaching session or class, catch up on admin, meet with a friend, or just go to the beach for a walk with the dogs.

I'm earning less now than when I was working in the corporate world, but I have so much more time. I'm constantly learning new things, and my lifestyle is way healthier without having to try so hard. My life before seemed healthy: I was practising yoga, exercising, and eating healthily. But trying to fit all that into my busy life was a stressor in itself, and I was beating myself up if I couldn't keep up. No wonder it all came crashing down!

Living in the sun most of the year has also meant that I don't get the winter blues so much anymore. Even though it rains here too, now I can choose when I go out to walk the dogs, do my grocery shopping, or go surfing. There's freedom in running my business—and my life. I can listen to my body and take a few days off when I want to. Of course, that sometimes means I'm working on a Sunday, but overall I've become better at living in sync with my body and its cycles. Living in Portugal, I feel I am making a difference for myself, my two dogs, and the clients I work with.

I don't know if I'll be here forever. If 2020 has shown us one thing, it's that you can't foresee the future and life will always throw you some curveballs. I really love living here, I feel part of the community, and have made many like-minded friends, so for now I have no intention of leaving!

My plan is to host more yoga and Ayurveda retreats in the future, and maybe one day that may include having my own retreat centre. I will continue to help many more burnt-out women on their healing path through my coaching, online classes, and programmes, in any way that is possible in this changing world. I really hope my story inspires others to think about how they're living their lives. If I can make changes to my lifestyle, anyone can.

✿ॐ✿ॐ✿

You can find out more about Irina's work on her website: www.foreversunday.org

10

Raising a Family in the Algarve
SUE ENGLEFIELD AND FAMILY

We are a family of four who moved to the Algarve in 2004, from Wiltshire in the UK. I left school at sixteen and trained as a beauty therapist at Farnborough College. I then worked in a beauty salon before moving on to work for some of the large cosmetic houses including Clarins, Lancôme, and Chanel. In my late twenties I fancied a change and started work for an American software company as a receptionist at their offices in Reading, Berkshire. That is where Chris, my husband, and I met.

Chris left school at sixteen as well and started work as a computer hardware engineer in Loudwater, Buckinghamshire. He then moved on to work for an American software company, heading up the European IT department.

We set up home in Winnersh, Berkshire, and in 2000 our daughter Alex came along. I gave up work to be with Alex, and we decided we'd like to move somewhere a little more rural. That way, we could get a larger family home for our money, but Chris could still make an acceptable commute to work in Reading each day.

We both enjoy renovating houses, so in 2001, we moved to a beautiful mill cottage in Wiltshire, situated alongside a babbling stream. We set to work on ripping out the kitchen, updating the bathrooms, and creating a utility room, doing all the work ourselves, before moving on to decorating it throughout. The garden also needed some TLC, but with neither of us being remotely green-fingered, we got the professionals in for that!

In 2002, our son Ben came along. We were enjoying living in Wiltshire; it was a great place to bring up two young kids, and we were happy and settled.

In 2004, Chris was offered an opportunity to take on a promotion in Boston, Massachusetts. We'd visited Florida on holiday twice, staying close to Fort Myers at Captiva Island, and had always said we'd like to move to the States one day.

With our children aged eighteen months and nearly four, we thought it would be the ideal time to make a big move like that before they started school. So we left the kids with the grandparents and flew over to Boston to check out New England, the properties, and the feel of the place. We decided it was an awesome opportunity for Chris to take the job and for us as a family, so we returned home and put our house on the market straight away.

Unfortunately, just weeks after we'd put our house up for sale, a new CIO started work in the Boston office that Chris was going to be transferring to. She shuffled staff around and the role Chris was to take over no longer existed.

We were absolutely gutted, having set our minds and hearts on a new life in America. We took our house off the market, but thought, what were we going to do now? Our current life didn't feel enough after the promise of something so different. Days later we received a note through the letterbox from a local lady, saying that if we put our house back on the market, she would like to buy it. A cash buyer, no chain! This had to be a sign, surely!

We decided everything happens for a reason and set our minds to thinking about alternative options of how we could move abroad and support ourselves. Where could we go that would offer a work opportunity and could deliver a good level of education for the kids? We wanted a reliably warm summer, but also a cool winter. It also needed to be a comfortable travelling distance from family in the UK.

We decided Europe would be the best option and, as luck would have it, we had already booked a holiday to the Algarve. It was our first time in Portugal; it was June, and we stayed in a villa on the outskirts of Carvoeiro. We immediately fell in love with the climate, the relaxed way of life, and the very family-orientated feel the area had. We quickly realised this was a place we could live and bring up our young family.

We thought we might prefer the quieter northern part of Portugal, and of course property is cheaper there than the Algarve, so we scheduled a couple of days to visit the Coimbra and Porto areas. It turned out it wasn't for us! Although our budget would go further, and the general way of life is slower and calmer, the 'toilets' at the service station we stopped at were enough to put me right off! They were outside, with walls that ended nine inches from the floor, and the 'toilet' was actually a hole in the ground. I laughed until I cried while crouching over this ceramic hole with tiled surround, thighs burning, and the breeze blowing through. The southern regions of Portugal were definitely more our thing!

So we focused our search on the Algarve with a view to living there. We checked out the central Algarve area, the non-touristic areas, the property market, and the schools, and chatted to a couple of expat residents about work opportunities. All of our research was very positive. The reason we chose the Algarve was for the facilities in general. The schools, the hospitals, the shops … and the 'proper' public toilets!

We were really impressed with the welcoming attitude of the Portuguese and the feeling of safety wherever we went, so we decided to just go for it!

We moved out in the October of the same year. We initially rented a villa from a local independent holiday rental company, the owner of which we are still friends with to this day. This gave us the opportunity to explore the region more whilst getting the children settled in schools.

We moved over to the area where we had holidayed so that it was familiar to us. In terms of work, there is a large expat community locally, which we knew would be beneficial to us for building a client base. With schooling in mind, the area also had a reputable international school.

After looking at all our options, we decided that the central Algarve would be best for us. This was mainly because of its good road links, schools, and centralised location, making it very easy to get to everywhere in the region within about an hour.

We enrolled our then four-year-old daughter into the International School in Lagoa, feeling it was important for her to have a good first impression of school. We thought it might overwhelm her to be thrown into a local Portuguese school, not knowing anything of Portuguese life, let alone the language.

After a relatively brief search, we found an old farmhouse near Silves which needed a fair bit of work. We fell in love with it and ended up buying it in 2005. It was in a rural spot amongst orange groves, but still within easy reach of the motorway, schools, beaches, and the airport.

Chris and I learnt basic French at school, and that's our lot. Before we moved here, we bought a Portuguese language course on CD and had a bash at it, but it wasn't particularly successful.

About a month after moving here, we had about a dozen lessons from a Portuguese lady at home. We found this to be much more useful, just to pick up the basics and to help us understand a little more of what was being said in day-to-day situations.

We have found Portuguese to be a tough language to learn. It is not helped by the fact that most Portuguese people know how to speak English, so it's often quicker and easier for both parties to communicate in English.

There are many times we have made a faux pas with the language, which has left people looking confused. My most embarrassing incident was in the post office when I asked for what I thought was 'two stamps' — *'dois selos'*, when in fact the lady explained that the word I was using meant I had asked for 'two breasts' — *'dois seios'*. The whole queue found it pretty amusing, so at least it brightened some people's day.

The kids however were a different kettle of fish. When we moved here, they began private weekly Portuguese lessons and picked it up a lot quicker than us! They were far from fluent before going to the nearby Portuguese school, but I think it gave them a base to work from.

I have asked Alex to tell us more about how it felt from a young person's perspective:

I feel that Ben and I both benefitted from moving here at a young age. It allowed us to better assimilate to both the culture and the language of our new home country. We began weekly Portuguese lessons with a tutor on top of the little rudimentary Portuguese they taught us in our time attending the English-speaking international school. However, even with these multiple avenues of language learning over the space of a couple of years, I feel like we were unable to become truly proficient in speaking the language. We were young intermediates at best, and lacked the immersion and listening/speaking practice that is necessary to pick up on the finer details of becoming fluent, the ones that are difficult to learn from a textbook.

Moving to a Portuguese-speaking school instead, surrounded me with a local way of life in a way which I was previously unfamiliar with. Before this, despite living in a foreign country, my life was largely confined to an anglophonic bubble. I watched English TV shows, read English books, and interacted with mostly English-speaking people.

It is essential, in my opinion, to break out of this bubble as early as possible, especially for the sake of younger children. Otherwise, they may grow up seeing themselves as being apart from the country they reside in, because of their lack of interaction with Portuguese media and individuals.

This can be done by ensuring that you slowly shift out of your comfort zone, and truly immerse yourself in your new home country, whilst still being aware of your own limitations and worries. Perhaps if you are tempted by the safe option of popping out for some lunch at a beachfront bar aimed at attracting tourists, go for the traditional-looking Portuguese-run café instead.

Ben and I only really gained a solid grasp on Portuguese when we moved to a school in which it was the only language spoken. In a very real sense, it was our only option. However terrible we were at rolling our Rs or spinning through our brain's Rolodex of textbook vocabulary, we simply had to make do to get through each week and ensure we got our homework done on time. This sort of deep immersion is marvellous for picking up not just the language, but understanding the more well-hidden societal and cultural complexities of living in a new country.

With all this in mind, I feel it is important to recognise that throwing oneself in at the deep end of learning a language can be a mixed bag of fortunes. It is certainly an excellent way to gain some rapid progress, but it requires resilience and determination. At the beginning you will regularly mess up your grammar, forget some of your vocabulary, and make all sorts of seemingly hilarious mistakes.

These are all things which an adult is likely to be much better equipped at coping with than a child.

If you are considering placing your child in a Portuguese-speaking school, as someone who has undergone the experience, I would heartily recommend ensuring that there is a strong support network in place beforehand, whatever their age. Social isolation and bullying are common in all schools, but the inability to communicate properly with other children of a similar age is only going to complexify the situation.

My advice to parents is strive to involve yourself in your child's education. Meet with the teacher to discuss how you're currently taking steps as a family to learn the language and express any worries that you may have. This will serve both you and your child well. Perform regular check-ins on your child's mood and general mental health. Arrange play-dates with the parents of classmates from school. All the above exemplify a more measured approach to popping the anglophone bubble that will take into account the unique struggles that a child may have in suddenly having to confront the experience of learning a new language.

✿ℬ✿ℛ✿

As parents, we are so proud of Alex and Ben, and the amazing young adults they have become.

Our favourite pastime as a family is eating out. I can honestly say we've not had a bad meal here in the Algarve. Our favourite super treat place to eat out is O Bovino in Quinta do Lago. The location, the service, the food, the golf cart that collects you from the car park and escorts you to the entrance. It's superb.

For a slightly less exorbitant treat Fim do Mundo in Ferragudo is absolutely awesome. The atmosphere is cosy and friendly, and the grilled meats and fish are to die for! Our go to day-to-day restaurant is a family-run place in Porches called Ti Teresa. Everything is freshly cooked, the portions are very generous, and they serve honest, home-cooked food which is terrific value for money.

We are still very happy with our decision to make the Algarve our home, with absolutely no plans to go anywhere else. For us, the air is fresh; the sun shines most days, and the pace of life is slower. But I can't reiterate enough how hard it is to make a living here. There are huge ups and downs which can challenge you and your relationships. Since arriving here sixteen years ago, we have seen at least seventy-five percent of the people we know end up moving back 'home'.

I think the key to our survival here economically has to a certain extent been down to luck. We have found that having multiple revenue streams that each bring in a small amount of money works better than having a single source that you have to rely on for your total income.

All of our work is intertwined. We cover computer support, website design, social media marketing, and run an online news portal.

When we first arrived, we started out by offering general IT support for home users and small businesses. After a relatively short time, we had built up quite a large client base that seemed to appreciate our honest and reliable work ethic. A few years later we had the opportunity to take over an established web hosting company that was run by a local man who had sadly passed away suddenly. This was the catalyst that started our journey into building websites and web-based applications, something we had experience of but never offered commercially before.

It was because of this that we were introduced to a local printed newspaper called *Get Real*, and its two owners. In 2009, they decided to cease printing the paper and shift to a completely online publication. At the time, this was quite a forward-thinking idea.

We built the first few iterations of the website which was renamed *Algarve Daily News*. Over time, we became more and more involved. When one of the original owners returned to the UK, we took on a much more responsible role alongside the remaining owner. We maintained and managed the website, adding and creating site content.

In 2019 the owner stepped back from the day-to-day running of the site to pursue other interests, and we took over full control and ownership.

Since then, we have continued to grow the readership. We gave the website a new modern look and ensured it was mobile friendly, and we continue to focus on building our social media audience. It is a great initiative with a strong presence in the Algarve, and we are at the forefront of both local and national news each week.

☼ၷჂⴄ☼

Visit the *Algarve Daily News* website for more information, including how to subscribe to their free weekly newsletter: www.algarvedailynews.com

11

Figs on the Funcho
CHERYL SMITH

The past shapes us, and our experiences, behaviours, and memories feed into the decisions we ultimately make. The Covid-19 pandemic that resulted in the first lockdown of 2020 stopped us from being on autopilot. We used the forced downtime period to recognise what was important to us.

Reflecting on the past and recalling our happy memories helped my husband, Graham, and I make the decisions that have shaped our new life here in the Algarve.

You can learn a lot from asking yourself three simple questions,

"Who am I?"

"Where do I come from?"

"And where do I want to be?"

Hopefully, I will answer these questions and tell you what made the Algarve so special to us that we came to live here.

Growing up in the southern hemisphere, me in South Africa, partly on a farm and partly in a town, and Graham in Rhodesia, now Zimbabwe; we both dreamed of exploring Europe's history and culture. After an enormous amount of research and planning, in July 1991, we set off from the UK in a Bedford camper van for a European road trip, with a planned route going through eight countries over three months. We crossed the English Channel intending to enjoy the lifestyle, culture, and history of a number of European towns and cities. We travelled as far as Turkey, where we met up with a group of friends on a yacht cruise along the Aegean coastline.

Our planned return journey to the UK included Portugal, but we encountered endless mechanical problems with our camper van, and sadly had to head back to England and skip a couple of countries, one of those being Portugal on the Iberian Peninsula.

Six years later in 1997, and now with two gorgeous children, Robert, and Lara-Ann, aged four and two, we relocated from South Africa, where we had been working as IT consultants, to make our home in the UK. When it came to choosing a sunny destination for our annual summer holiday, we chose the Algarve in southern Portugal, as this was the one country we truly regretted missing on that European discovery road trip. Listening to our friends' interesting travel stories about Portugal, with its scenic Atlantic coastline, culinary traditions, and historic villages, it increased our desire to visit the country.

In 2002, we watched the Channel 4 reality programme *No Going Back* on UK TV and that really inspired us to make Portugal our 'living the dream' destination. It was a documentary programme about UK families or couples escaping the rat race from their nine-to-five working days and forming a new, quieter lifestyle in a European sunny destination.

When we recalled the countries of our childhood, where we took our holidays, and where we enjoyed good food and wine, it was the Algarve that reminded us most of our home country within the confinements of Europe.

Back then, you would be lucky to find an Algarve tourist guide in a UK bookstore. External Portuguese promotion campaigns only began after the 1974 fall of their dictator, António Salazar, and choosing Spain as a sunny holiday escape was already a firm favourite with the British. Popularity for Portugal increased after the country won multiple tourist awards, including both Europe's and the World's Leading Destination. In 2016, Portugal won twenty-four awards that included the Algarve being singled out as Europe's Leading Beach Destination. It is truly the holiday destination where our family's best memories were made. The Algarve won our hearts over a period of twenty-three years of holiday vacations.

We purchased our first coastal property in 2005. It was ideal for our family holidays, with a huge array of facilities and activities to hand. Our children have some fabulous memories of holidaying there. My daughter, Lara-Ann, and I enjoyed the beach life, whilst Graham escaped to the golf course to play with our son, Robert.

With a view to purchasing a property where we'd like to live in the future, we found a waterfront property in 2007 that had two buildings: a one-hundred-year-old farmhouse with stables on either side and a barn with adjacent pigsties. Both buildings offered complete privacy with a 365-degree view of the countryside.

The farmhouse, now known as The River House, was restored into a modern, stylish, and spacious villa with five double bedrooms. We added an infinity pool overlooking the river, and decking areas designed for dining, entertaining, and most importantly—relaxing under the carob trees. Winding pathways were created in the garden to the water's edge for easy waterside access for canoeing, stand-up paddleboarding, and fishing enthusiasts.

We were not living in the Algarve, so it was an obvious choice for us to offer both properties as holiday rentals when we weren't using them. The self-catering villa became a popular choice for families looking for privacy and peace, allowing the guests to disconnect from their hectic lifestyle.

I became involved with taking bookings, marketing, and making recommendations about the highlights of the region to our guests. We were constantly maintaining and improving the properties, creating a 'home from home' holiday experience and taking great care that our visiting guests had everything they needed—from toddler and baby equipment, to kitchen appliances, and a DVD library for the children.

We have now started renovating The River Barn and when complete it will accommodate an additional eight guests, making the location well suited for small group activity holidays.

The two dwellings, The River House, and The River Barn, are referred to as Figs on the Funcho, as this is the name we gave the location. The river Funcho flows past the property and there are several fig trees on our land, hence the name.

Spring begins in February, when the almond blossom appears and it is a gorgeous time to be outdoors in the fresh air, exploring the countryside with its abundance of wildflowers, creating a feeling of renewal and energy. The hills surrounding us are filled with nature's bounty—the fragrant wild lavender, the white rock rose, with its floppy large white petals, aromatic rosemary, and sweet-smelling almond blossoms.

At the start of Spring 2020 we popped over to Portugal to oversee the pre-holiday season tasks, expecting a very busy few months ahead. Unfortunately, we (and the whole world) saw about half the world's population move into lockdown, with many businesses closed and a complete halt in holiday travel, something we, nor anybody else, ever expected. We encountered a flood of cancellations due to the travel restrictions imposed to contain the spread of Covid-19.

It was during the stay-at-home orders, and with no pressure to be anywhere, or in fact with anything to do, we were able to take stock of what we deemed important pre-Covid-19, and what we were enjoying doing in the moment.

During lockdown we had time to explore the self-guided walking route, The Via Algarviana. This 300-kilometre walking trail comprises fourteen sectors. We can easily walk sectors eight and nine of the trail as they run past our villa. This long-distance path also has secondary walking routes, one being the Percurso Pedestre Cultural (Cultural Walking Trail) that leads into our village, and travels past buildings of historical interest. There are several recognised routes branching out from the village, and The Via Algarviana has an excellent official website, with maps and information.

We all know that time in the natural environment is so good for our physical and mental health. Walking and enjoying the clean fresh air helps to clear out the mind of unnecessary chatter, and spring is the perfect opportunity to think about new beginnings. It was during this time that we realised we needed to break our current cycle. Running the holiday rental business from the UK was not fulfilling our dream of forming a new, quieter lifestyle in a European sunny destination that we set out to do over ten years ago.

Portugal's tourist board's 2020 campaign strapline was 'Can't Skip Portugal' and aimed to promote Portugal as a year-round holiday destination. We said to ourselves, why not turn it into a year-round living destination by making the Algarve our new home? It was time to make that leap of faith, and we had plenty to do before the Brexit deadline. We quickly made plans to sell our house in England, apply for Portuguese residency, and exchange our current driving licences for the Portuguese equivalent. Nothing like a deadline to get you moving!

Our riverside property nestles in hills overlooking the Barragem do Funcho, the local river dam. The outdoor views are an absolute gem, and it is this countryside location's peaceful and timeless characteristics that shaped our decisions in making Figs on the Funcho what it is today.

Many travellers now are seeking holidays that include a special interest. Portugal is not just a summer haven, but an all-year-round destination, and there are countless activities beyond the Algarve's sun, surf, and sand to explore. The Algarve tourist board is now actively promoting particular opportunities, such as walking and birdwatching, and the Algarve's traditional arts and crafts including pottery classes, basket weaving, and tile painting.

Having settled in the Algarve, it seemed right for us to move from a business model offering exclusively self-catering breaks, to a framework that promoted special-interest holidays. We also recognised that we have the opportunity to be environmentally friendly by introducing ecotourism and sustainable tourism practices. Our intention is to employ local walking guides, support environmental sustainability projects, educate travellers to be environmentally aware when exploring the countryside, and ensure our visitors are sensitive to the Algarve's long-standing water problem; a dilemma that is only expected to worsen in the future because of climate change.

As South Africans, we feel a connection with the Algarve. There are many South African seascapes and country landscapes that present similarities to the Algarve. In our garden we have several plants that were firm favourites in South Africa, such as the exotic bird of paradise flower, agapanthus with its rounded clusters of blue flowers, and the medicinal aloe vera plant.

If you have been on an African safari holiday, you would resonate with our 'Out of Africa' wooden decked area built around two mature carob trees. This is a bucolic idyll where guests can enjoy painting workshops led by experienced and qualified art tutors, for all artistic levels, from beginners to experienced artists. The artists explore various media, learn new techniques and experiment with their landscape painting; all from the scenic riverside deck. With breath-taking views of the river, countryside, and hills, the artists are never at a loss when choosing a theme to paint. Not only do our creative guests come away having improved their artistic skills, but they also enjoy the healing effects of nature.

We also host regular morning painting workshops and I prepare a wholesome vegetarian meal that we share after the art class, under the shady carob trees. Our painting meet-up groups are fun and supportive and great for people new to the Algarve looking to meet people that share a creative interest. Lasting relationships have been formed with people from all over the world, including South Africans, Americans, English, Dutch, and of course Portuguese, all living on the Algarve.

For those that feel energetic, we are wonderfully positioned in the countryside for exploring the walking trails on our doorstep. We can breathe in deeply and confidently fill our lungs with the clean fresh air as the air quality is so good because of our rural location and wide-open spaces.

We accompany our guests on the walking excursions, following the trails along the river, passing vineyards, orange, carob, olive, and cork oak trees, and aromatic lavender and rosemary plants. Our popular easy six-kilometre walks travel along the panoramic river Funcho to the 'secret pond', and thereafter to 'church hill'. On the hill, a large, interesting picture-tiled plaque depicts the historic 1834 Sant'Ana battle and shows the army positions and the site where they erected a field hospital.

You can see miles of rural countryside from the top of this hill. It is an ideal spot to enjoy the view and notice details in the landscape, such as the tumbling walls, farmhouse, ploughed fields, windmill, or the curved railway line tapering off in the distance towards Lisbon. Many art students have been amazed how their focusing skills have improved and have commented that they see trees and landscapes in a different light after practising the art of seeing and noticing during their stay.

Graham and I often walk part of the Via Algarviana's sector eight to our local village. Sometimes we pass Jorge attending his orange grove or vineyard, and he generously fills our backpack with oranges and clementines to enjoy whilst on our walk. This easy walk usually takes about forty-five minutes to one of the typical Portuguese cafés and restaurants in the village where we enjoy a leisurely lunch of grilled *dourada* fish and a glass of *vinho verde*; a green wine that is not named after a grape, but the region that is in the north of Portugal.

Our location is not only on the banks of a river, but is set in a protected nature reserve and attracts a wide range of bird species. Many nearby locals refer to our villa as the villa with the two ducks. We have one black and one white duck, which have been residents on our waterside since the beginning of 2020. We have named them Whitney and Winston, to the amusement of the locals. There is nothing more relaxing than having the opportunity to enjoy birdwatching from the comfort of our outdoor lounge. Other than keeping up to date with the activities of Whitney and Winston, we have a good view of the heron that spends hours wading in the soft mud picking up juicy bits to eat, and the exotic hoopoe and Iberian azure-winged magpie birds that fly around the garden.

We would like to leave the world a bit better than we found it and in doing so we are working towards implementing simple policies and procedures to help us gain recognition as a responsible travel destination, and in turn educate others to be environmentally aware. We identified several possible solutions and to start off we partnered with Vita Nativa, an association whose aim is to develop conservation and environmentally sustainable projects that will help us play a part in conserving our surrounding natural area.

Vita Nativa's project, 'Local Accommodation for Birds', aims to encourage nesting sites for birds in the Algarve region. It also promotes the important role birds have in the biological control of the pests the farmers have to endure, without having to resort to the use of poisonous products. They installed several nesting boxes on our site for the little owls, blue tits, hoopoes, and starlings. Whilst the team were fixing the nesting boxes to our carob and cork oak trees, they identified forty-one different bird species in less than two hours!

This is a very creditable bird spotting total for an inland site. The Iberian magpie and Iberian green woodpecker are of particular interest, as their habitat is limited to the Iberian Peninsula. Other species sighted that are not present in much of Northern Europe were the white stork, Eurasian hoopoe, Thekla's larks and crested larks, Sardinian and Dartford warblers, spotless starlings, and European serins. This bodes well for bird enthusiasts interested in visiting us.

The Algarve is a popular destination for guided birding and bird photography tours and is a major fly-way for thousands of birds migrating to Africa. One of the most important events in the world's birdwatching October calendar is the annual Sagres Bird Watching Festival, which has an awesome programme of activities. You can visit several bird hotspots with extensive bird lists without having to travel long distances. Of particular interest are the Ria Formosa, Salgados, Castro Marim, and the Vila Real de Santo António marshland nature reserve, and Alvor's nature reserve. The popular birdwatching town of Castro Verde in the Alentejo is only a forty-five-minute drive away for us.

Besides the stunning nature, there are also amazing towns and villages all around us. Our special-interest holidays include a visit to nearby places of interest; one being the historical town of Silves. This is an interesting town with narrow cobbled streets leading to one of the best-preserved Moorish castles in Portugal. After the guests have visited the magnificent Gothic cathedral, the archaeological museum, and completed their souvenir shopping, we enjoy a leisurely evening meal below the castle walls under mature jacaranda trees and marvel at the beautifully lit historical buildings.

※☙❖❧※

We also host weddings and Chris and Ellie, from the UK, were the first couple to choose Figs on the Funcho as their destination wedding location. They said they selected the venue for its beauty and privacy and that it was a blank canvas for them to work from to create their envisaged special day. They wanted to enjoy a relaxed garden party style wedding and they did just that!

The couple planned their colour scheme to be in keeping with the scenic views, so they chose neutral colours and the entire family got involved by adding special extras to make it a truly memorable day. Her bridesmaid's mum made rows of personalised hessian bunting to hang on the deck railings. Ellie's creative bridesmaid made rustic handwritten signs and posters and girlfriends spent hours making paper flowers. Her mum personalised the heart-shaped bunting that hung in the trees using a newspaper that was bought on the day her daughter was born. Square solar lanterns hung in the fig trees and her uncle made teepee tripods to hang white lanterns from in the garden, adding a nice touch to the countryside outdoor theme.

They wanted their wedding to feel like a big, relaxed garden party, so the guests sat down with a glass of bubbly prosecco or beer in hand for the civil ceremony held on the sunset deck where the couple made their own personal vows. Her uncle read a poem written by her ninety-seven-year-old grandad, and the groom's sister read out a short but sweet poem, and they had a light-hearted personalised verse to finish.

During the pre-party, Champagne and canapés were served near the pool deck, and impromptu photographs were taken of the wedding party that had the river and eucalyptus trees in the background. It was an ideal photo opportunity setting for the relaxed and natural style they were after. The party continued on the 'Out of Africa' riverside deck, under the canopy of the large carob tree that was lit up with solar lanterns. The guests enjoyed a delicious posh barbeque spread, feasting on lamb, prawns, and wonderful salads, dips, and paellas. The bride said that her favourite part of the wedding day was reading their vows with their friends and family against such a beautiful panoramic backdrop.

We feel blessed that we found 'a piece of heaven' in the Algarve, but we do not keep this location all to ourselves! We encourage others to create their own signature retreats with themes such as yoga and detox, creative writing, or walking holidays. A water activity that includes floating down the river in a canoe or balancing on a paddle board, is best organised during the period January to mid-July. This is when the water is at its peak after the winter rainfall, although some years, the water level has been a reasonable depth all year round.

A local goatherd regularly crosses through our property with his tribe of goats. On one occasion, he handed over a newly born kid, born that day, for me to cuddle! Another special moment was when he showed me how to cut the acorns into smaller pieces to allow the younger goats to feed from my outstretched bare hand. I felt it would be a wonderful experience if I could communicate properly with him in his language, and started making a list of phrases that would allow me to have a short conversation with him. My phrases included subjects such as the weather, references to his dogs and goats, and questions like where will the goats be grazing today? My pronunciation was so bad he did not understand a word I was saying!

Lucinda, a stall owner at our local fruit and vegetable market, is quick to point out to me the produce that is sourced and grown locally and she is also keen to help me communicate in Portuguese. She encourages me to ask for things in Portuguese, helping me build up my confidence in speaking and getting to grips with the pronunciation. Conscientiously listening to Lucinda when she talks to me will hopefully help me speak Portuguese without an accent.

I list words on a white board at home to help me memorise new words and I have a children's picture Portuguese dictionary that I often refer to. Each page has a theme, e.g. the farmyard page will have a visual of related Portuguese words for animals and farm machinery. All very useful as we live in a rural area!

My next step is to ensure that I make good progress in learning the language by signing up with a very enthusiastic language teacher that I recently met. She teaches a small group via the web on Zoom. I think committing to a weekly class with short assignments to complete will be the best way for me to keep on track and improve my Portuguese.

As Portugal has grown over the years, the facilities for living well, shopping malls, good doctors, dentists, and restaurants are in abundance. Portugal is a food haven, with a range of restaurants from the traditional Portuguese, seafood, international, French, or Asian cuisine to the best of the best restaurants on the Algarve. You can dine at your local favourite eatery, beach hut, or enjoy a formal gourmet experience, or you can even choose from one of ten Michelin Star Algarve restaurants. Vegetarian and vegan restaurants are becoming popular here too.

During the year there are several foodie festivals like the *Rota do Petisco* (tapas route) and we have our own annual Gastronomic Festival in our village, São Bartolomeu de Messines. Budding cooks can source anything at the Apolónia supermarket, now known as the 'The Waitrose of the Algarve', with shelves filled with a variety of foreign and gourmet products. The Algarve also brings sophistication with several upmarket hotels and award-winning spas. If you want a simpler lifestyle, you can find peace and quiet, but if you are looking for something more sophisticated, it is there as well.

For connoisseurs of fine wines, the Veneza restaurant, near Paderne, has a massive fifty-thousand-bottle wine cellar! After enjoying their authentic Algarvian cuisine, drop by the Côrte-Real art gallery nearby, or take a look at the ancient ruins of Paderne castle.

To help us maintain a healthy and balanced pescatarian diet, there are many restaurants that serve wild fish and seafood. *Dourada* (sea bream), is the everyday fish of the Algarve and one of my favourites. We do not live far from one of the typical Algarve fishing villages, Olhos de Água, where you can still find fishermen mending their nets in huts that line the shoreline of the beautiful Praia de Falésia.

Olhos de Água is one of many towns on the Algarve that holds an annual sardine festival in August. The promenade is lined with outdoor barbecues where the fresh sardines are grilled over glowing coals and served throughout the evening with salad, potatoes, and local farmhouse bread. It is a vibrant summer occasion, full of Algarve traditions and culture, with live shows on stage, plenty of beer, and wine from Portuguese vineyards. If you are not sure when to eat your sardines, it is easy to remember because if the name of the month in Portuguese ends in 'ro' you avoid them. The sardine season is between March and August, but I would wait until May when the sardines are at their best.

I love to explore the Algarve, finding new walking routes, restaurants, and activities, sampling different wines, and visiting nearby towns and villages.

I adore the hand-painted pottery that is for sale here, and I have accumulated many pieces over the years. If there is a particular style you like, it is best to determine the origin of the potter's workshop, as designs tend to be unique to family potters and the items are more likely to be sold only in their surrounding area. There are many pottery shops to explore in the market town of Loulé. It is a lovely place to discover culture and traditions by active participation in courses and learning experiences, be it handicrafts, art, or gastronomy.

Alte village is one of the most picturesque towns in the Algarve. If you are keen on wild swimming, the natural springs in Alte are a beautiful outdoor spot to enjoy a refreshing dip. After your swim, the tearoom, Aqua Mel, serves delicious homemade cakes—the Algarve orange cake comes highly recommended.

Living a healthy and safe lifestyle is important to us, and the Algarve fulfils these qualities in many ways. The air quality, according to the QualAr network of monitoring stations, is positively rated as either 'Very Good' or 'Good' across the Algarve region; and Portugal achieved third position on the 2020 Global Peace Index, which is very encouraging.

Moving to a new country can be challenging, but the Portuguese are lovely, gentle, genuine people and they are particularly welcoming.

We moved for the lifestyle, the sunshine, the gorgeous beaches, outdoor living, excellent food, and award-winning wines. In those respects, the Algarve actually reminds us a little of South Africa. Combined with the friendly welcome and relaxed style of the

Portuguese, it's not hard to imagine why we spent so many holidays here and eventually made it our home.

✧❀✧❁✧

Find out more about Figs on the Funcho, including information on their activities and holidays, on their website: www.figsonthefuncho.com

12

From the Swinging Sixties to the Present Day
BJ BOULTER

My given name is Barbara Jane, to friends and family I have always been just BJ. Whilst completing my college education in London, my family suddenly moved from Tanganyika to the south of Portugal. It was a little country attached to Spain that I had never even thought about. At Victoria station I found it was possible to travel there by train. It would take three days, various currencies, a lot of walking, and two ferryboat rides!

Having struggled through Paris from one station to the other, the transit from narrow to broad-gauge railway at the French/Spanish border of Hendaye to Irun was easy. It just entailed a long walk. A very slow and jerky train ride, interrupted by interminable stops in the middle of vast expanses of Spain, brought me to the border. After two lots of customs officials whisked away our passports to be stamped, the train chugged slowly across no-man's land into Portugal.

It was Christmas, 1962. The passengers, who were mostly Portuguese, had emigrated for work to France and Switzerland. We tumbled out of the train onto the platform at Vilar Formoso. I followed the crowd surging into the nearest café. Desperate for a proper coffee, their voices rang out, *"café"*, *"bica"*, *"cimbalino"*, plus all the other variations of a Portuguese cup of coffee. My request "with warm milk please" was easily met. I tasted my first *galão e pastel de Belem* ... and became addicted.

There was only one passenger on the journey that spoke English, an aristocratic young gentleman serving in the Portuguese diplomatic corps in London on his way home to Praia da Rocha. What luck! I, too, was on my way to the Algarve to join my family. The train connection in Lisbon was from the other side of the river Tagus, a boat ride away. It meant we had to wait until the next day for a crowded six-hour journey sitting on our suitcases. "Did I know Lisbon?", "Had I heard the Fado?" No! Soon I was walking slippery, cobbled streets, sipping heady red wine, and listening to the extraordinary singing voice of Amália Rodrigues.

My father was an engineer in East Africa, building railways, bridges, pipelines, houses, schools, and convents. My mother ran the business side. Our hometown was Dar es Salaam in Tanganyika. My father's work sometimes took us away.

At Sultan Hamud, in Kenya, we lived in rondavels, which were very noisy hexagonal tin cabins near the station, while he laid the water pipeline from Kilimanjaro. My one vivid memory is of climbing into thorn trees as the cattle roamed the plains, hanging from a branch to drop onto a Sanga cow for a ride. While holding fast to the hump, it would slow down, stop, shake me off, then pound off to join the herd. It sounds dangerous as I write it now, but I was never hurt.

From there we moved to Uganda, where my father built the railroad for the last phase of the infamous Lunatic Express. We lived on a remote hill overlooking what was then Lake George, with a magnificent view of the legendary Mountains of the Moon, the Ruwenzoris, where King Solomon was said to have built his mines. "Ptolomy was here," so father told us. His remit was to descend the escarpment and cross the papyrus-clogged lake to the foot of the mountains. This entailed building a spiral, one of the few railway lines in the world that circles under itself. I have wonderful memories of camp Ncongoro, for by that time I had reached the age of reason, seven years old and being schooled on a two-way radio. A foretaste of today's children coping with isolation because of the Covid-19 pandemic.

As I grew older, I was sent from wherever we lived at the time to boarding school in Nairobi, a long journey by boat, train, or plane, sometimes combining all three. Commuting to far-flung places became a habit for me that has never been broken.

Arriving in the Algarve after Tanganyika gained independence, my parents, Royston and Dorothy Boulter, sought to make a living in a country where very few people spoke English. They bought a small clifftop hotel, called the Solar Penguin. They added lots of bathrooms, created a bar, and welcomed guests. My mother took on the task and adapted quickly, commenting that a small hotel was not much more to manage than a family with seven children. My father propped up the bar. On the customer's side!

Portugal became home. From here I set out to discover the

world, always sure I could come home to the Algarve. Living here was an exciting challenge. The first hurdle to overcome was easy. Learning the language when few people spoke English, and being very young and gregarious, made it a natural thing. These were the sixties, the wonderful happy-go-lucky sixties.

In the summer, with friends on holiday from university in Coimbra, and adventurous young travellers from all over the world, we would buy *garafões* of red wine, light a campfire and grill sardines on the beach. That was fine, though the *Cabo do Mar* from the port authority who were policing the beaches for miscreants, would admonish any girls wearing a bikini and flagrantly baring their midriff!

Earning a living was not quite so simple. When Neville Roberts opened the unusually named 7½ discotheque in the little fishing town of Albufeira, I spent one summer as a disc jockey there. It soon became a fashionable getaway for luminaries of 'the swinging sixties' arriving in flashy sports cars, together with urbane young Portuguese in their fast motorboats, or chauffeurs having driven the long, winding road in the ubiquitous Mercedes.

I remember the Shadows, Frank Ifield, Jane Asher, Paul McCartney, and Cliff Richard visiting the venue. There were few English girls my age that I recall living here at that time, although one person who opened the fabulous little Anna's restaurant near the 7½ was Ana Graham, daughter of Brigadier Graham, then of Monchique. Albufeira then was the place to meet absolutely everyone.

One afternoon I went with friends to watch my first bullfight. The *Cavaleiros* had set up a wooden bullring in a corner of a sandy football pitch, with folding chairs and makeshift stands to accommodate the crowd. The bull pranced into the ring, became annoyed, and crashed through the ring onto the pitch. The entire audience scrambled into the ring, both laughing and terrified. I have not been to another bullfight since.

In the winter, I took a tutoring job in Lisbon. All that was required of me was to speak English with the three little girls and enjoy the good life. The following summer, back in the Algarve, I rebuilt the basement of my parent's small hotel and opened a restaurant overlooking the beach. Early each morning a horse-drawn carriage took me with the other restaurateurs to the fresh meat, fish, and vegetable market in the centre of Portimão.

There were few hotels back then. One of the finest was the beautiful Bela Vista, built in 1918 by António Júdice de Magalhães Barros as a wedding present for his daughter. She died in 1924, and the mansion lay abandoned until it was acquired as a hotel in 1936.

Opposite the Solar Penguin was the Pensão Sol, and nearby was the famous Hotel Viola which opened in 1912. Reputedly during World War Two, like Rick's Cafe in Casablanca, British and allied spies, and purveyors of conveyances for those seeking refuge, would meet there to arrange escape to the New World. Portugal was politically neutral during that period and served as an intelligence exchange site. Praia da Rocha had been a resort from the turn of the century, and with a casino in operation since 1910, it was a natural choice of meeting place.

By the next winter I was off again, this time to Argentina, returning by boat in the spring to travel around Europe. After one more summer running my restaurant, I was head-hunted to run a discotheque in Hong Kong. Being a trendsetter was great fun. There I met my first husband. Our honeymoon aboard ship took us to Sydney, Australia, where my design education paid off. Working at ABC Channel 2 television was the beginning of my career in the film business. Five happy working years slid by and a too youthful marriage gently fell apart.

Separated and far from family for much too long, I took a year's sabbatical and booked a berth aboard ship for Durban on my way home to Portugal. Once we set sail, with passengers crowding the deck to wave farewell to Sydney, I was surprised and delighted to find at my side the charming young Dane whose company I had recently enjoyed. How romantic was that!

At the end of a four-month stint in South Africa, my plan to visit my homeland of Tanganyika by travelling north on public transport had to be abandoned. With a baby now due, I could not take the required inoculation for yellow fever. Instead, returning by air to the

Algarve with my future husband, we opened a small restaurant in the unused open yard beside my parent's hotel. The idea was to set up a grill based on the South African *braaivleis*. It was a great success. People came from far and wide for a tender charcoal-grilled fillet steak with onions and a baked potato. Sadly, our success was short-lived due to the 1974 Revolution.

After two years of trying to make ends meet, now on my own again in a tourist vacuum with a small son, I set off for pastures new. This time to Holland, having been told that all Amsterdammers spoke good English. Which was quite true. I had to insist that people spoke Dutch so I could learn the language! Here was my chance to get back into the film industry. It was a wonderful time to be doing creative work in the emerging commercial film business. First in the studios and all over Holland; and then travelling to find locations and building sets around the world.

As soon as Portugal started to recover from the isolation caused by the 25th April coup, I began longing for 'home'. I wheeled my ancient Harley Davidson and my Yamaha 650 Special motorbikes into my Renault Estafette (remember those blue vans with the sliding doors used by the French gendarmerie in the Tati movies?!). I slapped a mattress on top of the bikes for somewhere to sleep, piled my lovely old deal tables on the roof rack, said my goodbyes, and returned once more to Praia da Rocha.

✡ ꙮ ꙮ ✡

This has been all about my travels. What about the Algarve?

When I first came here in 1962, there was no dual carriageway for a dash south to the sunshine and beaches. Quality entertainment, museums, art, and book stores meant the inverse; a trip to Lisbon. The road was tortuous, taking almost five hours from Lagos, winding its way among cork-oak forests through Odemira, Cercal, Santiago do Cacém and Grandola. At last you would reach the long straight stretch to Alcácer do Sal where the branch road to Faro diverged. From there the choice was to queue to catch the ferry from Barreiro or race up to Vila Franca de Xira.

The magnificent Ponte Salazar bridge was only just starting construction, and would not be completed until 1966, by which time there would be an airport in Faro. Both heralded the beginning of real and viable tourist access to the Algarve. Back then it was a little-known hidden gem of golden sandy beaches overlooked by soaring russet cliffs.

There were few hotels, no developments, no apartment blocks, no airport. Entertainment was centred around the monthly cattle markets, the yearly circus, Saturday dances in village halls and in the old casino in Praia da Rocha, with the lads on one side, girls on the other, mothers in black sitting gossiping with a wary eye on their daughters. Not forgetting football. Many beaches were completely deserted, sea-bathing was not popular, and the sandy expanses were used for football. In wintertime, the beach cafés were dismantled, and the rain and pounding Atlantic waves lashed the cliffs below our hotel, which crumbled, scattering great rocks onto the sand.

To get to the nearby tiny fishing village of Benagil one wound down a precarious track on foot, or as we did, on horseback. Alvor was a little fishing village with a great expanse of inland lake. There were no tower blocks and hotels back then. There were orchards of almond and fig trees along the cliff edge all the way from Praia da Rocha. We would walk to Praia dos Três Irmãos, picking figs to eat and getting scolded by a farmer wielding an old rifle.

The Penina hotel and golf course of today was a saltwater wetland. The EN125 main road was then a narrow lane. You would see donkey carts ambling along, and a couple walking shaded by the ubiquitous black umbrella. Faro, the capital of the Algarve, was a two-hour drive away. It was the place one went to for any paperwork. If there were other places worth a visit on the way, I never knew of them. Beyond Faro was a long, narrow road to a car-ferry river crossing to Spain, a journey only made to renew the three-month visas that were inspected regularly by the P.I.D.E. the secret police.

Our little family-run pension was popular with those Portuguese families from Lisbon and the north with relatives in the Algarve, touring couples from all over Europe, and brave young adventurers.

There were write-ups in guidebooks, such as this quote from *Vista Portugal*:

"The *Pensão Solar Penguim* is a tiny, civilised British island in the midst of bogus Portuguese Grand Hotels, and it comes as a surprise to read many famous names in its visitors' book."

Unlike the other two or three hotels in Praia da Rocha, the Solar Penguin was not at all bogus, grand or smart, but casual and welcoming, therefore popular, and not only with British travellers.

Serving two proper meals a day, which was required for the operating licence; the menu consisted of soup, fish, a main meat course, and a sweet with wine and coffee. The cosy bar overlooking the beach attracted locals and foreigners alike. My father insisted the front door remained open at all times to welcome the weary traveller.

Every guest had to be registered with the P.I.D.E. My mother naively assumed couples with different surnames had not yet been issued with new passports and were on their honeymoon. Mother took the hotel laundry to be hand-washed in the river on the Monchique road, and there spread out to dry over cistus bushes, where the A22 motorway now roars overhead.

Living in the Algarve was healthy. Pre-wrapped foods were unheard of. There was no Piri-piri chicken in Monchique as yet, where delicious cured hams hung dripping from the café rafters. Fruit and vegetables arrived daily in carts from the *hortas* to the Portimão marketplace, on what is now the *Alameda* in the centre of town. Butchers surrounded the market, offering every cut of pork imaginable. Donkeys and mules chatted nose to nose in stables behind the market.

As the *traineiras*, the classic Portuguese coastal fishing boats, were unloaded dockside in Portimão, sardines were tossed up in baskets. They were packed in boxes of grated ice to go to one of the twenty-one canning factories surrounding the harbour, or trundled up in handcarts to the *Praça do Peixe*, where the fish was plentiful and cheap. Small children collected those sardines that fell from the baskets, to be grilled over tiny charcoal burners on the doorstep, then eaten wrapped in a slice of bread. A portion was always generously offered to a passer-by who stopped for a chat.

That is most of what I remember before leaving for Hong Kong in the autumn of 1966. When I returned in the spring of 1972, much had changed. Faro airport had opened, and the tourism industry blossomed with charter flights. Holidaymakers appeared in large groups and resorts were built to accommodate them. Others arrived to make a permanent or seasonal home in the Algarve. People coming from other newly independent African countries. People running from their own problems to this little 'semi third-world country'. People seeking adventure, a challenge, a new way of life, and retirees looking for warmth in the winter months.

The glorious wilderness of the Algarve, with its small farms and derelict cottages, was being sold up and estate agents were moving in. White villas started appearing, dotted about the countryside. Before, a trip to the interior driving on bare murram and rarely tarred roads, revealed tiny homesteads with a solitary olive or palm tree among scattered figs and almonds. A farmer would stop and stare as one drove by. That was the biggest difference to the area, the visual change to the landscape.

The leap forward did not last long. Democracy was bound to arrive, and as expected in early 1974, one morning it happened; the Red Carnation Revolution, the 'Dia 25 de Abril'. On the same day we heard that two lads killed themselves off the cliff at Praia do Vau in an appropriated Mercedes-Benz.

Here in the Algarve, the idea of taking from the rich and giving to the poor took hold, be it from rich Portuguese from the north, or from enterprising foreigners. Soon, where enough staff were employed and courageous, owners were locked out, and staff took over bars, restaurants, and similar businesses. A few foreign owners fled the country, having lost everything.

The Solar Penguin, having changed from a full-board pension to a small hotel in 1972, now had just a few part-time maids and was only affected by the lack of guests. These were hungry years for us as the burgeoning tourism industry was adversely affected, the currency value dropped dramatically, and exchanging escudos for hard currency was not permitted until the country's coffers were filled.

Freedom meant that before settling into democracy, the country languished through six governments. Angola and Mozambique gained independence in 1975, immigrants arrived and were housed in local hotels. They were hungry for work. Making a living became increasingly difficult. In 1976 I headed north, to Amsterdam, with my three-year-old son. My preceding two years' worth of bar tips amounted to just 105 Deutsche Marks, which because of currency restrictions I sewed into the waistband of his trousers.

○ෆ☼ෲ○

Returning to the Algarve in 1981, to a settled, democratic country, meant I could welcome production companies to film here. Advertising TV commercials were popular, as well as music videos, and corporate in-house documentaries. The weather, the coastline, and the varied landscapes, all allowed winter filming in locations that could resemble almost any country. My design and set-building skills were sought after by American, English, and European clients, to create scenes representing locations from their own countries, or even places in Africa or Australasia. Soon I added line production to my quiver. Casting, crewing, accommodating, and hiring vehicles and film equipment, I showed them Portugal. Faro airport offered direct flights to many destinations in Europe and onward. I had my home in the Algarve and I was free to travel anywhere in the world. How lucky can a lady be?!

Much changed in Praia da Rocha in those few short years. It used to be a series of lovely sandy coves linked by tunnels where people could swim and sunbathe peacefully. One could only paddle round the promontories at very low tide. Spring tides even filled the tunnels, which necessitated swimming dangerously round the rocky headlands.

Then the port authority decided to deepen the harbour of the river Arade for cruise ships by dredging and widening the beach to encourage mass tourism. A Dutch company was engaged, laying concrete pipes along the cliffs to pump the sludge. Each year they poured more dark-brown silt onto the 1,500-metre beach. An entire flight of steps and the drinking water fountain below the Solar Penguin disappeared.

Soon the fabulous rock formations that gave the beach its name were submerged, and the sea was driven hundreds of metres from the cliffs. As the rain washed and the sun bleached the sand, it became a desert-like expanse. Where the tide crept in, shallow mirage-like lakes came and went. Children sailed toy boats. Lifeguards moved the sunshades and umbrellas closer to the sea. The sand was very soft and hot, making it difficult to walk. They solved this problem by laying concrete flagstone paths. Now, many years later, people still walk along those paths in crocodile fashion.

It was during this time, encouraged by the then Swedish Consul, Tomas Halberg, himself a fighter pilot, that I took my single-engine pilot's licence in a Cessna 172 Skyhawk at Faro airport, thus discovering our beautiful coastline from the air. The licence also gave me the opportunity to hire a plane and fly myself to hunt for film locations as far away as Alicante.

When location hunting in America, the Caribbean, or East Africa, on renting a small plane and pilot, I would only have to mention my little private pilot's licence and the pilot would sit back and relax. Notwithstanding, I did have a few scary moments; including a burst tyre at Scottsdale airport in Pheonix, Arizona. Also a late-night landing by four-wheel-drive headlights in Amboseli. And a herd of zebra racing across the bushland landing track at touchdown at the Tana Delta in Northern Kenya. Flying a single-engine plane is always an adventure.

By the mid-eighties, together with a good friend, I opened an art and picture-framing gallery in Portimão, holding exhibitions bi-annually. I re-opened the Terrace Grill restaurant, working with some wonderful staff that are still friends today, and commuted to film locations all over the world.

Running an open-air eatery has its moments. The British Navy docked regularly in the newly built deep-water harbour in Portimão. Very proper and correct naval officers flocked to the Terrace Grill. One evening a howling gale tore at the awning, yanking at the pillars, cracking the walls, and threatening to carry us over the cliff.

The officers leapt to the rescue. Hauling in the sheets, they became young, joyful sailors once again. Drinks were on the house that night!

On another occasion, hearing screams and seeing fisticuffs and struggles on the stairs below the terrace, we called the port authority. Their response was: "Come and get us, we have no transport."

One evening, I vividly recall Senhor Caracol, the fishmonger, walking between the fully occupied tables with an entire tuna fish on his shoulder and tossing it onto the galley floor. He wiped his hands on a dishcloth, and smiling proudly at the eating customers, asked for a beer. I underlined 'fresh' tuna on the blackboard. We got a round of applause!

The good times continued into the nineties. The Algarve boomed and learnt what development could bring. Marinas for pleasure craft, golf courses for punters and professionals, tennis academies, health clinics, and international schools, to name a few.

My son grew up, left university, and moved to Holland. I rediscovered East Africa. Tanganyika, now Tanzania, opened its borders and emerged as a fascinating, popular destination to film. My commuter flights changed direction, taking me through Amsterdam, south to Nairobi and Kilimanjaro airports. Memories merge into one long, busy, exciting, fulfilling, and happy time.

○ɷ✧ଔ○

Today we are living in a very different Algarve. Fast highways, shopping malls, vast hypermarkets, liveried cars, dapper salespeople, magnificent holiday resorts, cheap high-rise apartments, a new airport, and a world-class Formula One *autódromo*. Beach festivals, music venues, and entertainment cater for every taste.

Extending out into the countryside around each town now is a well-to-do, modern middle-class suburb, housing the influx of company owners and employees. Some smaller towns and villages have not changed quite as much. For the past thirty years, I have lived contentedly in a very small town on a hilltop with a beautiful listed heritage church.

My mother asked me to build her a house nearby, and she moved here from Praia da Rocha thirteen years ago. At a hundred and two years old, she has lived in the Algarve longer than any foreigner that I know of. The young couples that relocated to the new *bairro* built in the eighties are now grandparents. Their children refurbished and moved into the old houses in the original village when their grandparents died. They stay because work abounds in the resorts, the amenities services, and the building trade. The local junior school has a waiting list. The streets are cleaned, and the garbage is collected daily. It is a closely knit society of old feuds and friendships. For them, very little changes.

Myself excepted. Over the last twenty years I gradually withdrew from the commercial film circuit, became involved in stage design for local amateur dramatics, produced independent films, and more importantly, started to sketch, draw and paint, just for myself. Designing, drawing, and painting to represent and deliver film sets has always been a part of my working life, but for the client and the film director, not for myself. During forty years of making a living through creative productivity to fulfil someone else's story, the artist within was on hold.

During the last ten years, aside from producing a few independent films, I have started taking myself as an artist seriously. I have filled many sketchbooks and painted constantly, experimenting with many mediums; acrylics, oils, watercolour, and collage. My objectivity has become focussed and has evolved into a search for the portrayal of my expression as an artist. Derived from many years representing 'the real world', my work is naturally figurative and realistic, capturing what I see. The need to tell a story through each work is paramount. From a simple sketch in a notebook, to an ambitious giant dolphin created from plastic waste to remind us of the danger to our oceans, to a tongue-in-cheek social comment, every art work I create tells a story. I continue striving to escape the portrayal of just that which I see and to express what is in my mind's eye. For me, my creative work is an adventure of discovery on life's long, exciting journey.

Perhaps my contribution to a picture of the Algarve can be

exemplified by *The Right Juice*, my first and most difficult independent film venture. The movie gently and humorously characterised the various people I have already outlined that come to settle in the Algarve. The original idea was a script by David Butler-Cole, veteran of amateur dramatic plays and comedy shows, for whom I had enjoyed building stage sets since the millennium year. My son, Kristjan Knigge, living in Amsterdam, and now a father and film director himself, collaborated with David on the script and returned to the Algarve to direct the film.

Aside from the two English leads, we did all the casting here. The two Portuguese leads are stars of television, stage, and cinema. For smaller roles we drew on the local community, both Portuguese, especially the Seniors Theatre Group at Tempo theatre in Portimão, and for the British, finding important roles among the aforementioned expats.

Crowdfunding, securing backing, and arranging loans, was a long and difficult process taking two years. Locations were discovered and freely loaned for the duration of the shoot. Few local film crews were willing and available, so colleagues came from Amsterdam. Vila Vita Parc, the Holiday Inn, and the Colina dos Mouros hotel gave them all accommodation. The star department was catering. Friends rallied round to cook and serve. We borrowed tables, chairs, and equipment. Intermarché supermarket in Carvoeiro gave us supplies. Wonderful hot meals kept us nourished through the rainiest spring weather in years. With judicious editing, the sunny Algarve shines through the movie.

What's next for me, I wonder?

❦❦❦

Following a career in art, film and TV; Artist, Film Producer, Art Director, Set Designer and long-term Algarve resident BJ Boulter now spends her time painting and sketching and creating striking artwork and sculptures.

You can find out more about her work on her website: www.bjboulter.com

13

Under the Star-filled Sky
USCHI KUHN

My full name is Uschi-Ursula Brigitte Kuhn. I was born in Heidelberg, Germany, under the star sign Leo. Happy and full of mischief, artistic, different, crazy, a bird of paradise, always smiling, dancing, and very helpful. This is what people say about me. I am a big rebel and I am always fighting for those not as fortunate as myself, and for women's and children's rights. I am a strong and ambitious person.

I wanted to study art, but back when I was born my father thought girls didn't need to study. He said they should learn a skill to earn money, marry, and have children. I still cannot believe this way of thinking. Women were building up Germany after the war as the men came back ill or had died. It's not that long ago that women still had to get permission from their husband or father to go to work or start a business.

I learnt the hairdressing trade, but my interests lay with art and style. I completed a three-year apprenticeship in the most exclusive shop in Heidelberg, with a fantastic boss who always told me to memorise everything with my eyes. He said to me,

"You never know, you may need it one day."

How right he was. I was very ambitious, I wanted to learn more and to be a makeup artist for shows and competitions. I loved creating fantasy makeup with crazy hairstyles, and I made myself known locally. I won a lot of competitions in different countries and people recognised my style in my local town.

At one of the competitions, I met my husband, who came from a well-known hairdressing family.

Bang!!!

He married me on the spot.

I could not say no, he loved me and accepted me as I was.

I wanted to travel and explore the world. I was aged twenty when we emigrated to South Africa. You cannot believe how shocked my family, friends, and my boss were. At that time, you went to America, but not Africa. Nobody knew anything about South Africa, its people, and wild animals. We thought we would see elephants walking down the main streets of Cape Town. We arrived with two suitcases and enough money for one person to fly back to Germany.

The only question was who would stay and who would go home if it didn't work out? But we were young and in love, and we believed we could move the world around and achieve everything that we dreamt of. We established hairdressing and beauty shops with a partner and friend who was in the same position as we were. We eventually moved from a small apartment to a house. OK, it sounds easy now, but we worked hard to achieve our success.

We then moved to a new house under Signal Hill with two Alsatian dogs, several cats, and two children. Time went by and my heart belonged to South Africa. From being a teenager, I grew up to become a woman. I was successful and happy, and a free spirit.

After ten years, we took the decision, as hard as it was, to return to Germany. We wanted to give our children better and safer opportunities for their future. We had to give up everything, our house, business, friends, our lives, and it was very difficult. Children who are born and bred in South Africa live a wild free life, with beaches, the sea, lots of friends, and sunshine. My son asked me one day,

"Why does Germany have no stars?"

The sky was always so dark.

Get on with it, I kept telling myself. You have the forest, the wine, Heidelberg, and Leimen, my new hometown. I had a new business, a new house, a power job, and a name. I told myself to get on with my life and achieve something great.

In the evenings, I studied for my master's degree. In Germany you have to complete a three-year apprenticeship in hairdressing, and then you must work as a qualified hairdresser for a further three years. To open a salon and have staff and teach the trade you need to study for another year and after passing the exams you get your master's degree. After this you can study for a further colour and style degree. I went to Dale Carnegie to learn how to deliver speeches, then I got an extra job from Goldwell (an established hair firm) doing shows.

In Leimen, my shows and work were now well known. I was getting involved with running benefit shows to raise money for children, crèches, and cancer treatments for children. With the help of my friends, we organised the biggest convoy of aid to Romania to help children in homes and children with HIV/AIDS. This was in 1990, and I wanted to see for myself where all the goods, medicines, and help went. We were five women in total, and we travelled with the Red Cross to Romania. There was a lot of discussion before we were allowed to travel. We transported one hundred tonnes of goods and 500,000 Deutsche Marks' worth of medicine to Oradea, in Romania. We had a doctor for support and an ambulance. On the Romanian border we heard shooting going on, but we made it through safely, and we were a great group working together to help others. What I saw there I will never forget.

꩜

Working on my shows and starting to create art got me back into painting again. First, I painted on paper and then on bodies. I was working with Goldwell and Wella, and I found an article for entering a big competition which involved creating day makeup, fantasy makeup, and body art. My lovely daughter convinced me to enter and said she would sit as a model for me. After a lot of training and hard work, we brought home the trophy from Paris. I must give credit to my children and my husband for all the support they have given me.

Holding an exhibition was my next dream, and using the space in my hairdressing salon to market myself, the idea was born under the name 'Salon Kuhn'. I advertised 'Art on hair and body - Models needed!!!'. But then I ran into a problem. I couldn't paint someone and leave them standing around for two days in an exhibition! What could I do instead? My brain ran amok. I needed a solution. I created moulds from live bodies and used window dolls and mannequins. Nothing was safe anymore from my hands. After an entire summer working on these ideas, hairdressing during the day and working at night on my creations, with many sleepless nights, I was ready. September arrived, the month of the big annual wine festival in Leimen. My exhibition was ready for the opening night of the festival.

It was a tremendous success and all my hard work was worthwhile. "Wow!" was the reaction of the visitors. I was so grateful to my husband and my children, and our staff who helped such a lot. The news spread, the television crews came and did a film about me with the title 'Interesting People of the Region - Uschi Kuhn'.

I was working hard, but my mind kept wandering back to South Africa and I kept dreaming that one day I wanted to live in the sun again. My South Africa was calling me, but I knew it was too far away. My husband and I went on holiday to many different countries until we visited Portugal. I stepped out of the airplane and there was an instant feeling of coming home. The sun, the sea, the flowers, the countryside, and the mountains. It was my Table Mountain. We quickly bought a little house behind São Lourenço Church in Almancil.

I came out to furnish the house with two girlfriends. We were loaded up with bedding, cushions, and everything we needed for the first night. At the airport they asked us if we were going to fly to America because of all the luggage we had. Thank goodness we were flying with Lufthansa and not Ryanair!

The house had wooden windows and was not really made for winter. I remember the first night, we had a storm and heavy rain. It was a good job we had our bedding. I was so cold, the hair on my head was moving in the night, the house was so draughty. There was little insulation and no heating.

We were pioneers again. We built the garden and pool ourselves. My husband, myself, my children, friends, and parents all working together and we all had a great time. Seventeen years ago, the airport was small, the streets narrow with little shops and markets. It was lovely. We brought everything from Germany, which we could not get or did not find in Portugal. We loved the people, we started to learn Portuguese, we made friends, and said *bom dia*, and *obrigada* to everybody.

We tried to visit as often as we could. We loved the red wine and grilled sardines, the chicken Piri-piri devoured on the beach, Portuguese cheese, exploring the countryside, and nights sat eating under the stars and enjoying mega sunsets.

Then came the day to make a decision. I could not go on anymore. We had big discussions regarding what we still wanted to do in life. Our grandchildren were born whom I love dearly, but I was tired and wanted a break from working so hard. My husband decided he wanted a bigger property in the Algarve. He said to me,

"I have finished looking after this garden in one day, what shall I do for the rest of the week?"

He wanted to retire and have ostriches running in the garden. We needed to find a bigger property. The Deutsche Mark was very high against the escudos. Germany was talking about the euro. We started exploring up and down the Algarve until we found it. On the edge of Loulé, in the countryside, we found a ruin nobody wanted. We bought it in no time. My reason for buying the property was the view. I could see Table Mountain.

Once we had purchased the ruin, I asked my brother for advice. His reply was,

"Oh my God, I can only see work."

Very helpful!

Oh well, I thought, that's the challenge before us, because I can see how it could look. I have never experienced anything like this before and believe me, living in South Africa, I know.

I am talking eighteen years ago, today, maybe it is better or maybe not? I discovered that you have to be there on a building site all the time. The materials must be delivered, you have to deal with people not coming; you set a time schedule and people don't keep to it. Those stories could fill page after page; it was a very stressful time. But in the end we made it, and it was all worthwhile.

We ended up with a new house, because we had to knock down what looked like something you see in old movies. It was not suitable to live in. Gaining planning permission can take years, unless you know somebody who knows somebody else. It is not easy. We had a recommendation of a German-speaking building firm with architects. They were very helpful and nice, but it still took over a year of us flying back and forth to sort everything out. Whenever I came out, I always thought the building team must have contacted Frankfurt Airport to check the passenger list, because miraculously workers were always on the building site when we arrived. The site always looked like a rubbish dump until one day I lost my temper and started screaming out loud,

"*Isso é uma casa do porco?*" ("Is this a pigsty?").

The building project was giving me grey hair. It took another year to complete the house. For the garden I made my own plans. I read a lot of books, walked around the property, and bought plants in every season. Now I have flowers all year round. You have to learn which plants don't need a lot of water and which plants will survive and thrive in the strong sun out here.

The next step had begun. Leaving my children behind in Germany, together with my home, my town, my business, and my friends, I thought, what have I done? We moved to Portugal, and it rained, no, it poured, like heaven was crying. That first Christmas I walked into Loulé town. There were beautiful decorations everywhere, Christmas music was playing, and I thought to myself, did I really want this? Tears poured out of my eyes.

I started a hair and beauty business, but nobody knew me. At home I was a star—here I was completely unknown. This was the hardest start I had ever known. But slowly, mixing with people, going to women's afternoon tea parties, saying hello to all the neighbours, giving little parties, getting my name around with the German communities, I got some work.

The first show I did involving hair and makeup with models was a German October festival. My removal firm wanted some entertainment for their clients. What a surprise for them when the model bride wearing nothing more than a lacy body-painting came on stage. I had ten models and had forgotten that I had no staff to help me prepare them. The event went into the local *Algarve Resident* newspaper and *Entdecken Sie Algarve* magazine, and people started talking about me.

We then experienced big fires in Monchique. I had never witnessed such fires, and I knew we needed to help and raise funds for the people involved. Of course, I could put on a show!! I chose 'The Phantom of the Opera' as my theme. Friends from Germany flew in to help, and we had twelve models wearing black gowns with white masks walking to the music of the opera around my swimming pool. My neighbours thought the Ku Klux Klan were meeting up! It looked fantastic. Friends helped with a BBQ and we raised a lot of money to give to people who lost their homes.

Wella, the hairdressing company, then invited me to do a body painting show in the Casino Madeira. The show and subsequent workshops brought me back to life again. I could be creative, mad, crazy. It reminded me of my time back in Germany.

✥❧✥❦✥

As time went on, I was asked to join the Almancil International Rotary Club. This is a network of friends, leaders, and problem-solvers based in the Algarve. Their aim is to create a world where people unite and take action to create lasting change in our communities and in ourselves. It is an English-speaking community service organisation and its members are a network of business and professional leaders devoted to the Rotary's motto: 'Service above Self'.

For over one hundred years, the Rotary's people of action have used their passion, energy, and intelligence to take action on sustainable projects, including literacy and peace, fresh water, and health. They are always working to better our world.

Their guiding principles are:
"Is it the truth?
Is it fair to all concerned?
Will it build goodwill and better friendships?
Will it be beneficial to all concerned?"

My husband and I started to get to know a lot of people helping those in need, and raising money by organising events. They were good times, until 2013, when my husband passed away.

In 2015-16, I was elected as the first female president of the Almancil International Rotary Club. Well, being the first female president was not easy, but I had lots of help. The president has a board, there are five people who all work together. There is the president, a secretary, a treasurer, a master of ceremonies, and the next incoming president.

In the Almancil branch, we have about forty members of all ages. We organise a wide range of fundraisers, from golf tournaments, Christmas events, virtual dog shows, country music BBQs, visits to local attractions and sites and lots more. We support the local food bank to feed the poor, and fundraise for the local schools, autistic children, and charities that work with Alzheimer's disease, the environment, and summer camps for students. We join in with other Rotary clubs all over the world by Zoom; we have very inspiring speakers every week, and have our meeting point at the Conrad Hotel.

The year 2020 was a difficult year to raise money because of Covid-19, but we have continued to meet every week via Zoom to keep up the contact with each other. We have set up virtual events, supporting each other and other Rotary clubs all over the country. 2020-21 was also my time to become Rotary President again. This time around, I decided to focus on a big international project on plastic and our ocean. It makes me very upset to see what we do to our planet. This country is safe and beautiful, and has a lot of nature, culture, countryside, and seaside to enjoy, and the air is like champagne.

※☙✧❧※

I started to paint again and showed my paintings in a local art gallery. I believed in my angels and tried to heal from my loss with the help of my Rotarian friends and by meeting lots of international people. Portugal, the sun, the sea, and its people have been good to me and I bow my head to this country.

My life is displayed in the colours I choose to paint with, which show my state of mind and my feelings. I paint mainly landscapes and flowers. I try to create everything to find out if I can do it. I love to paint bodies and sketch, and have created sculptures for the garden—hanging shoes in trees—which makes me smile. I feel my angels around me and meditate with them. They help me. I have my art studio, a wooden house tucked away in the garden. This is my place to relax and forget everything. Overlooking the countryside, I feel much nearer to heaven and I am at peace.

In life and work, the show must go on. My garden developed like a park, and a new adventure was on the horizon. Loving art, painting, and mixing with arty people, made my life turn in a new direction. I set up an Art Retreat on site. I was ready to create body paintings again and give art classes. Art groups can now come and stay here and sleep in lovely rooms, or I can offer day classes. People come and relax on holiday, meditate, or simply do nothing and just enjoy the garden and location.

My life became filled with laughter, fun, a new partner, and travel again. My favourite thing now is to sit on the beach, have a drink, and eat fresh fish with the stars above my head. Life is good in Portugal. I would not like to live anywhere other than here.

❁ɕ❁ɕ❁

To discover more about the work of the Almancil International Rotary Club, visit their website:
www.rotaryalmancil.org

14

The Healing Touch
MARYANNE SEA

Hello, I am Maryanne Sea, and I am a Thursday's child. And 'Thursday's child has far to go!', as my great-aunt Josephine used to remind me often.

She was right. I have gone far—far from my hometown of Summit, New Jersey, USA, to a life in Australia, then Canada, back to the US, then returning to Australia for many years, and on to Ecuador, France, Malta, and now Portugal.

However, what Josephine did not know is that I would have to travel another journey, one deep within myself, in order to heal from extreme environmental illness.

At twenty-five, after just completing my master's degree, my life would change forever. I crossed a street in a Michigan blizzard and got hit head-on by a car that was accelerating at top speed to make it up a frozen hill.

Two years later, I weighed less than seventy pounds (about thirty-two kilogrammes) and was labelled 'permanently and totally disabled' as a result of extreme chemical, food, and inhalant sensitivity. In short, my immune system crashed after the accident and I became allergic/sensitive to virtually everything on this earth.

To recover, I had to live in a 'bubble', a room with nothing but two chairs and a lamp. I could not touch a pen, paper, books, my mail, or just about anything else associated with normal daily living.

The logic of this extreme isolation was simple—avoidance (of everything) would build tolerance (perhaps not of everything, but of something). This was the hope.

This journey through environmental illness took years, but it was, fortunately, not one I traversed alone. A wonderful man came to visit me one day and decided he wanted to return. He is still by my side forty-two years later.

After twenty-two years of living in various degrees of isolation from the chemically laden world we live in, I found my way back. As soon as I did, I started to champion a holistic (mind, body, emotions, and spirit) approach to healing, and began teaching doctors and nurses in hospitals and universities in Australia.

I was also blessed to discover that my sensitivity was a gift—it could actually help people. I became an 'intuitive', someone who calls upon their intuition to help others heal and grow. I work with people who have all kinds of challenges, physical, emotional, financial, and relational, and my goal is always the same—to allow my intuition to guide me to the content (emotions, thoughts, and traumatic events) stored in my client's body. I know that if we can see and feel and eventually release what is stored inside us, then it no longer takes such a toll on our bodies and our lives.

My most special work is with babies before they are born, as we know, without a doubt, that babies before birth are highly sentient, or capable of feeling, long before they are born.

Much as I love my work and am thankful for people's praise, what I am most proud of in my life is that I did not give up. Even when on many days I was so sensitive that I could not have anything —even clothes—near me, I somehow found the strength to keep going. And I will remain forever grateful to the countless sources of loving kindness who nourished this strength in me.

✧ↇ✧ↂ✧

My husband, Cory, and I moved to Portugal in 2013. We did not know much about Portugal. All we knew is that we needed to find a country to live in! We had been living in France but knew we could not stay there forever because we were not permitted (ever) to earn any money. We moved to Malta because it is English speaking and I had taught in universities and hospitals in Australia and thought perhaps I could teach in Malta. However, after arriving there to live for three months (the requirement for residency), we discovered the government programme for residency was now defunct. The person helping us did not know about the change.

That same day, we looked at a map of the world and wondered where we could go next. We thought, why not try Sicily? We called the Italian Relocation Centre and spoke to someone called Damien O'Farrell, which seemed like a strange name for someone advocating Italy. Quickly we found out that dear Damien was not advocating Italy, in fact he told us NOT to come to Italy, but to go to Portugal. And he gave us the name of a lawyer to call.

That call with the lawyer was life transforming. I come from a family of four lawyers and a judge, so I knew, within a second, that this was a special lawyer.

He spent almost an hour on the phone with me. I told him I was so exhausted from three international moves in less than three years, that I did not know if I had the strength to do another.

He simply said to me,

"Can you get yourself to Portugal on Christmas Day and be in my office at 9 a.m. on the 26th of December with your passports?"

I said we could. To which he replied,

"That's all you need to do. I will handle everything else." And he did.

After that, we came to the tiny village of Ferragudo, Portugal, in February 2013, and fell in love with this little village. The beautiful sunshine, the cobblestone streets, the square, the people, all touched my heart. We found Ferragudo in the same way we discovered nearly all the places we have lived—intuitively.

I relaxed, looked at a map of Portugal, and let my intuition guide me to a tiny spot on the map.

We 'just knew' that this little place on the map might well be the perfect location for us to settle.

We arrived in February and the town really was so quiet. It took a few days for me to learn that this was a place that thrived on tourism, and the tourist season did not include the winter months.

Yet its charm and beauty were everywhere, from the small fruit and vegetable shops selling the Algarve's own and very delicious oranges, figs, and almonds, to the town square encircled by cafés and restaurants. We loved the resplendent views from the cliffs, and the townspeople who graciously welcome a total stranger, like ourselves.

It was not difficult at all to make friends in Ferragudo, and we have found this true in all the Algarve. The Portuguese welcome efforts to speak their language, but do not judge any failed attempts, or even no attempts at all!

And I had no qualms about finding the correct words in Google Translate, writing them down, and if my pronunciation was wrong, showing my papers to those interested enough to read them.

It did not take long to feel like we belonged here. For me, this came through volunteer efforts with *animais de rua* (animals of the street), which drew me naturally in contact with the mayor and other Portuguese people who cared about animals. But I also joined various expat groups, including, of all things, a German choir!

I am passionate about unsprayed—bio or organic—fruits and vegetables. I enjoy finding them, eating them, and encouraging others to forego sprayed food. So, this was another easy point of entry for me here in the Algarve. I met those who shared my passion and joined the local community garden, taking my plot right between a German woman's and a Portuguese man's. And I found incredibly nutritious organic food across the river at various places in the adjacent town of Portimão.

We decided to rent and spent four years in Ferragudo and have now clocked up an additional three in Portimão, where we are blessed to live in a home that overlooks the river and the boardwalk.

We have fallen in love with the 'city life' of Portimão and enjoy being able to walk to just about everything here in the town. I like being part of a neighbourhood, which is not something we had in Ferragudo. We could sense this if we walked into the village, but did not necessarily feel this on the street we lived on. Our apartment in Portimão is near the boardwalk so we can walk by the river and enjoy watching children eating ice cream cones, and dogs walking briskly—or slowly—with their owners. We can say hello to all those whose kiosks offer boat rides, walk all the way down to the row of sardine restaurants, and finish with a rest right in the town square itself, which has a wonderful fountain crossing virtually its entire length.

We have again made friends quite easily and know lots of people who live or work near us. And, of course, if we want to appreciate the tranquillity of Ferragudo, it is only a five-minute drive away.

We love seeing the tourists come each year and, most of all, we are delighted with the local bio market and bio grocery, both of which are within easy walking distance of our home.

The bio market has two vendors, Carla and Paulo. Both manage certified organic farms in Silves, and both arrive on Saturday morning at 9 a.m. to sell their fruits, vegetables, nuts, seeds, wine, olive oil, dried fruit, beer, legumes and more until 1 p.m. The markets are busy. One owner has seen a six-fold increase in business in five years! More and more people want food that is not sprayed with glyphosate or genetically modified. Confirming this increased interest is the fact that one of the large grocery stores here in Portimão now has a vast bio section, offering produce, meat, groceries, frozen foods, and refrigerated items like cheese and butter. I can't comment in any significant way on the difference in prices, as I have only purchased bio (organic) food for many years. For me, the extra cost is worth it, as it means I stay healthy.

The local grocery store in Portimão, Bio Mercearia, is lovely. It has so much character and is constantly adding new items to its shelves, including bio nail polish and dishwasher tablets to its extensive list of regular items, which includes cheese, vegetables, fruits, grains, wine and beer, milks, cosmetics and more. The shop has an online business too, and delivers every week to people all over Portugal, not just in the Algarve. The grocery is also a café and I can't count the times I have met friends there and loved sitting either inside or outside near the river.

The expat community is strong here, and together we are able to help animals and humans in need. I am actively involved with a charity called Algarve Network for Families in Need. I liaise with my local coordinator every week and provide what they need for local families. The other organisations I have supported, primarily through donations, include several animal-focused organisations: the Refúgio dos Burros, (Donkey Sanctuary), home to around one-hundred-and-fifty animals of all kinds, APAA (Associação de Protecção dos Animais do Algarve), which offers an effective 'Spay and Neuter' programme and covers the veterinary care bills of the animals of families in need, and Algarve Dog Re-Homing, which has found new homes for hundreds of dogs since its inception.

For animal lovers, it can be upsetting to read or see stories of animal abandonment and mistreatment here. The good news is that there are many, many people who are highly dedicated to changing the situation.

We have lived, as I mentioned, in many countries and have truly appreciated all of them, but Portugal has a special place in our hearts for lots of reasons. Portugal offers the most beautiful weather you can imagine and the sun shines almost every day! The people are kind and welcoming—despite their less than ideal driving habits—and genuinely accept and appreciate those who have migrated here.

I think there are many things about living in Portugal that helped me become much stronger, and these include the bio food, and the temperate climate, the air quality, and most of all, the sense of community. Cory and I have made a lot of friends here, and I believe this sense of community is so important in staying well.

Though we are not citizens, we are free to work here. My husband, a retired psychologist and naturopath, can now pursue his love of music and art. He has been welcomed by many Portuguese musicians and has had some wonderful opportunities to play music, especially in the tourist season.

I now work as a somatic (body-oriented) therapist for people with challenges of all kinds, including those with a history of trauma. I also work with women trying to conceive and those who are pregnant. Finally, I run complimentary Powerful Intention groups for people all over the world who want to give and receive the power of strong, heartfelt intentions. All my work is online. It is quite easy for me to work at home using the internet, and I have not had any trouble with the internet signal here in Portugal.

I am so grateful that Portugal allows us both to work.

✧෨✧ൟ✧

My work with animals began soon after I got here. The woman who drove me around, before I purchased a car, had a dog. The dog looked terribly neglected and clearly had medical problems. And the owner seemed remote, lost in her own pain.

I felt I needed to help the dog, and in the process, perhaps help her.

I engendered her trust in me and then jumped in. With her permission, I changed the dog's diet completely, purchased soft bedding, and visited twice a day to take him out for walks and trips to the beach. He blossomed, and she seemed to thrive, too.

It was a real commitment as I never missed a day unless I was travelling and then I hired someone to take over for me.

Soon after, I noticed a dog lying under a truck in the centre of Ferragudo. I cried when I saw him. He was scared, with his ears almost completely eaten off by some disease, and he had rashes all over his body. And he was absolutely terrified of my approaching him at all.

I went to the *junta de freguesia* (the town council) and heard the dog's story. He had been badly abused by his first owner and left to wander the streets after the owner died. Later he was hit by a car and had no veterinary care afterwards, resulting in a terrible limp. He was now living in a dilapidated garage with a man who was an alcoholic, who had no money, but wanted to give him a home.

Again, I jumped in, but this move was more complicated. The owner spoke no English and had an 'old mentality' in relation to vets. In short, he believed vets were evil.

It took some convincing the owner, who was named Chico, but eventually the vet came and gave the dog, called Fiel, three months to live.

I was not comfortable with this prediction. I knew it would take longer to heal this dog's spirit.

So my 'Fiel project' began. I built more trust with Chico, so that I was allowed to visit his property every day with lots of homemade food, new beds, blankets, hot packs in the winter, and the medicine prescribed by the vet.

In the process, Chico was happy to shift the care of all his animals to me, which meant that eventually I was taking care of twenty-six cats, two chickens, and three dogs—every day, rain or shine—365 days a year.

I did this for three-and-a-half years, and after two-and-a-half years, my little Fiel finally relaxed and let me tap his head once very gently. By the time he died in my arms a year later, I could sit and massage him each day for as long as my hands and arms would hold out.

Great healing began to occur in that old, mouldy, terribly run-down home. Chico stopped drinking! His son, a troubled soul, started to let some love in. His son's dog, who had been badly neglected, was also given a whole new lease of life.

I spent almost four years on that property. Though I always tended to recoil from the squalor, I found a way to serve all the beings who lived there, and I am so happy I could.

I was there with Chico, when we both discovered that his wife had died suddenly in her bed. A year later, I went to the hospital and held this man's hand when he appeared to be dying too. But the greatest triumph was in the life of his son. After two years of demonstrating that he clearly did not like me, this young man allowed me to hold him in his arms as he sobbed after his dog's death.

And I learnt how to move beyond any ideas or expectations or judgments of what my life should look like and just follow my heart.

○෨✧ෆ○

My Portuguese language skills fall into the category of basic minimalist. For most of my time here, I have been working with animals who seem very happy to become bi-lingual. For the rest of the time, I have been on calls with my therapy clients, with whom my English needs to be very precise.

So I have not learnt more than the basics of Portuguese, though if a person speaks slowly, I surprise myself with how much I can understand.

And I must remember that most nights when I went to Fiel's home, I stayed half-an-hour and watched a game show called *O Preço Certo* with Fiel's owner. After that, I would watch ten minutes of news, and then 'Professor' Chico, who had never attended one day of school in his life, would quiz me.

Chico is no longer alive, but I do suspect he is looking down on me and is frustrated by my not moving beyond my minimalist basic level of Portuguese, but I also believe he is happy that all his animals were cared for to their very last days.

And I do have my husband to lean on. I am happy to say that Cory studied hard and passed the Government's A2 Level Portuguese language exam, which is no small feat!

It may also have helped him understand better the Portuguese love of bureaucracy and systems, which has always dumbfounded me. Like many, I needed to change my driver's licence from an Australian to a Portuguese one. This process got off to a great start! I hired a woman who handles these kinds of tasks for expats, and she happily handed me a piece of paper that said I was allowed to drive, and told me to expect my licence within a month.

The month came and went, but no licence. Two months, three months, then four months went by and still no licence. More papers permitting me to drive were issued, but no licence appeared.

I called and called the Licence Department and received various excuses ranging from:

"The photocopier is broken."

"Your photograph is blurry, please drive to Faro, (an hour away), so that we can take another."

"The photographer is sick—don't come to Faro for another photo, we'll use this photo."

"The photographer is better—do come to Faro, we can't use this photo."

"We already sent the licence to you, but it was returned, saying you did not live in Portugal."

And when these explanations ran out, we started at the beginning again, and I learnt that the photocopier, the apparently quite tired and dilapidated photocopier, was broken again.

Finally, the good news came—the licence was sitting on the director's desk waiting for him to sign it. Then they would send it to me in the mail.

Having been forewarned never to lose my patience with a government official, I politely queried,

"And will it take about a week or two for the director to sign it?"

"Oh, no, it will be at least three or four months!" came the reply.

Six months later, I finally received my licence. I held it in my hand and uttered a small gasp. Next to the section entitled

Nationality were the words: Reino Unido (United Kingdom). Overnight, I had become a British citizen!

I am not a British citizen, so I thought I should call and ask them to correct it, but my Portuguese friends thought better of it. Better to feign a British accent to any police officer who stopped me than to start the process all over again.

It took two-and-a-half years to change my driving licence, and with every renewal, I remain a British citizen.

However, the sunshine, the openness of the Portuguese, the freedom to do work that I love, and the opportunity to do some good in a country, whose people, generally speaking, are not rich, far outweighs the bureaucratic challenges.

I will always be grateful to Portugal, and hope I can continue to give back to a country that has given me so much. And I truly hope that all who come to live in Portugal have the same blessed life that Cory and I have had.

✿ෆ✿ඣ✿

For more information about Maryanne's upcoming book, *Love is the Healer*, the story of her journey through environmental illness and beyond, visit her website:
www.maryannesea.com

15

Creating Safe Communities
DAVID THOMAS, MBE, BEM, CPM

I was adopted at just a few weeks old. I lived in Carshalton, Surrey, England, in a middle-class area where all the streets were named after poets. I joined the local branch of the Air Training Corps when I was twelve. I remained there until I was twenty, by which time I was on the adult staff. I really enjoyed this as I flew in gliders and aircraft, and learnt how to fire a variety of weapons — not at people or animals, of course! We went camping and visited various RAF stations, which no doubt led to me eventually deciding to join the RAF.

In 1972 I met Jane, who was a children's librarian at Croydon Public Library. I should add this was not because I was reading children's books, but because her colleague had suggested that we should meet, on account of the fact that I was the proud owner of a Jaguar E-Type at the time. After six months of whizzing around in this lovely car, or should I say whizzing around in my car with lovely Jane, we got married.

For the first few months we lived apart whilst I undertook the RAF commissioned officer training programme, but upon graduation as a pilot officer we moved to Yorkshire. I completed my training in a Chipmunk aircraft and, upon passing that, moved onto the Jet Provost intermediate pilot training course. We lived at RAF Dishforth, in North Yorkshire, which was a dormitory station whilst I flew from RAF Lynton on Ouse.

However, I soon discovered that flying was not for me. Flying upside down in a jet aircraft fifty feet above the ground was not good as far as my digestion was concerned! I went for re-selection at RAF Biggin Hill and was offered the RAF Regiment. Sadly, during the processing of the application, Prime Minister Harold Wilson announced the defence cuts of 1974, and the course was axed. With limited promotion opportunities available, I decided to leave the RAF.

At that point I considered joining the British Army, the Canadian Armed forces, the Metropolitan Police, or the Royal Hong Kong Police (RHKP).

I attended the extended interviews for the RHKP in London. I was accepted, and on 8th November 1974 Jane and I were off to begin a new life together in the Far East. So began my thirty-year career as a police officer in Hong Kong. Over this period I covered security work, operational day-to-day policing; and police training, planning and development. My last post for three years was Assistant Commissioner – Training and Development. All of this no doubt held me in good stead for my future work in setting up the Safe Communities Portugal initiative.

Our two children, Shelley and Sophie, were both born at the British military hospital in Hong Kong. They grew up in arguably one of the most cosmopolitan areas in the world. There were around 130 mother tongues in their school. Both enjoyed life there with a good circle of friends from a variety of different cultures and backgrounds.

Both children learnt ballet and began swimming at a very early age, winning many awards. They were very energetic, particularly Sophie, who was very keen on sports, even learning the trapeze whilst on holiday at a Club Med resort.

We enjoyed great holidays as a family travelling to Sri Lanka, Malaysia, Singapore, Portugal, and India several times, and also China, where we took part in car rallies. In India we visited many regions from north to south enjoying everything the country has to offer, including of course the fantastic food. Hence my love of cooking curries.

Having lived in Hong Kong and enjoyed regular trips to Macau, it was perhaps inevitable that Jane and I would end up in Portugal after my retirement. Macau in the 1980s was a lovely place with a relaxed lifestyle and great food. It was here each year I raced a 1960 Triumph TR3A in the annual grand prix races, a car I had brought from the UK and rebuilt in Hong Kong.

It was not just Macau that influenced us, however, in choosing Portugal. In the 1970s and 80s we took long leave periods once every three years, and visited the former Portuguese colonies of Goa and Cochin on the south-west coast of India. Again we fell in love with the Portuguese culture and learned more about their history as well.

It was during a game of squash at the Hong Kong cricket club I saw an advert for a holiday property to let in the Algarve. Jane and I decided that for our next holiday we would travel there. This was in the early 90s and we really enjoyed ourselves for all the normal reasons, great food and wine, friendly people, fantastic weather, and culture. Where else could you buy a bottle of wine for two hundred escudos (the equivalent of one euro)?

We had also been on holiday in Spain and France, but for us, Portugal was the place. One factor in our choice is that having lived in Hong Kong for many years, Jane did not want to live anywhere where the temperature was less than twenty degrees centigrade. At the time of writing this, in winter, the temperature is just six degrees!

So, in August 1995, during one of our holidays to the Algarve, we saw an advertisement for an old quinta on the outskirts of the village of Alfontes, near Boliqueime. We decided this was the area where we wanted to live. There was no A22 motorway back then, and the road to the property was unsurfaced. Unfortunately, it was the last day of the holiday, so we returned to Hong Kong thinking about what to do next.

In January 1996, I travelled back to Portugal to have a look at the house again as well as others. It was one of the wettest winters on record, with some flooding in the local area. Of the thirty houses I was shown, regardless of age, most of them were leaking because of the heavy rainfall.

In the end, we decided to purchase the house in Alfontes. After undertaking quite a bit of refurbishment work, we rented the property out to help cover the restoration costs and to avoid the house standing empty as we were still living in Hong Kong.

We found Alfontes a good choice for many reasons: firstly it was rural which we liked; it was a short walk to the nearest shop and bar, and just one kilometre from a main road with some enjoyable walks and cycle routes nearby. Located in the central Algarve, it was also convenient for the airport and major shopping areas.

When I finally 'retired' and moved here to live in 2005, the A22 motorway had been constructed and we had a properly surfaced road to our property.

I say 'retired' with a wry smile, because at the time of writing this, sixteen years later, I have yet to retire because of my commitments as President of Safe Communities Portugal.

After leaving Hong Kong I was fortunate enough to spend five years undertaking very interesting work from which I gained valuable experience in international policing and security.

The first of these was my four-year role as a full-time consultant for Interpol. Just prior to leaving Hong Kong, the Secretary General of Interpol had offered me a job at their headquarters in Lyon, France; to help develop the organisation's training capacity. However, as we were about to move to Portugal, I became a consultant instead, based in Portugal, but travelling once or twice a month to Lyon or other countries overseas. From this I gained considerable experience of security forces work in places such as Africa and Russia. My work involved advising the Secretary General on training matters and creating Interpol's international training strategy.

I then helped to create Interpol's strategic plan before finishing in 2009. They were four demanding and fascinating years, and I gained great insights on how such international organisations work. I really enjoyed Lyon, especially the food and the friendliness of the people.

A few months later, I worked for almost a year as a consultant for the United Nations Office on Drugs and Crime (UNODC) in Bangkok.

I applied for a project which was to evaluate their ten-year programme of the establishment of border liaison posts in the Greater Mekong area of South East Asia. In the online interview with tight deadlines for answers, they suddenly asked me what was my understanding of 'triangulation' in the context of undertaking evaluations? My heart jumped as I did not have a clue—although it presumably had something to do with threes or triangles. My reply was,

"Conducting interviews, document research, and undertaking surveys in order to determine the desired indicators, outputs, and outcomes."

How about that? Anyway, they were impressed—I was surprised —and they offered me the job.

The next few months I was based in Bangkok. It was not a good time, as political protestors surrounded the UN building. They were organised by the National United Front of Democracy against Dictatorship (UDD)—commonly known as the 'red shirts'. It was a violent period, resulting in over two thousand injuries and eighty-six people killed.

I travelled throughout the region visiting remote posts and meeting police, military, immigration, and customs officials in places such as Laos, Cambodia, Thailand, Myanmar, and Vietnam. It was the sort of job I may have undertaken, even if they had not paid me! It was a great experience, and an opportunity to encounter many different cultures. It also prepared me for the work ahead in Portugal.

ೞ෨ೞ෬

In 2009/10 the Algarve had a spate of very violent residential robberies, which was most unusual for the area. Eastern European and Brazilian crime groups were targeting foreign nationals living in luxury villas in rural areas. This sent shock waves through the community, and some people were literally living in fear in the more isolated locations.

I met with the Civil Governor for Faro District at the time, Isilda Gomes, to offer any help I could, based on my experience in the police, as well as being a resident here. She was extremely receptive and also introduced me to the District Commander of the GNR police. I proposed the forming of a community association to work closely with them both to foster closer GNR public engagement. I established the Safe Communities Algarve website, which was written in English and included crime prevention advice and details about the GNR.

In 2012, we formally registered as Portugal's first crime prevention association. I formed a Management Board and recruited members including Jim Litchko, and Marianne Guerreiro. Jim was a cybersecurity expert having previously undertaken projects for the FBI and NASA in the US, and Marianne, a neighbour of mine, had previously worked in the military in South Africa.

Our first aim was to create greater awareness in the foreign community of the work, not only of the local GNR, but also the PSP who police the major cities. To do this, I started writing monthly features for the *Algarve Resident* newspaper, which has continued to this day. We established a Facebook page reporting on the work of the police; launched a newsletter, and created 'Crime Check', a Sunday feature on *KissFM* the local radio station. Our next strategy was to hold seminars throughout the Algarve, bringing together the foreign community and police. We held these in English and for the first time GNR commanders spoke in English, covering their work and answering questions that concerned residents. The seminars were extremely well received.

Due to their popularity, we expanded the number of speakers to include those from the Regional Tourism Board, SEF, and the Civil Protection Department for Faro District. We included the latter because of the risk of rural fires.

Our second aim was to ensure that Safe Communities Algarve had the foundation stones in place to secure its sustainability. We wanted to be properly recognised as a trusted organisation, supportive of the work undertaken by the Government and officials whilst at the same time representing the public safety needs of the foreign community and tourists. Safe Communities Algarve was unique, and everyone we met in government was very supportive of our work. We quickly put written protocols in place, setting the framework for lasting collaboration.

A decision we made at an early stage was that Safe Communities Algarve would comprise a nucleus of a small but dedicated number of volunteers with relevant experience reflecting the objectives of the association. We were determined that everything we did would benefit all communities, including tourists, and that all the information and services provided would be free to all users. I believe this is very important for an association dealing with safety and security—as these are fundamental rights that we are all entitled to.

This meant that our primary source of funding would be through donations. This volunteer-based model has served us well, and I am grateful to everyone who has supported our association through donations over the years.

Our official launch was in 2012 following our registration as a non-profit organisation. Clive Jewell, Vice Consul of the British Consulate in Portimão, invited me to a Consular Outreach event in Albufeira in the presence of the British Ambassador at the time, Gill Gallard. I have had the pleasure to work closely with Clive, sometimes on a daily basis, over the last nine years, and his support has made a considerable difference to our work.

After two years, news of our work had spread far and wide, so we changed our name from Safe Communities Algarve to Safe Communities Portugal to reflect the work we were about to undertake in other parts of the country.

Safe Communities started as a crime prevention organisation based on the needs of the area at the time and was designed to address the crime prevention challenges the Algarve faced. Much has changed in the Algarve since we formed. Crime has dropped over a quarter and people have become more reassured.

A major step forward occurred in 2017 with the launch of a Local Security Contracts programme, which mainly concentrated on the Algarve region and some areas of Lisbon. This was an initiative by the Ministry of Internal Administration, focusing on the elements and causes of crime, and bringing together various entities and non-governmental organisations in each municipality. This led to my first meeting with Dra. Isabel Oneto, then Secretary of State for Internal Administration. Her dedication and approach towards this programme and public safety in general was inspiring. Aided by her assistant, Angelo Marques, we drew up many new initiatives and she always made a point of attending these events herself.

Usually it was Angelo who contacted me, but one morning I received a call directly from Isabel inviting me to be a keynote speaker at a conference in Coimbra—which of course I readily accepted. She is that kind of person.

The start of 2016 came with a surprise to me, as they announced in the Queen's New Year's Honours List that I had been awarded the British Empire Medal for my services in Portugal. It was for 'Crime Prevention and Services to the International Community'. I was deeply honoured by this award because it reflected well on Safe Communities and our volunteers, and Portugal as a whole.

In May, the medal arrived, and it was presented to me by the then British Ambassador to Portugal, Kirsty Hayes, at her official residence in Lisbon. This was in the presence of Jane, and our two daughters, Sophie, and Shelley who had travelled from England with her partner John, together with colleagues, friends, and officials whom I worked with. This day brings back many happy memories, and I thank the ambassador for all the arrangements and supporting our work.

Having received one award, one does not even contemplate receiving another! But this is what happened when they announced in the UK Government Gazette on 30th December 2020 that I had been awarded an MBE in the Queen's New Year's Honour's List. It reads 'For Services to Public Safety and to British Nationals in Portugal'. This I can assure you came as an even greater surprise!

I feel particularly proud of this because it shows that volunteers who try their best to help the community are recognised. Again, it reflects on everyone involved and the hard work of our volunteer team, especially during Covid-19. At the time of writing, given the current pandemic situation, it has yet to be decided what the presentation arrangements will be.

I was also very pleased to receive a personal letter of appreciation from Eduardo Cabrita, Minister of Internal Administration, following the award. A very kind gesture.

✿෨✿ൔ✿

After the rural fires in the Algarve in 2012, it was clear that closer engagement was required between the public and the authorities, regarding fire prevention and protection. We established a protocol with the Algarve Civil Protection Authority and then with the National Authority for Emergency and Civil Protection in Lisbon.

Over the years we have worked closely with these authorities in creating greater awareness, especially concerning land clearing and how people should protect themselves in the event of fires.

After the major fires of 2017, we worked hard with the Government to improve the information available. At a national level there was no communication in English on matters that could prevent injuries and the loss of life in a catastrophe such as an earthquake or major fire. There was also very little, if any, communication with tourists should this occur. What we achieved, I believe, helped save lives in subsequent fires such as the Monchique fire of 2018. This was simply because the community and tourists were more aware prior to and during the incident, and given information in a language they could understand. We have worked hard to bring about a change in communication, but there is still more to be done.

When we think of fire of course there is well-deserved recognition of the monumental work of the bombeiros who are mainly volunteers. Sometimes forgotten, however, are those who are also on the front line such as those in the GNR who fly in helicopters to the scene of a fire and are involved in evacuations; the aircraft and helicopter pilots themselves; and the INEM emergency medics who treat people at the scene. Also the Army whose drivers plough through undergrowth to clear the way for firefighters, and the Civil Protection commanders and support staff who direct and co-ordinate the overall response to fires, together with many others involved in this dangerous work.

At the start of this journey some years ago, someone said to me that obtaining help from tourist boards in matters such as crime prevention would be impossible, as this is not what holidaymakers wish to hear. In my opinion, this is so wrong—safety and security are often the key criteria upon which people choose their holiday destination. We have worked closely with the local and national tourism boards and have undertaken over twenty-five seminars related to tourism, with many government speakers attracting audiences of over three hundred people.

Although we never know when the next crisis may occur, we at

Safe Communities Portugal have been preparing extremely diligently for any such event, being ready to provide a supporting role to the Government. We have increased the size and breadth of our capability, and built a team of loyal volunteers that can meet any large-scale crisis. We trained to become a statutory Civil Protection Volunteer Organisation, the only non-Portuguese association to achieve this status.

Our biggest challenge was yet to come, namely the outbreak of the new coronavirus in Wuhan, China.

When the news first emerged from China and the World Health Organisation in January 2020, it rang alarm bells, taking me back to Hong Kong in 2002 with the outbreak of SARS. As a senior police officer, I was inevitably involved in dealing with this outbreak, which killed almost three hundred people in such a condensed place. I learnt a great deal from that experience.

Safe Communities decided to monitor the developments closely; in fact, I believe we were the first organisation in Portugal to do this for the foreign community. One concern from the outset was false news and misleading information. We forewarned people about this at the time before the first coronavirus case was confirmed here. This was an emerging problem then, but is a larger issue now; not just here, but globally.

Our aim is always to help the Government in its efforts to provide informed official information and advice to the population, in order to help the community stay safe.

Specifically, we provide such information in English and other languages for non-Portuguese speakers and visitors. We try, where possible, to clarify government information and advice, help with public enquiries (and there are many), liaise with the Government and embassies; counter misinformation and make proposals to the Government where we consider a need to do so.

At Safe Communities we pride ourselves on being a trusted source of facts, especially in emergency situations, only dealing in and reporting official information. Our work is only possible because we have a loyal team of volunteers who work without pay 24/7 when required. I am grateful to all of them.

We all have strengths and weaknesses in our lives, and one of my weaknesses is languages. Whilst living and working in Hong Kong, I found Cantonese very challenging, although I passed my exams at Basic and Intermediate level. With learning Portuguese some thirty years later, little had changed. I undertook Portuguese lessons, and my reading skills improved, but I still find it very difficult when it comes to day-to-day discussion.

In meeting with various government officials, even if it starts with a few words in Portuguese, we usually revert to speaking in English, otherwise we would never finish on time.

A funny episode took place at a Civil Protection exhibition in Portimão in 2018 when the Minister of Interior, Eduardo Cabrita, visited the Safe Communities stand. He picked up one of our crime prevention leaflets, written in Chinese, and asked me a question in Mandarin. I do not speak Mandarin, so I replied in Cantonese. Neither of us understood each other! Today, after sixteen years in Portugal, my Cantonese is still better than my Portuguese.

We are lucky where I live in the Loulé municipality to have an excellent GNR Commander Captain, Daniel Fernandes, and also the head of the GNR Safe Residents Programme Corporal Daniel Dias.

They found out; I suspect through my daughter Sophie that I was celebrating a milestone birthday in May 2020. The big day came, and due to lockdown, I was working as usual from home. Suddenly I heard a police siren at my gate. I went outside to find they had both arrived at my house in a patrol car. They offloaded a cake onto the front bonnet of the car and then sang 'happy birthday' to me, much to the amusement of our neighbours! All part of the GNR 'Safe Elderly Programme', I guess.

The Algarve has many points of interest, and although the focus is often on the beaches, there are many, many other attractions as well. Two of our favourite places in the Algarve are the lovely villages of Alte, even if it can be over-burdened with tourists during the peak periods, and Querença, north of Loulé. There are lots of enjoyable walks around these areas with walking and cycling route maps available from tourist information centres.

The same goes for food. There are Michelin star restaurants in some of the luxury developments and of course British style food is readily available. That is one of the things about the Algarve, its diversity. However, there are also an abundance of fantastic restaurants serving traditional Portuguese cuisine here, and some of our favourites are Veneza near Paderne, A Casa do Avô near Guia and Gamboa in Almancil.

The tourist board has developed the '365 Algarve' programme, promoting the Algarve all year round, not merely as a summer destination. There are literally thousands of events, cultural shows, opportunities to learn something new, places of entertainment, and many ways of occupying your time. It is just a question of keeping track of what is on. One good tip is to visit the local municipal website, which has all the information available.

Moving to any new country means adapting to the way of life there and accepting the fact that you are no longer in your own country. My advice is always to learn as much about your new home as possible: its history, culture; and people, and the law as it affects you.

Jane and I moved from the most crowded place on the planet, Hong Kong, where everything was done immediately; to Portugal, which is traditionally rather more laid back and it can take more time to achieve things. However, we adjusted to this, but it is obvious from what we often see that for some *estrangeiros* (foreigners) this remains a challenge.

One of the things to consider if you move to live abroad is deciding how you are going to spend the next chapter in your life. For me, having the chance to continue to help communities regarding safety and security, albeit in a different way compared to when I was working professionally in my career, has given me tremendous satisfaction. However, I had to create that opportunity. This may not be for everyone, I readily admit.

But if there is something whereby you feel you can continue to contribute in some shape or form, look for the opportunities that could present themselves through creating your own business or undertaking voluntary work. As they say, keeping the grey matter ticking over is important.

I have had the pleasure to deal with many government officials over the last few years. Many in the foreign community seldom meet the people who have responsibility for protecting us, especially those at a national level. However, I have been privileged to do so, and I am impressed with the professionalism and skill they display in helping to keep us safe and secure in Portugal. This is no doubt one reason why Portugal is the third most peaceful country in the world according to the 2020 Global Peace index, and it has one of the lowest crime rates in Europe.

There have been so many people that have assisted me on this journey, and it would be impossible to name them all. I am grateful to every single official, volunteer, supporter, and contact that has helped to shape Safe Communities Portugal into the thriving association that it is today.

Safety and security are fragile things and can change in an instant should a major disaster occur. Being prepared and knowing how to deal with these issues with well-produced and rehearsed plans in place is vitally important. Based on my thirty-five years' experience in policing and security, I do not hesitate in concluding that we are in very good hands here in Portugal.

A high quality of life means a stable and safe environment, and we should never forget this—we all have a part to play.

✿ℬ✿ℛ✿

To find out more about the work of Safe Communities Portugal, visit their website:
www.safecommunitiesportugal.com

16

The Wedding Planner
ALISIA ALAO

I was born to Nigerian parents; I lived most of my early life in south London and went to school & college there. I trained as an audio-visual aids technician at Wandsworth College, though I kept this as a hobby and never really worked in the industry until many years later. If you are not sure what this is, think back to your school days. The AVAT was the person who set up all the projectors, cameras, and film development, and repaired the photocopiers.

After leaving college, I worked in the retail trade at Waitrose as a management trainee. I worked in several different departments in one of the best branches, King's Road, Chelsea. What a ball we had in between work. I met some great people in and out of the store, too many to name!

There are two incidents I remember clearly. The first was an opera singer who popped in for a quick shop who thought he was quietly singing to himself. The store came to a complete standstill whilst he was singing at the deli counter and he got a massive round of applause.

The second was the customer who passed out at the till with a tremendous crash. We thought she'd had a heart attack, but we then discovered a frozen chicken hidden under her big woolly hat. I don't know if she shoplifted elsewhere, but she definitely didn't come back to the shop again!

I left Waitrose and worked for Cullens Convenience stores, which was a luxury corner shop. This was followed by a short stint at Sainsbury's and then Woolworths, where the free pick-n-mix sweets were irresistible! I went on to be deputy manager of their Lewisham store, with the highest sales per square foot in London. It was also the first store to introduce a 'night fill' team, which was my idea. They were responsible for replenishing stock overnight ready for the next day's trade. This was quite unusual in those days, but it's pretty much standard now. The general manager left me to sort this out just at the time our staff scheduling and payroll became computerised. He was terrified of anything with a keyboard, including his mobile phone. His wife used to call me because he didn't know how to use his own phone—he was such a technophobe!

In the summer of 1995, I left retail to attend college. I'd been out of education for around ten years, but I wanted to retrain for a complete career change. I had always been interested in health and fitness, and I was obsessed with going to the gym and attending fitness classes. I'm a little different now, though!

The second time I went to college I did a sports coaching diploma, then I went on to university to study sports science and American studies. Then I did a postgraduate diploma in health promotion, which was basically a course to guide you to working within the NHS. During this time I also completed vocational qualifications within the health and fitness industry, including a personal training diploma, exercise to music certification, and aqua aerobics, where I created a format called 'silent aqua'.

Lots of the classes I taught at that time utilised microphones as it was very difficult to be heard above the noise of the swimming pool. This was when I developed throat problems, something that affects me to this day.

Initially, when I moved to Portugal I taught group classes, but it was very poorly paid work compared to the UK. However, through these classes I met many new clients and was able to develop my own personal training business.

I had never been to the same country twice until 2001, when a friend persuaded me to return to Portugal on a girlie holiday. Having lunch in Vilamoura Marina one day turned into something else when I met my partner! We emailed each other for a few months, then I travelled back and forth from London until December 2002 when I moved out here to live. We had lots of fun in those days living across the road from the marina. However, every party must come to an end and mine did in 2005 when I had my little boy.

A typical weekend for me now is a dinner at mine or a friend's house. I love Sunday lunch somewhere nice—but never a roast dinner—yuck!!! The Algarve is a great place for kids, it's fairly relaxed with minimal crime. Sadly, the public transport leaves a lot to be desired and turns most parents into part-time Uber drivers, especially if you live in a village, which we do.

After the economic downturn, I changed direction again and fell into planning events. I organised events in clubs and bars then I moved into planning weddings when the woman I used to work with returned to live in the UK. Wedding planning has been challenging, hard work, rewarding, and extremely good fun!

Being a wedding planner is one of the craziest professions ever. Each wedding is different. Initially, I get to know the couple via phone or video conversations. Then they usually come on a 'site visit' after being presented with a range of venue details that match their criteria, number of guests, budget, and desired location—beach, hotel, etc. Once they have viewed the venues, they select one. They then make most of the other decisions via email or phone. This will include an introduction to suppliers.

They may come back a second time to do some food tastings and meet all the suppliers and make final choices about the décor. They return a few days before the wedding and do a rehearsal. I am with them throughout their special day, making sure everything runs smoothly and according to plan. I then meet with them after the wedding to hand over their marriage or blessing certificate if it is ready. I wish them well and they are on their way!

Running a business in the Algarve is like being a sailor with lots of navigation. It involves building great professional relationships (which can take ages…'eye roll') and requires the ability to stay calm when faced with rules that are complete nonsense!

I'm totally into online marketing, be it via social media platforms, working with venues, or advertising on a wedding website. There are literally hundreds of sites to maintain a presence on.

Finding suitable locations is like seeing a nightclub in daylight. You need a trained eye and a very open imagination!

There are so many stories from the weddings I've arranged over the years. We did a wedding in Quinta do Lago, and within an hour of the guests dining I realised that quite a few had some sort of eating disorder and they kept the cleaners busy! I don't think I need to break it down any further…

I can also vividly recall the family that were all on anxiety medication and loved to drink. What a mess! Then we had the wedding with the nurses. Most of their guests were in the medical profession, and during the reception, clients from the adjoining restaurant came and sat outside their marquee. One of them, a pensioner, wasn't feeling okay. The next thing I knew, she vomited on the floor and had a stroke! The bridal couple and their friends assisted, we called an ambulance, cleaned up the vomit, and the party went on!

Medical mishaps are sadly quite common. We had a wedding where a guest took over a large bongo drum and broke his thumb playing it. He ended up stuck in the Algarve for another week before he could fly home.

Another wedding ran until 5 a.m. The bride's sister brought her two kids, and by the end of the evening all the kids were asleep in a makeshift crèche. As the last babysitter was about to leave, she told me that one kid was left behind. We had to call the guests in turn to find out who owned the 'leftover kid'. We discovered it was the grandmother who was so drunk that she had only taken one of her grandchildren home with her!

At one wedding I had a bride whose uncle was Russian. He was there at the wedding with his wife in tow, but he still chased me for most of the day. I pointed out the security cameras with the help of one of my team who spoke some Russian, and eventually got him off my back!

I might not be able to speak Russian, but my Portuguese has really come along since my child started secondary school. He has always been educated in the Portuguese language. I'm not fluent, but I've come a very long way.

I have found it useful to chat to older people who have no interest in learning or practicing their English. They respond to you in Portuguese rather than 'helping you' by responding in English. They often speak with a 'local lingo' which can vary within a ten-minute drive, and make a lot of small talk about the weather, food, and everyday subjects.

I also like to talk to young children. They will repeat, repeat, repeat the same words and phrases until you understand what they are talking about. They don't get into the grammar of everything, they just speak to you, keeping it simple. I read kid's books and watch kid's videos, and listen to Portuguese radio and TV as much as possible.

I also like to watch a movie with the sub-titles switched on. It's such an eye opener to see things spelt correctly, especially as we live in the south where they lose half of their words in the back of their throat!

It was inevitable that I would make some mistakes along the way. Taxi drivers couldn't follow my directions until I found out that the Portuguese words for 'straight ahead' and 'turn right' sound almost the same. I once asked participants in a fitness class to 'stay in a hotel' not 'stay on the spot'. It pays to check your verbs, they use different ones for staying still and staying at a location or venue. I learnt the hard way…

I have even asked someone about their 'sex life with themselves' instead of asking about their blood pressure. And yes, I did it in front of a lot of Portuguese people at a BBQ. It was only then that I realised I had previously asked a doctor to check my 'masturbation'. I have never mixed up those words again. It really pays to know the slang terms!

I have one piece of advice if you have children that are in a foreign school. Your child may speak and understand English very well, but make sure to keep up with their reading and writing. We have always paid for extra tuition and exam costs. It keeps their options open for the future.

※※※※※

It's difficult to pick just one restaurant I like as I visit so many due to work. The best restaurants are any that are by the beach or serve authentic Portuguese food, especially seafood (I'm a pescatarian). Any restaurant that serves *arroz de marisco* (seafood rice) or free-range grilled fish Xerém (it's a kind of polenta) with lobster or crab is a definitely a winner in my book. Washed down with a jug of wine, it's heaven.

One of the problems of living in Portugal is the bureaucracy, and sometimes people are too laid back. Everything takes a long time, and it often feels like you need twenty forms signed by fifteen different people. The Portuguese love numbers and codes. You also need to show your ID just to buy a loaf of bread, well it feels like that sometimes. I also miss being able to purchase ingredients to make Nigerian, Angolan, or Mozambican food.

The waiting times in the health service are terrible. I had a friend wait almost a year for her smear test results. Before I arrived here, I wish I'd known about how many insect bites I would endure. I have had so many infections from insect bites, worse than anywhere I have ever visited on holiday.

I love spending time on the beach and horse riding. It was not something I did before as it was too expensive (I was also scared of horses back then!) but it is very affordable here. There are some great stables, and they are less pompous here than in the UK.

My son is growing up here with so much freedom and variety. He has friends from all over the world and he is learning so many languages, Portuguese, French, Spanish, and even a sprinkling of German and Russian.

I would never say 'forever' but for now this is a wonderful place to call home.

✥✥✥✥✥

For more information about Alisia's wedding planning service, visit the website:
www.algarveweddings.eu

Almost an Artist – Possibly a Poet?
DAVID TRUBSHAW

I retired to the Algarve, with my wife Penny, in 2004. We had both visited Portugal many times on holiday and loved it—the beautiful beaches, months of sunshine, friendly locals, good food, delicious wines, and not forgetting the port. It ticked all the boxes.

We were both hooked on books. I was a director in a publishing company and Penny worked in the famous Foyles Bookshop on the Charing Cross road in London. Then, in 1982, we decided to open our own bookshop, Unicorn Books, in Epsom. This grew into a successful chain of seven bookshops and a small school supply unit. We said goodbye to Unicorn Books Ltd in 2003 and moved to Portugal in 2004. We both love the Algarve and have definitely put down roots here.

I started to paint again with private tuition under the expert eyes and professional guidance of two German artists, Kerstin Wagner, and Gudrun Bartels. This has resulted in exhibitions in Portugal and Germany. I paint both abstracts and landscapes in mixed media. Trees and leaf structures feature in many of my paintings and prints. I am intrigued by trees, their shapes, textures, and leaf patterns, and how they blend, mould, and merge with the landscape. Even dead plants and fallen leaves have a unique structure and design. Perhaps this has something to do with my early ancestors. The name Trobeshawe has been traced back to Saxon times and comes from the Saxon words trobe (tree) and shawe (shade). One of my very early ancestors fought in the Crusades.

I also enjoy writing poetry, especially haiku, the Japanese style which aims to capture a feeling, in three short lines, and evoke images of nature. Shortly after we came to Portugal, I joined a creative writing group which helped me develop my writing.

My favourite word is serendipity, which can be defined as 'making unexpected and delightful discoveries by accident'. There is a quotation attributed to the Greek poet Simonides of Ceos, who said,

"Painting is silent poetry, poetry is eloquent painting."

A simple but beautiful summary. I would not suggest that my paintings are silent poetry or that my poetry is eloquent painting, but

I can empathise with this comparison and by coincidence or serendipity, painting and poetry came together for me.

After I started to paint again, I decided to write a book using some of my earlier haiku poems with a selection of my paintings. I titled it *Haiku for You – A Celebration of the Four Seasons*. In our garden, my favourite tree is a beautiful, large white poplar and watching this change with the seasons inspired me to paint it and compile the book. We printed two hundred and fifty copies, all of which sold, and I made a donation from sales of the book to a local children's charity through the Silves Rotary Club.

I enjoy writing haiku for the challenge and discipline of composing a poem of only three lines divided into two sections. The first a short one line, called the fragment, the second, two lines called the phrase. All the words and letters should be written in lower case.

Here are a few examples from my book:

spring sunlight
new leaves shimmer
branches swollen with buds

algarve spring
pink almond blossom
fills the hillside

summer fireworks
flowers burst
colours explode

sunlight
between the leaves
warm silence

autumn
strong winds trees sway
leaves tremble

autumn around the trees
leaf carpets burn
red and orange

winter
naked trees
raw wind iced snow

bare trees
calligraphy
of twisted branches

On a different level, I also like writing, hopefully, humorous poetry. I am not suggesting Global Warming is a humorous topic, quite the opposite, but I wrote the following poem just after we came to Portugal, fifteen years ago, when it was not hitting the headlines as it is today.

Around Monchique

"The rain in Spain falls mainly on the plains." They said.
"The Algarve never sees the snow, last time was forty years ago."
They said.
So to Portugal, some years ago, we both retired, we came to stay.
Departing from the cold UK, bid farewell to the freezing fog,
dropped off our thermals in the local Oxfam shop.
Now we could go, Algarve beckoning, warm and welcoming
free from frost, black ice, and snow.

Five years ago, around Monchique, one morning bright,
a blanket, white, had fallen silently in the night.
A strange, fine, crunchy, powdery stuff – real snow!
"Last time was over forty years ago." They said.

Many here had never seen real snow.
Many more with cameras, videos and kids, jumped into cars

Raced down from Lisbon to record this rare and ghostly sight.
Because the weathermen had said – "It might be forty years again
before snow falls around Monchique."

Last year – Guess what? Yes, quite right –
One night snow settled, silently, around Monchique.
But then came frost and hail, for days on end,
torrential rains, strong winds and sleet!
We wished that we could grow webbed feet, around Monchique.

P.S. Urgent email to UK to family about to stay –
As well as P.G. Tips (large size) bring winter thermals!
Surprise, surprise – for we both fear
Global Warming's tracked us here – Around Monchique.

✧৯০✧ଔ✧

We bought our house in Portugal in 2004. It had been empty for over three years and needed serious attention and repairs. There was no garden, and most of the land surrounding the house was overgrown with weeds and brambles. The previous owner was a builder and the large area of land at the front of the house was filled with old pallets, broken tiles, bricks, and piles of rubble. The only plusses were the orange and lemon trees which filled a strip of land at the side of the house. I can still remember the beautiful perfume of their late blossom during our first visit in early May.

So why did we buy it? Our daughter was already working and living in the Algarve, and we asked her to find us a property that would allow us all to live together. This house was already divided into two separate dwellings with separate entrances and we saw the potential and so went ahead with the purchase. Our daughter moved into the house for a year, surrounded by a team of builders, while we stayed in the UK until repairs and renovations were completed on the house. A year later, we sold our business, retired, and moved to the sunshine of the Algarve and the perfumes of the almond, orange, and lemon trees.

The next challenge was the garden. After several large skips, days of clearing, and a little blood, sweat, and tears, we had an almost blank canvas on which to design our new garden.

When we originally bought the house, there were three large, beautiful palm trees, but sadly, despite regular spraying, all died, victims of the dreaded Red Palm Weevil beetle which ravaged through Portugal. The sole survivors were three iceberg rose bushes, which after serious pruning surgery, have now developed into beautiful shrubs that flower twice a year. They produce a mass of white scented flowers, which actually won a prize at a flower show one year.

I have always been interested in the Feng Shui of gardening, which is probably the oldest form of garden cultivation in the world. It dates back thousands of years to China, which was already a great civilisation, while we in the west were still largely barbarians. It is based on the simple philosophy of man and nature living in harmony, and that life is infused with an invisible energy, the Chinese name 'chi'. This is a life force that circulates through our environment and is essential to our well-being, health, and happiness.

Paths, an essential part of any garden, should not be laid in straight lines, but have gentle curves or winding pathways that facilitate the passage of natural energy. We have used *calçadas*, (Portuguese stone blocks) to make several curved walkways, paths, and circular areas on which to stand pots.

Balance is also a vital element, and we have mixed the shapes and sizes of the plants in our garden. Massed beds of colourful flowers are popular in western gardens, but Feng Shui recommends subtlety, with a few delicate colours and plenty of green leaves. This is a far better conductor of the chi.

Trees are important, so we planted several, and my favourite is the white poplar. It was about two metres tall when first planted, but now (ten years later) it is over twenty metres in height. It has white and green coloured leaves and a beautiful trunk covered in orange lichens, a sure sign of unpolluted air.

Gardening in the Algarve is a rewarding challenge and well worth the effort, whether you are experienced or a beginner.

Depending on where you live, there are several gardening clubs who will help, advise, and provide friendship. The Mediterranean Gardening Association promotes Mediterranean plants and gardens, produces a newsletter, organises lectures and events, and sells a range of gardening and wildlife books in English.

The Algarve is famous for its hundreds of beautiful beaches, but there is so much more to discover and enjoy. If you are interested in birds, wildlife, orchids, or fungi; or just wish to explore the wonderful scenic walks in the Algarve countryside, then the website www.algarvewildlife.com is worth a visit. The site shows you all you need to know with maps, books, and online information. Each nature site or walk is illustrated by Google maps with facilities to zoom and scroll, plus directions and pictures to help you find your way.

My wife and I are particularly interested in wild orchids and fungi. As members of a gardening club in Monchique, we were able to go on two organised walks by the authors of two delightful and informative books.

Wild Orchids of the Algarve, by Sue Parker, gives you the how, when, and where to find wild orchids with over one hundred beautiful colour photographs. One April we met up with her and explored an area near Benagil and saw many wild orchids growing and in flower in the fields.

One special orchid which was both beautiful and caused amusement was *Orchis italica*, commonly known as the naked man orchid or the Italian orchid. Why? Well, it gets its name from the lobed lip (labellum) of each flower which mimics the general shape of a naked man.

I wrote a small poem about it:

The Naked Truth – Orchis Italica

Ladies, in April
For a special thrill,
A certain field near Benagil
Is worth a visit.

During that month
That is when
The field is full of naked men!

Fascinated by Fungi, by Pat O'Reilly, is an amazing book exploring the majesty and mystery, facts, and fantasy of the fungi world, with over one thousand colour pictures.

We were again very pleased to join our gardening club and go on a guided tour by the author around an area of woodland in Monchique. This was an ideal site for seeing many varieties of fungi growing in the wild. Some members took baskets to collect mushrooms to take home to eat, after the author had confirmed they were safe and edible! Before our fungi foraging expedition, we had an illustrated talk by Pat, who warned all of us never to eat fungi unless we were certain they were not poisonous. Some wild fungi are deadly poisonous and can kill within minutes!

The pictures and descriptions of these deadly fungi intrigued me, and I had to write a poem about them:

Mushrooms To Die For?

Fungi are fascinating, inspiring and interesting.
90,000 species and still growing, so maybe worth knowing –
Some are decidedly delicious – gastronomically auspicious.
But fungi aficionados beware! Some are murderously malicious.
"Never eat an Amanita!" sound advice, do not ignore.
Not all angels are angelic – Destroying Angel, for example.
Panther Cap and Fool's Webcap, two species you must never sample.
Dead Man's Fingers, bent and beckoning, could tempt you to your final reckoning.
Fly Agaric, the Fairy Ring with a deadly sting!
Murdering Magpie - not just the birds…
So fungivorous followers, please remember, when out fungi foraging,
However tempting, smooth and sweet –
If in any doubt - NEVER cut and eat!

Almost an Artist – Possibly a Poet? • 235

❁ೞ❁ఴ❁

I have been a Rotarian for over twenty years, both in the UK and now here in Portugal.

The Rotary International was founded in Chicago in 1905 as the world's first volunteer service organisation and has 1.2 million members in over 35,000 Rotary clubs in more than two hundred countries. It aims to conduct projects addressing today's challenges including illiteracy, disease, hunger, poverty, lack of clean water, and environmental concerns.

PolioPlus is Rotary's flagship programme, aiming to eradicate polio worldwide. Rotary club members have contributed millions of dollars and countless volunteer hours to immunise over two-and-a-half billion children in one hundred and twenty-two countries. Rotary is a spearheading partner in the Global Eradication Initiative along with the World Health Organisation and UNICEF, and is now concentrating on the last two countries where polio is still endemic, Afghanistan, and Pakistan, to make them, and the world, polio free.

On a local level, Rotarians also aim to help associations, groups, and those in need in their local communities, by raising funds through donations and charity fund-raising events.

There are two projects I helped organise and was pleased to be involved in. The first was through the Almancil International Rotary Club, which I joined when I first arrived in the Algarve, supporting the Lar de Crianças Bom Samaritano in Alvor. This is a children's home for about forty children aged from three years to teenage. All the children have been placed there by court orders as they were deemed in need of protection. We helped by providing bedding and duvets, a new sewing machine for their seamstress, beach parties, and organising a Father Christmas to give out presents.

But a different and unusual request, by the director, was for me to write her a special poem. She had a beautiful painting by a local artist hung on a wall in her office, and this painting was to feature in a leaflet asking for donations. But how do you write a poem about sad and damaged children in a care home? I used the painting for inspiration, and here is my poem:

Bom Samaritano

Cold darkness gripped me.
Another night alone, afraid, trembling.
My tears transformed, turned into a dream.
Strong arms reached out
Warm hands enclosed my fingers, guiding me
To the large door – bright, ajar, beckoning.
We pushed together, bursting into sunlight –
Laughter, love, new life surrounded me.
Please help me live my dream.

The other ongoing Rotary project I am involved with is with the Silves Rotary Club, of which I am now a member. Our objective was to raise funds for the charity Casa do Povo, in São Bartolomeu de Messines, to help them instal a sensory room in their new building. This is a special room with lighting, music, and objects used as therapy for children and adults with limited communication skills.

"Every child is an artist - the problem is how to remain an artist." - Pablo Picasso

I enjoy encouraging children to paint. They are small goldmines of creativity, they just need a little stimulation and out it pours! So, in 2012, I started to visit local schools to organise art workshops. These were a success, welcomed by the children and their teachers. Art is not a set subject in many school syllabuses here, often it is only an optional choice for out-of-school activities.

In 2016, with the help of some fellow artists, we organised an art project for local schools. We chose sardines as the theme—what could be more Portuguese than sardines?

With the help of two teachers, we produced a video in Portuguese and English, inviting pupils to paint or make models of sardines. The response and results were incredible. Over fifty schools submitted over two thousand individual sardines! These creative children and their teachers used an impressive range of materials including bubble wrap, bottle tops, paper towels, coffee beans, grains of rice, sweet wrappers, and even pencil sharpener shavings. We created thirty collages in total from their entries, stretching over fifteen metres. They were displayed in the Lady in Red art gallery in Lagoa, Silves city hall, and several local schools. They are now on permanent display in the Casa do Povo building.

In 2017, we asked students to paint a picture or write a poem, and we published the best entries in a book entitled *Arte e Poesia - Art & Poetry*. This book included one hundred and fifty paintings, in full colour, from primary, junior, and secondary school students, and forty poems in Portuguese. It also featured the top twenty paintings from the Sovereign Art Foundation Student Art Prize competition in 2018.

We priced the book at ten euros. Because the editorial and printing costs were covered by sponsors and private donations, we can donate all the monies collected from sales of the book to the Casa do Povo charity. To date; we have raised just over six thousand euros towards the cost of the sensory room.

✧✵✧✵✧

One of our favourite places to visit is Caldas de Monchique, which is a spa town in the Monchique mountains, the highest point in the Algarve. It has been famous since Roman times for its waters, which supposedly have healing properties. You can buy bottled Monchique water in many supermarkets. Portuguese royalty also used Monchique as a seasonal retreat.

The journey by car up to Monchique is a delightful drive on winding roads through wooded hillsides, and this is one of our favourite ways to escape. We start and finish our day in warm sunshine, enjoying the scenery and views over the Algarve, and end with a relaxing meal.

There are many places to eat around Monchique, but we love to visit a small family restaurant called Café Império. Prices are moderate and it sets a high standard for food, hygiene, and service. The menu is simple and basic but they serve chicken like nowhere else! Start with the local *presunto* (smoked ham) and cheese while you wait for your freshly cooked chicken (with or without hot Piri-

piri sauce), chips, and a tasty salad. To finish, mother's home-made mango mousse is delicious.

Parking is relatively easy along the side of the road. Seating is limited though, so I suggest you book in advance. *Bom apetite!*

We have been living in the Algarve for sixteen years and our only regret is we wish we could have moved here earlier. We are very happy and settled, and have no regrets about moving from the UK and making the Algarve our home. Yes, we have definitely put down roots here.

To anyone reading this book, I hope our stories may help you decide to make the same life-changing decision.

All we have is now. Please check out the art of mindfulness, which will encourage you to find stillness so you can stop living on autopilot and consciously choose which thoughts to appreciate. So when you feel yourself rushing again, you can slow down, be grateful, present, and totally immersed in the moment, and you'll start living a more mindful, joyful life.

Here in the Algarve is the perfect place to do just that.

✿ൠ✿ൠ✿

If you wish to order a copy of the book *Arte e Poesia - Art & Poetry*, please email David Trubshaw for more information: davidmtrubshaw@hotmail.com

18

Matching the Right Properties to the Right People
SUSANNA GROSS

I am originally from Germany with a French grandmother. I was raised in Germany in a nice environment and I had a fantastic childhood within a large family. Family was, and still is, very important to me.

I love nature: mountains, trees, long walks in the fresh air, animals, and good cuisine, especially from my own vegetable garden. I used to play tennis and loved skiing, any outdoor activities where I was next to nature. The only thing I really hated was the date of my birthday, the ninth of January. None of my schoolmates or friends could come to any birthday celebrations because the weather was always so bad. Everywhere was covered with snow and ice! I am a sort of 'Heidi' from the mountains.

I completed my high school certificate and studied languages, sales and marketing, then continued my education working as an industrial clerk, which was my mother's wish. Unfortunately, this was in a bigger town away from my family and friends, and my beloved nature, but my mum always wanted me to have a 'Plan B' so if something happened, I could still have other options. That was typical of her! She never wanted me to do anything that was 'risky'. It took time for me to learn that I am different and that it is ok to take risks.

Besides my education, I loved to paint and to write poetry in different languages. I was alone in a bigger town, and it helped me to pass the time learning and studying. I have family abroad and I was also curious to travel to different countries. My language skills made this easy, and I never felt lonely or lost.

I visited my cousin in London and stayed there many times, attended language courses, and met a lot of interesting people. I worked as an au pair and visited a cousin in Spain and I also stayed in Paris which I really loved. What a great, romantic city! My hunger to visit and explore other countries continued. My cousin in the UK married a wonderful and beautiful baroness and they wanted me to stay in the UK, offering me the opportunity of a different life. However, through some contacts I had been presented with a huge and marvellous adventure … the chance to stay in Malaysia for one year with a Chinese family. Wow!

I didn't tell my mum about my possible plans immediately. I knew too well how she would feel and tell me to "stop this nonsense!", but nothing could prevent me from following this dream, even at such a young age. I continued with my studies and worked five evenings a week in a restaurant to save money for the trip, which I was really excited about. After six months with my education complete, it was time to move on.

I didn't want to spend too much money, so I decided to travel with the Russian Aeroflot airline—a strange adventure! My destination was in the suburb of Petaling Jaya in the capital Kuala Lumpur. I was immediately immersed in a new and different way of life.

My Chinese family were lovely. I knew one of their sons in London from when he was studying there, and most of the family spoke English. I worked as an au pair and helped the father during his exhibitions, translating and interpreting. I became a member of a large Chinese family—me, the only blonde one! I loved Chinese home cooking and tried to learn a little of the Chinese language, which was mission impossible for me—it was just too difficult! I learnt about their culture, how to approach other people with respect, and how to eat correctly (because there are different rules between the Malays and the Indians).

This was one of my best experiences, and I learnt a lot about myself. I was able to live in a non-European country and I had survived, I wasn't 'homesick', and I had made lots of friends. The only negative points were there were too many dangerous animals and the heat with ninety-eight percent humidity nearly killed me, but I became an adult there. I grew independent and strong, and had plenty of good ideas for my return to Europe—which I missed.

From Malaysia I applied for jobs back in Germany and had interviews in the largest European region for Japanese companies—in Düsseldorf, a city located on the River Rhine and close to Cologne.

I was offered a great opportunity with a big Japanese company. I think they felt I had a natural talent for connecting with Asian people. At the time it wasn't obvious to me, but after two weeks they said to me,

"Forget your high school certificates, your education … we will give you a trial period of six months, if you succeed you can stay. We will pay you the same salary as a man in your position."

So, of course, I went for it and learnt great skills, tactics, business strategies and more about Japanese people, their culture, and lifestyle. I have never really worked for German or French companies, but it's doubtful that they would have given me the same opportunities I received working for the Japanese firm, and I was very grateful and happy.

It was hard work. The first thing they said was "no boyfriend and be on duty nearly 24/7!" So, since I was alone in the big city without friends there, I agreed and never regretted it. They became like a second family and even invited me to their seasonal celebrations. Over time, I developed a greater understanding and skills in marketing and sales. My products to sell were boring—huge industrial printers—but with the help of my peers and my Japanese colleagues, I was a successful sales consultant and marketing adviser, and earned a wonderful salary.

I was responsible for national and international exhibitions, and this is how I met my future husband Peter, who was a competitor at the time for another big Japanese company. We dated for a long time in secret, before finally revealing our relationship. Together we went on many international journeys and weekend trips. Finally, after seven years, we were married in a small wedding chapel and my Japanese team was there.

Because Peter also worked for a big Japanese company, we lived in different countries, like The Netherlands and Belgium. We both enjoyed being abroad and loved exploring different lifestyles and cultures. I used to play tennis, which I loved, but Peter was more interested in golf! One day, in the late nineties, he surprised me with an impressive trip to the Algarve at the end of November. We stayed for one week in the wonderful, romantic Vivenda Miranda boutique hotel in Porto de Mós, Lagos. The stay included one week of golf, superb dining, and excellent service. Every day we enjoyed beautiful warm weather, meanwhile, it was very cold back home in Holland.

That week changed our lives. From then on; things seemed to pull us towards Portugal and the Algarve. It was our first trip to the Algarve, everything was new to us, but it felt good and we had both fallen in love with the region, climate, people, surroundings, the ocean and nature, the superb cuisine, and fabulous wines!

✧ဢ✧ଓ✧

We were working hard back then, and we didn't have much time to think about the Algarve—but we couldn't forget it after our first trip. We kept recalling the beautiful landscape, beaches, golf courses, towns and villages, friendly and helpful people, and the sunshine.

Not long after we returned to Holland, we purchased our first holiday home near Lagos. At that time, we only knew Lagos and its immediate surroundings. We dealt with one real estate agency that showed us eleven properties in one day! After the first seven, I nearly gave up because I could not remember them all. It was very confusing, but finally we saw property number eleven: a simple, nice rustic house with three bedrooms and a pool on a big plot. We loved it and bought it immediately as our holiday home.

From that moment onwards we spent all our holidays in the Algarve and began to explore the different areas, made friends, and were very happy with this beautiful area. We also loved other parts of Portugal such as Lisbon, which is a fantastic and historical city. Eventually, Peter's work commitments became so much that he couldn't find time to travel with me to the Algarve. Spending time alone in our holiday home was not what I expected and wanted, so we decided to sell it, because we didn't have the time to enjoy it together.

We wanted to work with one sole estate agent, but that was not successful. After one year there were no clients … it was a good quality property, not luxurious, but on a great plot, with a pool and in a nice location (even without sea views). In those days the demand for properties to buy in the Algarve was huge, so we couldn't understand why it hadn't sold. After further attempts with other agencies, we gave up and decided to sell the property ourselves. Finally, we succeeded!

Back in Holland it dawned on me that we had a lot of money and no time to have fun and spend it. For much of the time Peter was abroad on business trips, for short meetings to Tokyo and then to the US. I was suffering and it wasn't only me. One day I looked at Peter and realised just how pale and tired he appeared—though he was still young. I started to think about our lives and our future, and one day we began to discuss this more seriously. We had owned three properties in three different countries, and Peter asked me,

"Where do you want to live? Germany, Holland or in the Algarve?"

I immediately nodded and said,

"The Algarve."

The dream destination was born, but the reality of getting there with Peter took a while. What would we do in Portugal? Peter was a real businessman and used to hard work and success, he had one hundred employees in Holland so what would the two of us do in the Algarve? We were too young to retire, and we were too active to relax! We needed a new challenge.

We moved to the Algarve, rented a house, and explored the possibilities for work in our new home. Luckily, we had time and enough money to find the right idea and it took us a while to realise that it was the real estate sector which would suit us, especially after selling our holiday home near Lagos.

We both had a passion for properties; having purchased homes in different countries, renovated some of them and sold them with a profit, so from here a new idea was born! We gathered information and started to plan and research the necessary licence and documentation required, the language, and the area. We wanted to think big and cover the entire Algarve, not have just one small local agency. We looked from east to west and I started gaining experience working with property rentals. It was a difficult business, with a lot of work, long hours, and little money, but it brought me experience in the beginning.

Then in 2004 we decided to take the big step to become a licenced real estate agency—studying for the licence, learning the language, and improving our knowledge of the Algarve. It took us one year to manage everything and put our properties abroad up for sale. I learnt the business language whilst Peter set up our company. In the first few months we didn't sell a single property and we were disappointed. The property market was good, but we were new to this and no one had heard of the real estate agency called Togofor-Homes.

But Peter and I worked hard from our first small office in Alvor and kept motivated. We kept costs low and worked together with the help of our years of sales & marketing knowledge. In addition to this, Peter was a qualified engineer, so he helped me with all the technical stuff. Our business developed step by step, slowly, but with increasing acceptance in the market and steady success. We discovered what is necessary for this job: money to invest, excellent sales & marketing knowledge, a solid grasp of languages, an open mind, a strong work ethic, the ability to work long hours, good networking skills both nationally and internationally, adaptability (particularly in the digital age), as well as the philosophy 'Never Give Up'.

Today, in 2021, we can say that we are a well-established real estate agency with three company-owned offices throughout the Algarve; in Lagos (Marina) in the west, Vilamoura in the central region, and Tavira in the east. We are proud to have a very good team working for us. We have gone through a lot of ups and downs, especially during the crisis of 2007/2008 which we overcame with the programme from the Portuguese government to sell 'Golden Visa Tickets' to non-Europeans. I have to admit our solid experience of working with Japanese companies has helped immensely. Our sales and marketing background aided us and the fact that we do love our work. I adore communicating with many people of different nationalities, I love to speak different languages, match the right properties to the right people, pass on my knowledge and train new colleagues, and motivate and support them. I am open-minded and happy with my international team.

As I mentioned, initially we bought a small holiday home near Lagos as we were both settled in Holland and had not thought about moving to the Algarve. We renovated our little Algarve home nicely and started a big garden project. We decorated and furnished it with lovely things from home, and it felt comfortable and cosy. Friendships were made through our golf pro and we got to know a lot of people in the Algarve, mostly British. I even made friends at the Meia Praia beach in Lagos through my sweet puppy called Bianca—dogs network too!

We love the Algarve with its beautiful, very different landscapes, the beaches, mountains, friendly Portuguese people, incredible food and wine, and of course the climate!

We invited our family and friends to the Algarve to stay with us in our house. My mother and my family have visited lots of times and enjoyed the environment and beauty of the area as well as the good food. My uncle even managed to do a video film of the Algarve and Lisbon for the German television stations.

It is a big decision to give up a secure life in your home country and start a completely new life in Portugal. If you are retired and can live from a pension, it is much easier. But Peter and I were still young and needed to continue working. Luckily, we both belong to that category of curious and brave people, and we had good financial stability. We had plenty of experience and no fears too, and we have never regretted our decision!

I didn't learn the Portuguese language in the beginning at all. I speak several languages; and short term it's not a problem to survive with just speaking English in the Algarve. But if you want to work or really make an effort with the community or go further inland, it is wise to learn some Portuguese. When we decided to open the real estate agency, I registered at the language school in Lagos, which I can recommend. I learnt the language bit by bit over many months, which was tough! It was—and still is—a very difficult language for me. It was hard, but I made it in the end, however I did not have a choice for this particular job—it's vital.

Peter and I divide our tasks; he is not the language person, but he can organise companies and is an engineering and technical person. For me, it has always been easier to learn languages because of my family heritage.

Once I passed my exams, I tried to speak Portuguese with neighbours, in the supermarket, the post office, in restaurants. Daily training is necessary, because the language is difficult, especially understanding the 'Algarvian' dialect.

Oh yes, I have many funny stories of our time here. I had to check with my lovely husband to make sure he didn't mind me telling this story. Of course, I told him about this one at the time!

In the early days, when we were renting a villa on the outskirts of Portimão, I was shopping at the local Lidl supermarket. I came out of the supermarket and pushed my trolley towards our Jeep. A nice-looking Portuguese man walked over and followed me to my car. I was initially a bit concerned and taken by surprise; I have to say. Then he said to me (quite loudly),

"Are you interested in an adventure?"

I was shocked and looked at him and said,

"I am married and have four children."

He replied,

"So what! I am also married and have five children."

We both started to laugh. People in the car park heard and were laughing too and watching to see my reaction. I left the car park waving at him and the people who were clapping their hands. It was a really funny incident.

My beloved beach is Meia Praia, Lagos. It is a long and flat beach with many restaurants. I loved to walk and jog there right from when we had our first holiday home in the town. In the winter I love walking there with my dog and meeting other animal lovers. When we opened our small real estate office in Alvor, we would often walk the long sandy beach there. When we lived in Portimão, we loved to go to Praia da Rocha (it is also a great beach for sports — we used to jog there). We have visited a lot of different beaches in the Algarve, for both work and pleasure. We are so fortunate to have a wide choice of beaches and we love to explore more and more, especially the islands in the east, but my favourite beach is still Meia Praia.

We love all the beach restaurants and have tried many of them. Because of our work, we have experienced a lot of wonderful food in different restaurants and areas from east to west. Besides the typical Portuguese restaurants, we love Italian cuisine, and Japanese restaurants like Happy Sumo in Lagos.

Now we live in the Serra de Monchique. We have two favourite local restaurants: Foz do Banho on the main road to Monchique near Caldas de Monchique, and A Charette in the town of Monchique which serves authentic food from the region.

I spend my leisure time either in our large garden or on our land. I adore being outside, gardening, and walking in the hills and mountains of the Serra de Monchique. I love pets, swimming, picnics, and exploring other areas of Portugal. We enjoy the Alentejo region, long beach walks, cooking, entertaining friends for lunches and BBQs, and getting to know new areas of Portugal.

At first, way back in 2003 when we started living here, I felt the Algarve region was like living approximately fifty years back in time. That was my feeling compared with when we were living in the UK, Germany, Holland, Belgium, France, and Italy. But this gives it a kind of nostalgic and romantic feeling which adds to its charm. It did not really matter to me as I fell in love with the Algarve!

I still remember the many power cuts here when it rained. This has improved a lot, but there are still things which could be upgraded and better maintained. I have noticed one other problem so far in Portugal. Everything takes longer, for projects or questions at the council or appointments—you need to allow much more time in the Algarve to get things done. Your documents must be stamped and approved again and again. You must be patient, especially when interacting with local councils, authorities, and banks. But most of the people here are stoical and wait, especially the Portuguese.

I miss my family and friends who live in different countries, but I love living here in the Algarve. I am tall and thus cannot buy most of my clothes and shoes here. I can order them online, but it is not the same, I need to try shoes on and feel the cloth. But the Algarve has become our home, and Peter and I do not wish to change that. We are Europeans and have found a wonderful place to live and work.

The Algarve is an international region with many different nationalities living peacefully together. You do not have to be isolated and on your own; it is not difficult to meet people and make friends. You can join a sports club, walk or cycle in a group, walk your dog and meet animal lovers—there is a lot to offer in the Algarve. It is a safe place, which is very important these days. I do like that people follow the rules of the country without any doubts. They have trust and confidence in their government and police. I am happy and grateful to have received the chance to live here.

ఇలంలు

For more information, visit the Togofor-Homes website: www.togofor-homes.com

19

The Inspirational Senior Solo Traveller
JUNE MADILYN JORGENSEN

I was born in the wild and lush forests of Northern Alberta, Canada, in the oil sands trading post town of Fort McMurray. My birth father was a Hungarian fur trader and my mother a Metis, a mixture of Scottish and Aboriginal (Cree) heritage. I was a one-year-old baby when the family split up. A loving Danish couple, Ruth & Bruce Jorgensen, eventually adopted my twin sister and me. They were the only mom and dad I knew.

I grew up in Lethbridge, in Southern Alberta, a wind-swept prairie town one hour north of the US border, on the edge of the Canadian Rockies. At nineteen, I married a Swiss man and had my only child, Marc. Two years later we moved to Klosters, Switzerland, where I experienced my first taste of living in a foreign country. Besides being a mom, I was a ski instructor and private English teacher. Years later, we returned to Canada, where we divorced.

I studied and worked as a reporter and photographer for a local newspaper and on documentary films. After going back and forth between Europe and Canada, I settled in my home country, living in Calgary, Canmore, Alberta, and later Vancouver Island.

Over the years, my life was busy with family, careers, several business ventures, a second marriage, art, and theatre. In between, I travelled extensively.

Always up for a challenge, I travelled solo to Thailand, China, and Italy. I spent three winters in San Felipe, Mexico. I visited Germany, France, the Netherlands, Greece, the UK, and Hungary, plus Asia and North America (the western and central states including California and Arizona), and travelled across Canada, coast to coast.

In 2015, recently retired and now a single mature lady looking for some stability and an easy-going lifestyle, I was searching for a winter retreat in Europe. I also wanted to be closer to my son Marc and grandson, Rafael, who live in Switzerland. So I crossed the pond once again from my home country of Canada.

It was a chance encounter that brought me to the Algarve.

I thought of returning to Majorca, Spain, where I'd spent three sun-soaked weeks drinking margaritas a few years back, but a conversation with a friend changed all that.

We were enjoying a drink in an outdoor café in Winterthur, Switzerland, my son Marc's home city, on a warm August day. I had just finished a month-long tour of Italy and was contemplating my next step for the winter.

"What sort of place are you looking for?" my friend asked.

"Somewhere warm, sunny, close to the ocean, and inexpensive," I said. "And with a good flight connection to Switzerland so I can see Marc and my grandson Rafael often."

"Why don't you try Portugal?" he replied.

I was surprised and curious as I knew little about the country, even though I was a seasoned traveller to most European countries.

Asking him why Portugal, he said,

"Because the people are friendly, the food and wine are superb, the climate, especially in the Algarve, is sunny and warm in the winter months, and it's affordable to live."

Now in my mid-sixties, it was becoming a little harder and more daunting having to start all over again in a foreign country that I knew almost nothing about. I wasn't sure I could take that big step again, especially being on my own.

But, after mulling it over, I decided to give it a chance. If it didn't work out, I could stay somewhere in Europe that I was familiar with or go back to Mexico for the winter.

Two weeks later I was on a plane from Zurich to Faro, with no real plan, not knowing anyone, and going solo. Flying over Faro and descending towards the airport, I thought we were going to land on the beach! All I could see was water and coastline.

Soon I was heading west on a shuttle bus towards Porches, a village I picked because I liked the look of the hacienda-style hotel I had booked into. The sun was setting on a warm mid-September evening, and as we drove towards it, I thought it was the most beautiful red sunset sinking into the Atlantic Ocean that I had ever seen. I was in the Algarve, but at that time, I had no idea what that meant. After a few days, I searched the internet for a smaller village closer to the ocean, and Alvor came up. So I hopped on a local bus, and an hour later I trudged my suitcase to the entrance of Camping Alvor just as music began playing in the local bar. Settling into an apartment with a glass of wine, I was serenaded to sleep with Portuguese music ringing in my ears.

The next day as I wandered through the quintessential Algarve village of Alvor, I savoured the scenes of everyday life in Portugal — locals drinking coffee in the little cafés dotting the cobblestone streets, or sipping wine in the many colourful flower-decked restaurants down by the harbour, fishermen hauling and gutting their catch and selling it to the local restaurants. I enjoyed buying local fruit and vegetables at the nearby market, taking in the natural beauty of the beaches, and swimming in the frothy ocean while witnessing the most amazing red sunsets. It just felt right. It was all that my friend had said and more.

I stayed the winter at the camp in the apartment and loved being able to walk into town and to the harbour and beaches nearby. Growing up on a ranch and living mainly in small towns in Canada and Switzerland, the fit was perfect for me with this fishing village lifestyle. I bought a caravan in the spring and settled into camp life. It reminded me of living in Baja, Mexico, so the adjustment should have been easy for me.

At first, however, I felt a little lost and timid not knowing anyone and on my own. For some strange reason, my childhood shyness resurfaced, and I found it hard to go out and talk to people or walk alone into a restaurant. In retrospect, I think there were a few things that affected my self-confidence. I knew very little about Portugal, the country I wanted to spend my winters in. I think this was the key factor for me to acknowledge, I was here to 'spend the winter' which is a long time, it wasn't two weeks or a month then return home. Not knowing anything about Portugal before I came made me apprehensive. Would I like it? What were the crime rates like? What about the people, the accommodation? Of course, I could go back to Switzerland or Canada, but I wanted to make it work.

I don't think I was entirely afraid of coming here alone, having been to Mexico, Thailand, and other places solo and managed fine. I can only attribute it to being older and wondering what others thought of me beginning a new life at my age. Wow! I had never considered myself as being old and knew that I looked younger than my age, but my confidence was waning—just a little.

Finally, I think I was also tired of moving, picking everything up and starting over again. If I added it up, not including my early years, I had moved over thirty times, sometimes to other countries. I could handle going back and forth to my home city of Ottawa, where my sister Joan and niece Julia lived, but beginning a brand new life in a brand-new country made me question my motives. I wanted it to work so badly, but wondered if it would. I made a conscious effort to give it a try.

When I walked around the town and saw the friendliness of the people and found that English was spoken in the stores and restaurants, I started to relax. Slowly, I integrated with the people living in the camp and although there were expats from many different European countries there, plus Brazil and China, the US, and my home country, English was the common language. Once I realised everyone was more or less here for the same reasons—retired or semi-retired and looking for a warmer climate and around the same age as me—I began to open up and make friends. I have to admit there are 'cliquey' groups and even though it's not openly acknowledged, 'couple's groups', but I learnt not to let this bother me and instead sought out other like-minded individuals.

I joined lots of classes, which were not hard to find. One day I saw an advert for a fitness group at the local community centre and joined in, meeting other ladies who were friendly and supportive. A wonderful teacher named Marie led the class. We not only broke sweat together, but everyone was encouraged to go for a coffee afterwards in the downstairs café. We often socialised together, and I have made some lasting friendships through this group.

By word of mouth I heard about other activities and before I knew it, I was line dancing on Thursdays, tap dancing on Fridays, show dancing on Mondays, and swimming at the camp pool and fitness classes in between. I also joined the Algarve Writers Group, and we get together or meet virtually once a month to talk about the stories we've written for the class and to socialise. As with everything, the pandemic has put restrictions on most activities, and

I look forward to getting back to some form of normality soon. I have found if you make the effort to meet people and are willing to try different things and have an open mind, you can make friends easily and life becomes much better.

I do cherish my solitude though, and often meditate by the ocean, listening to the sound of the waves with the clear blue water lapping at my feet. My fears subside and my spirit soars and I marvel at the beauty that surrounds me.

"Every morning we are born again. What we do today is what matters most." Buddha

I love the contrast here between the new and old Portuguese. You can find white, tall, modern, five-star hotels on one side of the street, and rolling green pastures with old ruins and a bearded Portuguese sheep herder tending to his bleating flock on the other—all in harmony with one another.

✿෨✿ଔ✿

I now have a lovely two-bedroom static caravan at the camp with a beautiful garden. I enjoy the community ambience here and if I'm feeling lonely or need some intellectual stimulus, I just step out of my door and there is always a friendly face to greet me. I often walk around chatting with friends or stopping for a coffee. I can wander up to the bar or restaurant and see a familiar face and a welcome nod to sit, play darts or pool, or join a quiz. In retrospect, I'd say approximately a third of the people I know here are single, and half of those are men. I say this because statistically women normally outlive men. I think part of the reason there are more single men is the lifestyle—men seem to be more independent here and overall more active, hence they live longer. This is only my point of view—maybe it's the good wine too! Although it would be nice to share a meal or a glass of wine with the opposite sex, and I have dated, over the years I've come to enjoy my independency, but 'never say never', I say.

Living in the Algarve inspires my creativity. My writing has become more imaginative and intense since moving here. Writing for most of my adult life, it wasn't until I came to the Algarve that I took it up seriously. Working since I was a teenager, through several careers, three businesses and two marriages later, I never seemed to have the time. Since coming to the Algarve, I've gained inspiration around every corner.

But what gave me the final kick was a medical situation. I had a dual hip operation almost two years ago after my hips deteriorated from osteoarthritis, and I ended up having to use a walker and scooter. After trying to see an orthopaedic surgeon in Portugal, and being re-scheduled time and again, I returned to Canada for the operation in Ottawa. The recovery was long and difficult, but I recovered completely. It made me realise that health and life are precious—we're not guaranteed tomorrow. So I made myself a promise there and then to follow my dreams. One was to finish writing the stories I had started at some point but never finished, or that needed more work. And to explore fresh ideas. I had a story I had begun thirty-five years ago. Writing it started off as an emotional journey for myself, as it encompassed a traumatic part of my life. I decided to write it as a memoir.

After a couple of difficult starts, in January 2020, I finally made up my mind to face the pain and anger I'd repressed for many years. In the end, it was one of my hardest accomplishments. Writing the story brought with it healing and forgiveness, and bountiful peace. I felt it was a story that needed to be told. With the help of a writing coach and reading countless books and memoirs, I wrote my first draft, and the words began to flow. When Covid-19 took over our daily lives, it only enhanced my passion.

I now focus my days around my art. I concentrate on my chores and fitness until early afternoon, then at 2 p.m. my creative molecules kick in. I write for at least four hours, take a break, then either paint, write short stories, read related books or work again on my memoir. The day could end with a good movie at 9 p.m. or a drink with friends, or I might burn the midnight oil revising my manuscript until late.

My first memoir book is planned for publication in the spring or early summer of 2021. I think it will find an audience because it's a story about a mother's love, loss, healing, and forgiveness.

Another passion is painting, which I enjoy as an artistic expression and partly to record my heritage. I focus on Cree indigenous peoples in Canada and Haida Aboriginal art, and paint landscapes and abstract art in watercolour and oils. I'm setting up a studio in my home and would like to one day exhibit my paintings and sell online.

I was also involved in amateur theatre in Canmore, Canada, for over twenty years, and was pleasantly surprised to discover The Algarveans theatre group in Lagoa. I often go to their productions (when Covid rules allow), and volunteer when time permits. I am also a member of the Algarve Film Collective.

✿ஐ✿ରஐ✿

Being raised on a farm, I have a deep love for animals. I would often help a mother cat give birth to her kittens; or bottle-feed baby lambs and bring them into the house to wrap them in blankets when it was cold. Over the years I have volunteered with many animal charities, in Western Canada, Mexico, and now the Algarve.

When I moved to the camp, I had my first encounter with feral animals who would come in search of food. Asking around, I was put in contact with a lovely, dedicated Portuguese woman named Zélia Santos, who helped me sterilise and re-home them. The funding came from private donations, the APPA animal charity, fundraisers, and out of our own pockets. I also drove to Lagos every Saturday morning for two years to feed the cat colony by the harbour with a friend through an animal charity called Nandi, until my arthritis debilitated me.

After my hip operation, I began focusing my time more at home. One Easter Sunday in 2019, I was sitting on my deck-covered patio when a neighbour came over and asked if I would speak with two ladies about some kittens. I said sure, and I met Sally and her sister Penny. They said they were walking nearby and had seen two baby kittens in a ditch with no mother around. Not knowing what to do, they walked to the restaurant above the camp and asked Melvin (the former owner of Moley's restaurant) if he knew anyone who could help. He told them to 'try the cat lady', and they were directed to me. I became an overnight 'mama', bottle-feeding a three-week-old brother and sister every two hours. Their eyes had barely opened, and they wouldn't have lasted another night. And if this wasn't enough, a friend from the other side of the camp told me there was a litter of kittens born under a caravan and asked if I could help.

Now I was the surrogate mother of six! Because the mother was still feeding that litter, we left them with her, but then I noticed their eyes were infected. Off they all went to the vet and before I could say 'meow' I was babysitting six kittens. Thankfully, I had help from some kind people. Sally and Penny bought kitten milk and helped with the bills. Neighbours Anne and Liz helped to feed the new bunch. One little ginger was so sick we didn't think he'd survive, so I nursed him round the clock. After two months, they were ready for adoption. Remember the brother and sister? I put an advert online with a local animal charity and a very nice young Portuguese couple came and immediately fell in love with them. The two kittens, now called Ben and Billie, happily went off to live with their new family.

Now there were four little brothers left with their mother. They were old enough to be adopted, so I brought them to my place and Zélia gave me a big cage. We sterilised the mother and put her back into her environment. It was time to say goodbye, but I just couldn't part with Bo-Bo, the little ginger who was now a playful, healthy, and oh-so-cute boy. One of his brothers, a black-and-white kitten, looked at me with the most begging eyes as if to say, 'take me'. It's true that cats sometimes choose their owners—only an animal lover would understand this. He puffed out his little chest and smiled at me, and that was that. Bo-Bo and Scooter were my new fur-babies. They joined Bella, a sweet female who I rescued from the colony in Lagos. When I'm away in Canada, I usually get a cat sitter to care for my babes. There are also neighbours and friends who generously step in to feed my cats if it's for a shorter period of time.

The remaining two brothers were adopted, and all were sterilised. I organised a fundraiser with Zélia's help and raised enough money to cover their costs. I haven't been a 'surrogate mama' for a while, but I regularly donate to Isabel at SOS Alvor and the APPA charity, and continue to feed and care for rescue cats in the area. Compared to others, my help is modest. Many volunteers have given so much of their time and money helping not only cats but dogs and other animals in the Algarve and Portugal. With little or no Government funding, I don't know what we would do without these dedicated and caring people.

"The kindest thing you can do in life is to give selflessly of yourself."

༺꧁༒꧂༻

The first couple of years here I struggled with the language and still do. I planned my grocery shopping with a list where I had written what I wanted in Portuguese translated into English. I thought I was learning the words quite well, until one day I saw a package of what looked like chicken with the name *peru* written on it. After checking the price, it seemed to be quite reasonable, but wanting to buy locally, I put it back. One day a young girl at the store was stocking the packs of *peru*. Out of curiosity I asked her, in English (oops, sorry!), why the chicken was always fresh looking and inexpensive when it was shipped all the way from Peru? She turned and laughed so loudly a couple stared at us.

"No, it's not from Peru, it's the name for 'turkey' in Portuguese," she explained.

We both chuckled together, and I still do when I think of my silliness. And boy was I happy, as I love *peru*.

When I first heard Portuguese spoken on the local TV, I thought it sounded like a Slavic language, and nothing like Spanish, which I spoke a little in Mexico. Some words were the same as Spanish and I tried to understand them, but I was completely lost. I took lessons but found the pronunciation very difficult. The other problem with learning the language is that the majority of local people speak very good English and they teach it in the local schools. We expats sometimes become lazy in learning Portuguese because we know we can get by speaking English. I keep trying to learn Portuguese and use a habit I learnt in Switzerland to learn Swiss German. I read the local paper and tried my skills out in restaurants, often getting strange looks. I believe it is out of respect to a country to learn their language, even if it's just the basics.

Five years on, I'm still here. I spend my summers in Canada, with trips to Switzerland, and plans are in the making to see India, Bali, South Africa, and Tibet, and to walk solo on the Camino de Santiago. My son has visited five times and loves the Algarve, and my grandson has visited once, and, true to form, flights are frequent and inexpensive to Switzerland (and reasonable to Canada too)!

I also love the close proximity and accessibility Portugal has to other European countries. Overall, it's an easy country for a foreigner to live in, even with its minor drawbacks. But if you are thinking of living or retiring here, do your homework first. Come for a short holiday and explore the area that might attract you. Educate yourself as much as you can online about the town or city you would like to live in. Of course a job will bring you to a certain location unless you work virtually or from home. Or do what some foreigners do and buy a campervan and travel around until you find the perfect place. This is not always easy as a single person, therefore renting an apartment or small house for a month or so at a time might be more suitable. Give it a year and you will fall in love with this country, as I have.

"The only regret we'll have in later life is not finding the courage to follow our dreams."

Bem-vindo!

༺༺༺༻༺

You can find details about June's upcoming memoir and other writing on her website:
www.junebugmjorgensen.com

The Algarve - My Happy Place
GUIDA PEREIRA

I am from Macau, a small Far East territory originally under Portuguese administration, and I am Macanese, the daughter of a Portuguese and Chinese mixed couple. I'm a member of probably one of the smallest demographic groups in the world, the last generation of what was considered true Macanese. Mixed-race children born during the Portuguese administration, as Macau is now China, no more born under the Portuguese flag.

Today, Macau is the biggest casino city in the world, making around four times the money of Las Vegas. Like all casino cities, there is good and bad. The good—there is a lot of international investment, diverse cultural experiences, it is multicultural, and unique. But with gambling, also comes mafia, prostitution, loan sharks, and drugs, all of which I was exposed to at a very young age and to which I am quite accustomed.

It is also the place that I believe was the origin of one of the first fusion foods in the world, combining Portuguese and Chinese flavours and foods together. It originated from the fact there was a lack of Portuguese spices available, and the people tried to duplicate Portuguese dishes using some local Chinese ingredients that were available to them. The result was an explosion of delicious fusion food, called Macanese cuisine, which is unique. They created the food not only with a Portuguese influence but also with African and Goan characteristics and even elements from the Strait of Malacca too.

It is this tiny territory with its unique mixture of Portuguese architecture and Chinese temples blended together, unlike anywhere else in the world, where I was lucky enough to have a very fun, amazing childhood. Macau is a special city with a total blend of different religions and cultures, and today, a political system which China designates as the 'Special Administrative Region of China', following the 'One Country, Two Systems' ideal. I grew up exposed to a multicultural mindset, full of experiences and different behaviours, with a blend of religion and nationalities. I would say this prepared me for globalisation very early in life.

I am the third child of four. My mom always said she only wanted two, and I came along to mess up her perfect pair, but then she had the fourth one, which made it all OK again! I guess this set the path for my self-described third child syndrome and extra complexes. Hence all my childhood photos show me looking cranky. These insecurities most probably stemmed from the constant jokes in my family of me being dark, hairy, and looking like a monkey or a black olive. Weirdly, I hardly possess any hair today—anyway—this tells you I was definitely never the favourite, but often the one that stood up to my parents. I figured I had nothing to lose and as a result got beaten up the most.

I guess to my family it was a harmless source of entertainment, but to me it was the foundation of my feelings of inadequacy for years to come. On the plus side, I guess it made me more creative. I loved my imaginary world and often disappeared on a fantasy path of illusion in my mind.

As a child I played mostly with my little brother, we were very close. We understood each other the most. I worshipped and feared my older sister, and adored and respected my big brother. So just through my siblings, I had already experienced a welter of emotions by the age of ten.

The opinion we have of ourselves is too often formed at a very early age by those around us. Unfortunately, sometimes, regardless of what the reality is, or where our path later on in life takes us, the way we feel about ourselves is so ingrained from our early childhood, that it is very difficult to run away from.

Today, of course, I look back at it quite differently. Maybe I was a bit self-victimising as it suited my dramatic personality, but back then, because my big brother was my mom's favourite, my sister my dad's, and my little brother my aunt's, who also lived with us, I felt displaced. I spent a lot of time in friends' homes, attaching great importance to friendships at that age, as I felt it was where I was most liked and accepted.

Being mixed-race and speaking Cantonese fluently, we got to play with Cantonese, Macanese and Portuguese kids, all in different groups. Already at a young age, I had a very elaborate and diverse social interaction with others.

I lived in Macau for most of my childhood. We also travelled a lot to Hong Kong, which was only about forty-five minutes away by Jetfoil. I would spend many weekends growing up and most of my teenage years clubbing and shopping there.

We enjoyed what many would call a privileged lifestyle. My dad was a captain in the police force and my mom a maths teacher and also a businesswoman. Her family owned an import business, it was actually one of the first import companies of alcohol and olive oil from Portugal. We had a warehouse in our home supplying supermarkets and hotels with our products. Surprisingly, none of us drink that much considering we had readily available wines, spirits, ports, brandy, you name it, in our house.

Living in Macau in such a diverse community, even back then in the 1960s and 70s, I was fortunate enough to have been exposed to, and educated about, different cultures, religions, and political and social differences. At a very early age, I learnt how we can harmoniously coexist, respecting and learning from each other. Even with my friendships, being of mixed-race, I actually had three different sets of friends. I had pure Chinese friends that I used to hang out with mainly in my neighbourhood and through my swimming team, most of whom were Chinese.

At school, I played mostly with Macanese children. With my parents we met Portuguese and Macanese families through social gatherings in the military club, the police department, the social club that my parents belonged to, and the tennis club. There were also a lot of government functions which were attended by Portuguese and some Macanese people.

Growing up, I only spoke Portuguese and Cantonese. Having said that, when I was very little and first learning how to speak, my parents went on a tour of Europe and took my two older siblings with them. Apparently they asked me if I wanted to go, but I had answered no, so at two years old they decided I was mature enough to decide my fate and left me in the care of my aunts for a year. When they returned, I only spoke Cantonese and when my father spoke to me in Portuguese, I answered him back rudely in Chinese, saying that I didn't speak Portuguese. One slap later (a very common practice back then, child beating), according to them, I found myself instantly fluent in Portuguese, so I guess I spoke Portuguese all along.

English came into my life at a later stage, and today it is my first language. I think and communicate in English; I dream in Portuguese the most, and I definitely get angry and swear in Cantonese.

Because my parents did not get along too well, as a child I focused most of my time on sport. Training was my escape, and that is what I did to stay out of the house. Originally, I started with ballet, dreaming of becoming a dancer one day. That was short-lived when mom pulled me out of class, because of my father's extreme friendship with the then only ballet teacher in town. Then, around the age of ten, I turned to swimming. I trained morning and afternoon; it was my safe space, and I became quite good at it, making it to Asian-level competitions. Before I knew it, that's all I was doing. When all my friends were hanging out as teenagers and going to parties, I was training. One day I went to a party around the age of fifteen and a boy in a slow dance said I was so muscular that it was like dancing with a boy. That was it for me!

I stopped swimming overnight, started wearing makeup, smoking, going to parties, and living my best life. I was partying every weekend and going to Hong Kong a lot with my friends.

This is around the time I started realising that I could speak and understand English. I guess I was lucky that my parents made us watch Sesame Street and the Mickey Mouse Club as children, so subconsciously there was always some knowledge of English.

My initiation into practising English was actually quite embarrassing. I was invited to a very posh cocktail party full of American and English stars and went up to a group of English-speaking women, trying to blend in and engage in conversation. One of them had very cute dimples when speaking, but with my little knowledge of English, I got the words confused and told the woman I thought she had very cute nipples. She looked down at herself, non-plussed. Thank God, by then, they were all highly intoxicated and found it hilarious. I decided there and then that the way forward in trying to speak English was not to care if I made a mistake. At the very worst, they would find it funny or correct me, and since I had an accent, it didn't matter. It meant it wasn't my first language, and that gave me the courage to be more daring. By the way, this is the same advice I give to friends for learning and speaking Portuguese.

✿ৡ✿ಐ✿

Around the age of sixteen I was sent to Canada to further my education, which I was not impressed with because I was not only loving my life in Macau, I was also in love. My parents had split up by then and I was used to living in Macau with mom, so I was not happy to move to Canada where my dad had been living. So much so, it wasn't an easy time, which ended up with my dad kicking me out one night when it was minus 30 degrees centigrade. I was sixteen and homeless, only a few months after moving to Canada. Thankfully, that only lasted for a few days.

Being new in Toronto, I didn't really know many people. I did have one phone number of a girl called Nicky. She was a foreign student I met during my flight to Toronto. I called her; she was then sharing a basement apartment with two other Chinese foreign students and they took me in. For the next few months, I lived with them, sleeping on throw cushions on the floor. I found a job in a Chinese restaurant, pushing the Dim Sum cart. I must say, mine was an extremely popular cart. I was the only mixed-race girl any Chinese restaurant had. People enjoyed ordering from me, so they could listen to me speak Chinese. I was also lucky to be the darling of the chefs — they fed me the best food for six months.

Nicky and I were eventually thrown out, and I was again homeless until we settled in a room in a house on the outskirts of Toronto. These were very hard times, but also one of the happiest in my life. I learnt basic human kindness, strangers helped me, and gave me the strength to continue. I actually finished high school at the same time because I was determined to prove to my family that I could do it and would survive, regardless.

They were very difficult months, and it was a struggle, but somehow these strangers and new friends saw the potential in me and not only fed me, but encouraged and helped me. They gave me the strength and love to believe in myself and think that I was worth something. I managed to work and finish high school despite living a very basic lifestyle with very little money or material possessions.

And then my boyfriend came from Macau to take me home. I showed up in Macau and my mother was not impressed. Because I was still a minor, she put me right back on a plane to Toronto. I then had to make a really hard decision to either marry my boyfriend or never see him again. I chose to marry him, by applying for him to be my fiancé from Toronto and I married him within two months. I was only eighteen and six months later; I became pregnant.

Things were great for a year or so, we were a young couple in love with a baby. I had reunited with my siblings and some of my family in Canada, but life was difficult for both of us in a new country with new habits. I guess I adapted, and he didn't. Being so young, the marriage started to fall apart. By the age of twenty-two, I was divorced with a young child.

I often say, I am precocious in almost everything I do. It is not always a good thing, but having said that, I'd completed my 'Masters Qualification in Life' by the tender age of twenty-two. From then on, it was me and my daughter Vanessa, with a few turbulent relationships in between, until one day the idea of moving to Portugal was planted in my head.

Canada was supposed to be my forever home, at least as far as my parents were concerned. I loved Canada, Toronto was a great city, I adored my friends and family there, but there was always something missing, this feeling of 'home'. It wasn't like I was unhappy there, I just felt there was somewhere else I was supposed to be.

My mom had sold a house in Macau and she invited me, my daughter, and my older brother to visit Portugal on holiday. We could stay with her in the beach house she owned in Ericeira, a small town north of Lisbon.

My childhood best friend and my daughter's godmother had also just moved to the Algarve to live, so I took a brief trip down there to see her. When I arrived, my first thought was, this was a place where

I could see Vanessa having a wonderful childhood with freedom — the type of freedom I had enjoyed as a child in Macau.

Because things were not great in my personal life at the time; the minute I arrived in the Algarve, that feeling of 'home' came flooding in. It gave me a fresh perspective on how and what our little family really needed, at least until I figured out where our future would be.

I thought this was a place where I could take my time, reflect, and make the right decisions for our future. At the same time Vanessa would be exposed to fresh air, wonderful weather, and a lot of outdoor activities — something living in a big city like Toronto she was somewhat deprived of. I was constantly working to make ends meet and travelling endless hours commuting to work every day. I was spending very little time with Vanessa and knew this was not how I wanted to live.

I convinced myself that we needed this change for us. I also had a strong feeling that I was doing the right thing, so I packed up and with the help of my big brother and his partner, we took the leap. I thought to myself, I have nothing to lose and if it doesn't work out, I can always go back. Armed with 2,000 Canadian dollars, we moved to Portugal. At least for a while I could then contemplate life, so to speak, and decide calmly what to do next.

It wasn't supposed to be a forever place; it was just where I felt I could find some peace and make the right decisions while my child grew up in a safe and free place.

✲❀✪ଔ✲

When we first moved here, things were hard. Being unemployed for six months, adapting to a new life with a small child, having no car and no phone, was challenging; but as I watched Vanessa play, feed the pigeons in the square, and join the pony club, I knew I had made the right decision. I focused on looking for work. I knew everything else would eventually fall into place.

We first rented an apartment with Vanessa's godmother and her husband, thus cutting down on expenses and sharing costs. This made it easier on my 2,000 dollars, and it gave me an opportunity to understand my surroundings better. I would recommend to anybody considering moving here, to do the same. First rent and get a feel for the area. Take your time to discover where you most enjoy being, where you make friends, or end up working, or starting a business, before taking such a big step as buying a property.

My mom later bought a small apartment as an investment in a resort in Albufeira, which I then lived in. I could go to work and Vanessa would play in a safe environment with the reception and resort staff always around and looking out for her. This gave me a lot of peace.

Being in my twenties, the Algarve also offered an impressive nightlife. I had always enjoyed dancing; and clubbing in Macau, Hong Kong, and Toronto had been a constant activity on the weekends for me, and now in the Algarve it was just as much fun. There were many people like me, looking for a good time in a place that felt like a permanent vacation. I guess because I looked different, I got in everywhere for free and best of all never paid for a drink. Sadly, I can't say the same now I am in my fifties. I retired from the club scene by the age of forty, and now if I go anywhere I'm immediately asked to pay for drinks, which I'm not impressed with!

Back to the apartment, and although it was very small, there was no closet space, it had only one bedroom and Vanessa's room was a bunkbed in the hallway, we were very happy. We didn't have much money, but her life was free and outdoors. She spent endless hours in the pool and on weekends she would mostly have a friend stay over or she would go to sleepovers. She also joined the pony club, which in Portugal is quite affordable.

Although the bureaucracy at the beginning and getting used to the Portuguese way of life was sometimes difficult; the lifestyle, the air, the food, and the simplicity of the Algarve made up for all of it.

I was very attracted to the Algarve not only because of the obvious good weather and space, but in certain parts of the old towns I sensed a vibe very similar to old Macau, before all the big casinos arrived. There was also another attraction to me, being of mixed-race the Algarve had a lot of different nationalities living here in perfect harmony and I felt very comfortable.

Originally, I settled in Albufeira, solely based on logistics. As a single mother, I didn't know where I was going to find a job, so I thought it would be easiest to place ourselves in the middle. That way, I would be able to travel in either direction for employment.

Finding a job with a young child was not easy. It also was probably one of the strangest experiences I had here, because having worked in corporate Canada, I was not prepared for the different work culture at the time in Portugal. In fact, since I did not have a car for the first six months here, I found it almost impossible to find work. Public transport at the time was almost non-existent, but once I got a car, it made things a lot easier and I started working in sales. After a couple of bad experiences, I found work in an English medical clinic and ended up working there for twenty-two years as the Practice Manager.

Socially, it was a very new and interesting place to be at that time. Because I was young when I arrived, I managed to make new friends through work and going out. I also made friends through all the different sports offered. In my case, it was tennis, or I should say, my attempt at tennis. I guess because about forty percent of the population is foreign here, everybody is from somewhere else, so I found people quite receptive and friendly.

When I first arrived, there were only two things I missed, and one of those was Chinese food. I managed to meet all the Chinese people that lived in the area, so they could feed me and I, in turn, became their translator for local authorities. The second thing I missed was the city vibe, however, travelling to Lisbon or Seville on weekends provided all the city I needed in exactly the dosages required.

So, I wasn't actually missing much and today, with all the flights offered from Faro, I can be anywhere in Europe in a couple of hours or so. It has made living here even more enjoyable and easy.

I started thinking, why was I trying to figure out where to go next? I had already found a place where people worked their whole lives to settle in for their retirement, and I had the possibility to do that while I was still young and enjoy it. I didn't know if there would be a long tomorrow, none of us do, and that was when and why I decided Portugal was going to be my permanent home. I have never regretted it since.

The only downfall to living in Portugal for me was the low income in comparison to Toronto, which did not allow me to travel and go on holidays abroad much. Conversely, it gave me a quality of life-work balance that I did not have in my previous day-to-day life, where I would work nonstop for months to go on holiday for two weeks to somewhere like the Algarve. My twenty-something-self told me to choose quality of life over quantity.

Like everything else in my life, my love life had always been, let's say, quite colourful and turbulent. Portugal was also a place where I found love. Soon after my arrival, I was in love. It lasted seven years, but it didn't work out for me when he left to work elsewhere. I guess I wasn't 'the one'. Three years later, I fell in love again, moved house, and set up home thinking this was going to be it, but it wasn't to be, ending in terrible heartbreak, despair, and depression.

Sometimes, it's not the situation that brings us down, it is the last action that creates a tumbling effect and brings everything down with you. Things not dealt with before are shoved into the back of our minds, and then suddenly it just takes one incident for things to come crashing down, forcing us to deal with everything. That is what happened to me. Following six months of what I can only describe as existing as a non-functioning person, the end result was a terrible car accident that almost took my life in 2003. I lost three-quarters of my forearm and had to have skin grafts. The skin on my entire left leg replaced the skin on my left arm. There was a lot of physical pain, but the emotional pain was even greater.

The only positive thing about it was that I was alone and have no recollection of what exactly happened with only a few flashbacks of what occurred in the emergency room. I remember losing a lot of blood and almost losing my life.

I understood at a very early stage of my recovery that I had two options moving forward. The easy one would be to just feel sorry for myself and everything that goes with that, including resentment, hate, and fear. The harder and longer path, but ultimately the better one for me, involved understanding and forgiveness. I had to learn to deal with it and be grateful that nothing worse had happened and to appreciate the second chance I had been given to live. I chose the latter and really understood from then onwards the importance of gratitude.

Sometimes I think today, besides the scars that are a constant reminder of everything, it was probably also a blessing. My entire perspective on life started changing as of that day.

After spending a month in the hospital and another at home with daily medical care and physiotherapy, I started slowly healing physically, and I could move my hand again.

Painting came into my life then. Suddenly I woke up one day with the urge to buy paint brushes and canvas, so I did, and I just started painting and have never stopped. It started as a hobby, guiding me through the healing process, not only from the accident but from everything else. Painting offered me solace, warmth, comprehension, strength, and love, but mostly it made me feel alive and taught me that I still had a lot to say through it.

Abstract painting feels to me like there are no rules, no limitations, no guidelines. I can just express myself. Some people will get it, others may identify with it, some will hate it, but it is ultimately the place where I come alive and can be myself.

This is also the time when I discovered yoga. I was told at the hospital that I would only be able to recover at the very most seventy-five percent of my mobility in my left arm. My worst fault became my best ally. Thanks to my stubbornness, through yoga, I recovered all my strength and I can happily say the doctors were wrong. I now have one hundred percent mobility.

In 2012, I was made redundant overnight. Suddenly I had become too old and expensive to keep. Trying to figure out what I was going to do next, one night I had a dream where I met with my aunt. As a child I had always asked her for advice; and in a very matter-of-fact way, she said to me,

"Of course you know what you're going to do, you're going to paint."

When I woke up, my brother was here with me on holiday at the time, and I just announced to him I was going to start my career as a professional artist.

And I must say, it has been the best career decision ever, not so much financially, in fact barely, but I have never been happier. What resulted was the start of a collection of paintings demonstrating my love of bold colours, fuelled by uninhibited emotion, learned experiences, and nostalgia. Being an abstract painter, there is no end to where my expression can go, and it is my favourite escape.

We always make excuses for ourselves. Oh, it's so difficult, I can't adapt, I have to do so much to just get up and go. I truly believe that mostly, we are just scared of the unknown or simply of change. We settle for the not-so-great lives we feel we have, but if we can remove the fear, I believe we can accomplish anything, or at the very least, know what doesn't work and live life with no regrets.

✧ℰ✧ℛ✧

Having already lived in three different continents, experiencing a range of environments, financial situations, cultures, weather, and foods; I found that being in Portugal gave me the best quality of life, not only because of the historical and beautiful aspects of this country, but mostly the simplicity and humility of its people. Whether to work or to retire, Portugal, for me, definitely offers the best balance. There's no place I've found being broke easier to deal with — the sea and sun don't cost you anything, and a coffee in an esplanade is affordable to anybody.

Independently of the reasons anybody chooses Portugal to live, whether being for business, quality of life, family, friends, change, or retirement, I would recommend getting involved in some local activities. This always offers us a very good perspective on the place we have chosen as our new home and also forces us to understand the customs and language, and if we are lucky, meet new and different friends.

One of the biggest mistakes I found I made, and people in general do when moving to a new country, is that initially I kept comparing it to Canada, and to Macau. I criticised everything that was not working the way I was used to, and then I recognised that attitude was preventing me from adapting to my new life.

I realised there was a reason I chose Portugal. I wasn't one hundred percent happy with my life previously, so why was I analysing it now, what was the point? The sooner I stopped comparing the services or ideas or behaviour now to where I was before, the quicker I adapted and integrated into my new life. That, to me, is one of the most important things when moving to a new country.

With hindsight, having lived here since my early twenties, I have experienced many levels of lifestyle in the Algarve.

In my twenties and thirties, it was a great place to go out; it has a fabulous night life. At the same time, the beaches, sun, water sports, and activities, make it an excellent place to raise children. It gives them a carefree and outdoor childhood, where it is still safe to play outside, ride horses, play tennis, or simply go to the beach. Most importantly, it is all still very affordable. It is a wonderful place to implement new ideas. It is also one of the fastest growing locations in the country for young Portuguese nationals looking for a good work-life balance. For those who want to start a new life with fresh ideas away from the big cities, it is still quite an untapped market.

The Algarve still feels today like a place rife with new work opportunities. The market is still very new here for any business other than tourism-related. Services and businesses are growing daily, run by Portuguese themselves looking for a better quality of life down here.

I have a cute memory I recall of my clubbing days. I drank mostly gin or martini, I could drink tons of it and hardly ever got drunk. I would drink and dance and mostly not even engage with the people. If I had a couple of glasses of wine, I was the happiest girl ever and the bartenders of the clubs I used to go to knew that. One night I walked into a small club and the cute bartender just instantly brought up a barrel of wine, placed it on the counter and smiled at me. No words were necessary!

The best chat-up line I have heard so far in Portugal? Once outside a nightclub, I was told,

"You know something, I have beautiful toes."

I thought it was original and hilarious, so my interest was aroused. He removed his shoes and out came the most perfect toes I had ever seen in a man. We became instant friends.

The time through my forties and into my fifties has been a path of self-discovery, but these are also the decades when we realise or know what we want. Having been able to live here, discovering my love of painting, yoga, food, space, and environment has actually been what has made this place so magical.

If you have a job, you can finish work at 5.30 or 6 p.m. and it is still daylight. In the summer you still have hours of daytime left to enjoy your life, with no stress of commuting, or traffic, so your home and work balance is so much healthier. Here you can have a life after work.

Portugal has given me an appreciation of good grilled fish, tomatoes, onions, oranges, olive oil, the extremely good wine, love, hope, and happiness. Most of all, it has provided me with a sense of contentment and peace, and I really don't want to be anywhere else.

I have since found love again, with a like-minded artist, that I am very grateful for. He is my love, my friend, my companion, and we understand and respect each other; making me the living proof that as long as we are open to it, love is ageless and it can happen at any time.

To conclude about me and my journey in Portugal, my most prominent accomplishment and what I am most proud of, is my daughter Vanessa. I believe that maybe, even at a very young age, and sometimes not able to make the best choices, that at least I was able to provide her with a childhood full of outdoor activities, sand, sun, and a lot of love. And by making this move, I have also realised that the courage to change was one of my most important qualities on my path to discover happiness.

As for the Portuguese people, in my opinion, they are like their traditional Fado music. They are emotional, dramatic, but passionate, sometimes melancholic, but loving and kind, and kindness is for me, the best description of how I have been received by Portugal.

I have no regrets moving here, Portugal is a country of constant discovery, inspiration, and nature. It is a place of reflection, delicious food, serenity, contentment, and ultimately peace, and what I can only describe as My Happy Place.

༚ഩ༚ര༚

You can view Guida's artwork on her website: www.guidapereira.com

21

A Rewarding Life in Travel and Consular Service
CLIVE JEWELL

I appeared on the 11th June 1957 at St. Helier's Hospital in Carshalton, Surrey. My early years with my younger sister, Karen, my Mum, Sheila, who worked in a bank before having two kids by the age of twenty-one, and my Dad, Steve, a scaffolder, were spent in Colliers Wood, near Wimbledon. It was there I developed my lifelong love of football. We lived near Wandle Park, and dad would take me to watch Colliers Wood United FC. Afterwards I could earn a penny cleaning football boots in a bucket of water. Years later, I returned to play against Colliers Wood for Ashtead FC. Nobody offered to clean my boots!

We moved to Ashtead, Surrey, when I was seven. Dad was so proud to move us from a maisonette in a working-class London borough to a semi-detached house in leafy Surrey. It had a huge lawn which was converted into The Oval cricket ground in summer, and Wembley in winter. It is amazing how a small boy can play an entire FA Cup Final on his own! Those sports became the focus of my young life.

The cricket action, however, led to strained relations with Mr Sears next door. If I was served up a long hop by his son, Brian, it was too great an invitation to dance down the wicket and smash it over mid-off—straight through Mr Sears' beloved glass greenhouse!

I passed my eleven-plus at interview, having been a borderline pass in the exam. Not for the last time in my life, I got through on personality and chat rather than intelligence and academic talent! Aged eleven, I started at what was then Wimbledon College grammar school, commuting to school by train. On my first day Mum came with me and we sat in a carriage where another boy was wearing the same college uniform, accompanied by his Dad. We became friends and Mark and I would travel to school together for the next few years. His dad worked in London and always had a stack of newspapers on which he would write notes. I discovered that Mr McCaffrey, later Sir Tom, was press secretary to the Home Secretary and later Prime Minister, James Callaghan. I doubt that he would have foreseen my joining the Foreign and Commonwealth Office as British Consul in the Algarve some forty years later!

Learning was a serious business at The College, but fortunately for a young Mr Jewell, so was sport. They had a fantastic pedigree in athletics and rugby. I was enthusiastic about athletics, becoming county champion at 800 metres but scared to death of rugby. Only when I was introduced to sevens did I warm to it, and that was because I could outsprint anyone on the pitch. I eventually played scrum-half or wing for the school team, having grown up in mind and spirit if not much in body! Academically, I was neither the best student, nor the worst. I enjoyed English, history, and languages, especially Spanish.

Outside school, it was all about sport and music. At thirteen, I started going to Ashtead youth centre. One of the adult volunteers was an inspirational guy who encouraged us to do voluntary work like gardening or decorating for older people in the community. He also ran our Sunday football team. Many of the lads I played with in that team have remained lifelong friends.

I left school with seven 'O' levels, realising I did not have the commitment for 'A' levels. Neither did I have a job. In the end, dad fixed me up with an interview at Midland Bank Trust Company in London through a fellow patron at the local pub. It was not remotely what I wanted to do, but I had to start earning and contributing. I was miserable and quit after seven months. What happened next did not please my dad. I had decided that I wanted to go travelling, but I needed the cash to get started. I had worked a couple of summers at dad's new scaffolding firm. I wasn't scared of physical labour and could handle the lads' banter. I was always a bit quick of tongue as a teenager, often a bit too quick for my own good! So, for the next six months, I worked on a building site. It was good money, and I saved … not a penny! One job was near Heathrow airport and I remember watching Concorde flying overhead on a test flight. It was magnificent.

By then I was also working as a DJ. I had been playing at being a DJ at home since I was nine or ten years old. I would use Mum's record player to play her old 45s, recording them onto a reel-to-reel tape recorder. A pal at the youth centre, Mick, wanted to get a mobile disco going. Was I interested? Not half! Mick was a Post Office Telecoms engineer, yellow Morris van included, and he built the kit and did the driving. He was the brains and the roadie, as it were. I was the music man and DJ. The mouth to Mick's brains. Nobody found that difficult to understand!

Mick continued upgrading the gear and we kept it going for eight years. We DJ'd many a wedding reception, birthday party, Christmas and New Year celebration, plus regular spots at local venues like Leatherhead Football Club. By then Mick was married and I was heading off to my first overseas posting as a holiday rep in Menorca.

I had read a silly book by Stanley Morgan called *The Courier*. The book was part of a series where the main character, Russ Tobin, worked a lot of different jobs. In *The Courier* he became a tour guide on the Spanish island of Majorca. I realised that here was my career. This would be my ticket to Spain. I was going to be a 'courier'.

○୨୦♡ଓ○

February 1976 kicked off a career in travel that would last for thirty-three years. I retrieved my 'whistle and flute' from the wardrobe and joined the admin department of Global of London (Tours & Travel) in Tottenham Court Road. After six months, I went on a short visit to Majorca that cemented my determination to work in Spain. It was an educational trip. I still remember the amazing scent that wafted up as we left the aircraft. It was different. It was Spanish! The trip was hard work but great fun. As in very late nights! For this nineteen-year-old it was spectacular. We flew with the wonderful Dan Air. And if you have just said Dan Dair aloud, you are banned from reading the rest of this chapter!

Despite this, after a year I was bored stiff and looking for another job. By now I was meeting colleagues in the pub after work, and I became friendly with the operations team. One evening, their boss, Steve, said he had heard I was thinking of leaving Global.

"Yes," I said. "I need something more interesting."

"Fancy joining Ops?" shot back Steve.

And that was that. The shortest interview in history! It also lit the blue touch paper to the rest of my life.

There was nothing 9-to-5 about life in operations. It was the epicentre of the company, and we had daily contact with our overseas offices, our UK and Ireland branches, airlines, and other tour operators. If there was a problem with hotel overbooking, a flight or a crisis anywhere, we were involved. French air traffic controllers striking was a regular issue. I did a few exciting stints at Gatwick airport, where I learnt what it was like to face hundreds of angry customers while wearing the company badge.

Spanish hotels routinely over-contracted their rooms causing overbookings. It was my job to manage these at our end, notifying colleagues in our UK offices and Dublin of the customers who were affected. I may have thought it was a challenge handling this from my desk in London. I would learn all about handling it at the overseas airport a few years later. The four years I spent in the Global Ops department laid the foundation for my career working in the travel industry.

April 1981. Sunday morning. Ciudadela town square. I'd been in Menorca for two weeks. At noon, I raised my San Miguel beer to my mates back in Surrey who were playing football in our local Cup Final. I had scored twice in our semi-final victory, my last game before my transfer to Spain. I looked around the intoxicatingly Spanish scenery, wondering if I had made the right decision. I knew already. The lads lost the Cup Final by the way.

I learnt the job on the hoof. My main property was an overrated 3-star hotel and I spent the entire season facing enraged customers who had plenty to be unhappy about. I never stepped out of the firing line and quickly realised that if I was there for them, listened respectfully to their grievances and did my best to act on them, they would accept I was doing all I could. It was a baptism of fire, but I am eternally grateful for that. I had a fantastic season. The job was all I wanted it to be, despite long hours and a six-day working week. I was using my Spanish, and my social life was on another level. Life for a young person in a holiday destination, even the relatively docile Menorca, was a blast.

I spent an uneventful but pleasant winter season in Crete and then returned to London, now engaged to be married! We didn't make it to the altar. Long story. In 1985, I returned overseas and have never lived in my home country since.

Before returning to Menorca, as a newly promoted Deputy Area Manager, I visited my parents. They were now in Plymouth, Devon, running a hugely popular little pub called The Shipwrights Arms. Dad had been in hospital. I knew it was a blood issue, but my parents were a bit vague about it. My dad looked well, although he was on the customer side of the bar, and we chatted a lot over the weekend. I thought he was on the mend. A few weeks later, I spoke with Mum. Dad was back in hospital. The penny dropped. I asked Mum straight out, "what is it, Mum?" It was myeloma, a type of bone marrow cancer. At best he had six months, at worst, maybe six weeks left to live. It was less than that. He was just fifty-eight. My lasting memory of being with my dad was leaning on the bar, having a natter and a chuckle over a pint. Honestly, I have never, ever felt that I would change that.

Twenty-five years later, as British Consul, I laid a wreath on behalf of the British Embassy at my first Remembrance Sunday service at St. Luke's Church in the Algarve. It remains my most humbling experience in this job, and possibly of my whole life. When I gave a short speech at the lunch afterwards, in the company of the wonderful people of the Royal British Legion, I mentioned that my dad had been a 'sparks' in the Royal Navy and how proud he would have been of me that day. The emotion surged up my throat and I choked on my words. I looked around the faces looking towards me with such kindness and knew that I was in the best possible company to get emotional about my dad.

I spent three amazing winters in the Italian ski resort of Livigno, and the intervening summers back in Spain. By then I had left Global and was working for Falcon Holidays, part of the Owners Abroad Group (OAG). They later morphed into First Choice Holidays. I was Area Manager for the Costa Brava, based in Lloret de Mar. We had hotels in L'Estartit, where, twenty years earlier, I had been on holiday with my family, and I had fallen in love with Spain. I went back there to have a recce and see if it was familiar. I found our little hotel and made my way to the beach. I experienced the most astonishing wave of nostalgia. Then it suddenly dawned on me that this was the exact place where my whole career, my future, had taken shape, all those years before. Cue emotions! L'Estartit is forever in my heart.

My wonderful boss, Elaine Swann, a great friend, and Algarve property owner all these years later, had asked me to take on Ibiza. This was a further promotion and essentially another clean-up job as there had been all sorts of shenanigans the previous year. Another long story. It was an incredibly busy but successful season. Midsummer, I took a call from our Overseas Director. We had acquired a company called Martyn Holidays, a big player in Portugal. The plan was to merge the Martyn resort operation with ours. On top of that, we were to launch our own Portuguese handling agency to self-manage the local administration. It would be the company's first. He wanted me to head it all up.

✿૪ᗃ✿ᙠ✿

I arrived in the Algarve in February 1989, and was initially based in Albufeira. My then girlfriend and I had found a nice apartment near Olhos de Água. I was Regional Manager for Portugal and Madeira and I knew we had our work cut out for us. We were merging the resort operations of two very different companies. Owners Abroad was the UK's third largest tour operator, and Portugal would now be their biggest overseas operation, with 65,000 customers that year. I worked with Margaret Bailey, who was already Falcon's Area Manager, and we were joined by our colleague Ronnie McGregor, who had taken over from me in Lloret. We would be running multiple brands with around sixty staff. Uniquely, we were launching a new Portuguese handling agency that was to be staffed and launched from scratch in under two months. No pressure then!

Martyn Holidays was a specialist company, run in Isleworth by its enigmatic managing director, Martyn Harrison, sadly no longer with us. Martyn was understandably intent on protecting his brand's operating model from the interference of the big bad parent company, which was exactly where I came from! I realised I would sink without Martyn's support, so I launched a charm offensive to convince him his operation was in good hands. He saw right through it, of course, but we got on well. I knew there was a maelstrom of boardroom politics beckoning between Martyn and the OAG board. And that yours truly would be piggy in the middle.

With extraordinary teamwork, resilience, blood, sweat, tears, a can-do attitude, some near misses, and many epic, late-night strategy sessions in the Kings Castle bar next door to the office, we made it through the first year. It had been a monumental effort, both mentally and physically, and I was stressed to the max. Within twelve months, OAG had merged with Redwing, triggering another round of territorial shenanigans. The new management and I were not a good fit for each other, and I moved on.

I was enjoying the Algarve's winter sunshine when, out of the blue, Martyn got in touch. There was some chit-chat, but I knew Martyn well enough by then to wait for the punchline. No prizes for guessing he was going to start another company. Did I fancy getting involved? We would be launching an Algarve programme the following summer so needed to get accommodation contracts in place quickly, with photographs and brochure descriptions. As he was still attached to OAG, he needed me to front it here. It was known locally that I was professionally unattached, and my colleague Margaret had followed me out of OAG, so we quietly set about putting things in place. The villa owners soon rumbled it, but we held the line!

This remains one of the most fulfilling things I have ever done professionally. To be in at the conception of a new business, to help shape it, and give it your own DNA was an incredibly exciting feeling. Going all 'Secret Squirrel' about it just added to the buzz. I went back to London, and we launched in January 1992 from a tiny office in Isleworth, West London. Style Holidays was up and running.

My colleague Clare Gough and I recruited our first reps, and Clare bought the inaugural uniforms off the peg in Oxford Street. Back in Albufeira, Margaret sourced an office, between the Praia da Oura 'Strip' and Kiss Disco, that would be our base for the next sixteen years.

It was heady stuff. Anyone who has been an employee, and then become involved in a start-up, will know that you are convinced you can do it better yourselves. We were, and we did, because we had the freedom to carve out our own image, identity, and strategy. Martyn rightly had his own ideas as MD, giving Style the appeal of a small, specialist company that genuinely cared for its product and its customers. He knew how to make things appealing to travel agents and was acknowledged within the trade as a genius at what these days is known as yield management. Most of the office staff jumped ship from Martyn Holidays.

He allowed those of us on the overseas team the space to shape the resort operation. We could impose our own standards of excellence, customer service, and staff support measures. We set the bar high and those who joined us had to commit to our ethic. Our reps were recruited for their ability to operate in the field on their own initiative. I did not want them to be doing the job 'by the book'. I had done the job myself and I knew how enthusiastically I responded to being trusted to solve problems, while, of course, being clear on exactly what was expected of me and knowing I had all the back-up I needed, when it was required.

From a standing start we sold 10,000 holidays the first year. We eventually peaked at 145,000 holidays to our European destinations and Florida; with Portugal by far the largest programme. I had the great fortune to live here and have to travel to so many wonderful destinations! We launched another Portuguese handling agency, Jeropa Travel, and were the Algarve handling agent for various other UK operators including Inspirations, Direct Holidays, and, for one summer only, Richard Branson's European tour operator, Virgin Sun.

That got me an invitation, with others, to a cocktail party and a quick meet-and-greet at his mansion in Holland Park one evening during the World Travel Market expo. Richard Branson could not stay long as he was off to China. He stayed long enough to give a short but sincere speech to thank us for our efforts in supporting Virgin Sun through the summer. He was wearing a dodgy jumper. And he paid for dinner!

On a massive coffee table in the living room was an amazing chess set. The main pieces were recognisable carvings of famous politicians including John Major, who was a rook, and Margaret Thatcher, who was a knight I believe. The Queen was, well, the Queen! One of the guests was the director of a car hire company in Menorca. He knew the Branson family well as they owned a villa in Port Mahón. He moved one of the pawns forward a couple of squares and placed his business card under it. Brilliant opportunism!

In 1999 our main shareholder, Carlson, had merged with Thomas Cook, then in 2001, Thomas Cook was itself acquired by the German group C&N Turistik which promptly took on the famous old British name for its worldwide operation. Cook's pretty much left us to get on with things until eventually, in 2007, they absorbed Style Holidays and closed Jeropa Travel. We were all made redundant, but they handled the situation with kindness and sensitivity. We closed the doors to our agency in Praia da Oura in July 2008. So many fantastic colleagues left their personal mark within those doors. We were an amazing team, and we all shared the same unique DNA. It had been an extraordinary period of my life, and it was a privilege to have been involved from the first day to the last.

✿ఌ✿ଓ✿

By the end of 2009, I was restless and out of work. Then, in January 2010, the British Embassy came calling out of the blue. Or, rather, out of the Algarve Resident newspaper, where I saw the position of British Consul Lisbon advertised. After checking the job description and the skills required, I knew that this was the job for me. The application process was extensive and the interviews challenging. It made me even more determined to succeed. I have never in my life prepared for anything as thoroughly. As it happened, the result was even better than I could have expected, as I ultimately secured the twin role that had become available in the Algarve, and in July 2010, I became British Consul Portimão.

I joined an experienced consular team based on the Portimão

waterfront. During my first week, my predecessor, Paul Rodwell, was still in post, handing over to me and preparing for his move to Alicante. Paul had been incredibly helpful to me in the period between my appointment and start date. He brilliantly suggested playing nine holes at Salgados Golf Course, where, between shots, he gave me a great introduction to the Consulate, the British Embassy, and what is now the broader Foreign, Commonwealth and Development Office (FCDO). I got an inkling of the personalities and the hierarchy in my new circles, which ranged outwards in rings from Portimão to Lisbon, out to Madrid, where the Consular Regional Director for our Europe South region is based, and, of course, over to London. Getting used to working in an extensive hierarchy was going to be one of my early challenges.

I knew that while I was a rookie in terms of consular work, I was confident I would be able to learn the ropes. It was important that my colleagues and I got to know each other, and I was eager to soak up as much knowledge from them as I possibly could. What I was bringing to the party was my experience as a team leader. That was why I had been given the job.

Paul had drawn up a spreadsheet with the key topics to be covered in the coming weeks and months. There were over three hundred items! It was somewhat overwhelming. Over time I learnt you can simply never know it all. One of the great things in the FCDO is there is always someone to help and support you, either from experience or as a specialist, and there is a fantastic range of training, some of which was mandatory in the early days. I also learnt that no two days are the same in consular work and to be prepared for the unexpected.

Knowing key people in the local authorities with whom we work so closely, and on whom we depend to assist our customers with their difficulties, is critical. Our relationship with them is of paramount importance. The consular team works incredibly hard to nurture and maintain relationships with hospital social workers, who are the unsung heroes of Faro and Portimão Hospitals, the Legal Medical Institute which conducts all autopsies following a death, funeral directors, social services, the police, civil protection, the court clerks, mayors, and their town hall teams, airport management and many more.

I made my first visit to the Foreign Office after three months. Even as a bloke in his fifties, I admit that my excitement was off the scale. While walking the labyrinthine corridors of the King Charles Street building during the one-week induction course that every consular officer must cover, at whatever grade you start, I now had the unmistakable feeling of 'wearing the shirt'. I felt very proud.

During 2011 there was a review of our regional structure. This was normal procedure. Any organisation should regularly analyse its functional shape and purpose. The result that impacted on me was the decision to reduce from two British Consuls in Portugal, to one, based in Lisbon. It was exactly the conclusion that I would have come to had I been in my Director's shoes. I was perfectly happy in the Algarve, did not wish to move, and so applied successfully for the revised Vice Consul role in Portimão. Life went on.

I became accustomed to the incredible range of situations that result in a fellow British citizen requiring consular assistance. Hundreds of people lose their passport in Portugal every year and need an emergency travel document. A sudden illness or tragic accident can leave a family mourning a loved one. Though Portugal is one of the safest countries in the world, crime still exists. There are British nationals who fall victim to rape and sexual assault or robbery. People inexplicably go missing from one day to the next. Others who live with challenging mental health situations can suddenly find themselves vulnerable. So vulnerable that occasionally a consular officer will need to liaise with a family in the UK whose loved one has taken their own life here in Portugal. Others find themselves detained or imprisoned. It is not our business to be judgemental, that is for the courts. We ensure detainees are treated within the law, can get support from the Prisoners Abroad charity, and keep in touch with their relatives back home. These are but a few examples of consular assistance circumstances, and they can become incredibly complex.

There are also major crisis situations to face from time to time, such as brutal forest fires, major road traffic accidents, or airline failures. When Monarch Airlines sadly collapsed in October 2017, the Embassy team went into action at Portugal's airports and assisted on the repatriation of over 12,000 Monarch customers to the UK.

If it all sounds doom and gloom, it is not. There is no doubt that anyone working in consular service does it because they want to do a job where they can help and support people in the toughest of times. I am inspired by the dedication of our consular officers and their willingness to go the extra mile. But we do have some fun too!

I enjoy outreach events, when I get the chance to meet fellow British community members around the Algarve. In my early months in the job, we embarked on a series of local meetings with the theme 'Consular in the Community'. After the Brexit referendum result of 2016 these became almost exclusively Brexit-related of course, often with British Ambassador, Kirsty Hayes, then Chris Sainty, and British Consul, Simona Demuro, in attendance, as we endeavoured to keep people aware of developments and stressed the particular importance of being properly registered for residency in Portugal.

Of course, public events dried up during the Covid-19 pandemic of 2020. The pandemic has dominated much of our work since it broke in Portugal. From the middle of March to the end of the summer we were flat out dealing with a multitude of situations impacting on British people in Portugal, many of whom faced difficulty in returning to the UK, causing obvious distress. We also handle consular cases in Cape Verde, where similar problems occurred.

Excuse the name dropping here, but I have had the pleasure of meeting Prince Charles four times now, twice in Lisbon, once in Madrid, and Rome! On meeting him and The Duchess of Cornwall at the Embassy in Rome, as Prince Charles reached me in the line-up, I mentioned I had had the pleasure of meeting him in Lisbon some years ago. He replied,

"Good Lord! You must have a very good memory to remember that!"

Watching them greet hundreds of people individually, I was struck by how they brilliantly manage, for a short period of time, to make every person feel the centre of their attention.

Every year the Embassy holds a Queen's Birthday Party in the grounds of the Ambassador's official residence. This is a grand garden party, normally attended by around eight hundred people. It is an opportunity for the Ambassador and embassy and consular teams to invite members from within the Portuguese Government, the diplomatic world, key trade partners, charities, consular stakeholders, community representatives, and a whole range of people with whom the Embassy has regular contact. The event is always sponsored by British companies or businesses with strong Anglo-Portuguese links and is generally a jolly affair, albeit with appropriate recognition given to more serious matters in the Ambassador's welcoming speech.

In the Algarve there are two events that I especially enjoy attending. The International Algarve Fair and the Better Living in Portugal (BLiP) exhibition, allow us the chance to meet people face to face for a chat, to give advice, and to hear anything people have to say. It was so disappointing to lose these, and many other events, in 2020.

Within the greater scheme of things, I know I am a tiny cog in a massive wheel, but the history, context, and responsibility of my role hit home the first time I set foot in the British Embassy in Lisbon. It still does, and I look forward to my work every single day. How fortunate am I?

✵ ❦ ✵ ❦ ✵

I now speak Portuguese well, and have managed, as a mimic, to acquire a decent accent, or so I am told. I arrived in Portugal as a Spanish speaker, with reasonable Italian and some French. I have always had an ear for languages, but I couldn't find my Portuguese ear for ages. I could read it relatively well, there being many similarities among Latin languages, and I generally understood TV news presenters, because they articulate their words clearly, but, looking back, I should have taken lessons immediately.

I adore the beach, whatever the weather. It is a tonic for my wellbeing and equilibrium. I draw inspiration and calm from the sound of the waves, and in difficult or stressful moments, that is where I head. I often call into one of the beach bars for a quiet beer on the way home, just to gaze at the ocean, and offload the day's stresses. I try not to take work home in my head, especially upsetting situations we may have handled.

Living six kilometres from the outstanding beaches around Praia da Galé, I love walking the boardwalk beside the beautiful Salgados lagoon. For chilling and strolling around stunning rock formations, I like Pedras Amarelas, which also has a great beach bar with a DJ providing summer chillout and sunset sessions.

Restaurante Os Salgados at Praia dos Salgados and Restaurante Lourenço at Praia de Manuel Lourenço are my standouts for fantastic quality food and personal service every single time. Living in Guia, the enticing aroma of grilled chicken from the Piri-piri restaurants is always wafting up to my balcony of an evening, and frequent, easy going nights at one of those eateries is often compulsory!

So, my greatest joy in the Algarve is the quality of life, the happiness, wellbeing, and gratitude I derive from living near the ocean and beach. And, by the way, those things are free!

✧ℬ✧ℛ✧

Find out more information about living in Portugal, including guidance on residency, healthcare, and passports, here: www.gov.uk/guidance/living-in-portugal

22

Living the Algarve Dream
ALYSON SHELDRAKE

It all started almost twenty years ago now. Although it's hard to believe all that time has passed. In my head I'm still in my early thirties, proudly wearing a police uniform and chatting to friends. My husband, Dave, and I must have looked tired as our friends told us about a fabulous holiday they had enjoyed in the Algarve.

"Never mind," they said, "you're going away soon, aren't you? You'll be able to have a nice rest and recharge your batteries."

"Actually, we've just returned from a trip to Spain. Do we look that bad?!"

I asked them to tell us more about where they had been.

"We have a friend that owns a little fisherman's cottage in a tiny village in the Algarve. It's beautiful and very peaceful. You'd love it."

I was intrigued. Our friends were glowing with health and certainly seemed enthusiastic about a country we had never visited.

"I don't suppose your friend would let us rent the cottage for a week, would they?" I cheekily asked.

"I don't see why not, she only charges us £100 a week. I'm sure she wouldn't mind you staying there. I'll give her a call and ask her, and let you know."

A week later, we had booked our flight to Faro airport, and we were clutching a key and a scruffy set of directions.

Our holiday motto had always been 'never go back to the same place twice', and we had enjoyed exploring a range of different countries and places since we had first met. Venice, Hong Kong, The Caribbean, and a memorable and wonderful honeymoon in Cape Town, South Africa, had all been highlights of our travels. We were interested to see how Portugal would measure up.

We set off in the hire car from the airport, heading west along the Algarve. There was a moment which is still set firmly in my mind as one of those 'gasp' moments when we rounded a corner into Ferragudo, which was to be our home for the week. The bay opened out in front of us, and we saw the village reflected in the glistening water of the Arade river. Painted boats were tied up, bobbing with the tide, the houses seemed to tumble down to the riverfront, and the majestic whitewashed church sat proudly above them keeping watch. It was idyllic.

It was a good job there wasn't a car behind us as we slowed down, took in the stunning view in front of us, and rather inarticulately and ridiculously both said "Wow!" at the same time.

Ferragudo still has that effect on me today. It is a pretty little traditional fishing village with winding cobbled streets, a harbour full of boats, a central square with little cafés and restaurants, and a beautiful long stretch of beach tucked around the corner from the lifeboat station.

Every time I drive to Ferragudo and the village comes into view, it still makes me say 'Wow!' inside, and gives me a sense of calm and peace that nowhere else has quite managed to achieve.

We were hooked from that moment on. The initial belief that this was going to be 'just another holiday' quickly turned into a magical week of exploring and discovery, as every day gave us new things to enjoy and experience, and every red circle on the map we drew led us to ten more places that we wanted to visit.

We discovered the west coast with its stunning coastline, dramatic cliffs, wide open skies and beautiful unspoilt beaches, hidden traditional villages, gentle friendly people, wonderful simple food, and a slower pace of life. We were smitten.

That was the start of our love affair with the Algarve. We returned to 'our' fisherman's cottage seven times in the subsequent two-and-a-half years. It became the only place that we wanted to visit, as we started doing repair jobs on the cottage for the owners when we visited, and left small items behind in storage in the spare room. We travelled back there more often than the owners themselves, who had become friends, and laughed every time we rang them up to enquire if the cottage was being used at all that month!

Dave and I had been holidaying in our adopted holiday home for several years when suddenly the defining day arrived. We sat in the sunshine in the square at Ferragudo, looked around and both said to each other at the same time,

"I could live here."

I think until that point it had probably been just a silently voiced 'one day' distant dream for both of us, however, once we had said it out loud and agreed with each other; suddenly it became one of those 'well, why not?' ideas that refused to disappear.

It wasn't long before we were house-hunting and purchased a modern property on the edge of the village. We still had the slight problem of working back in the UK, but we spent every spare minute we could in our new home in Ferragudo. Finally, after five more years, Dave retired from the police, I handed in my notice (a scary moment!); we packed up the car and moved to live in the Algarve.

Our new life in the sun could begin.

We warn people when they come to stay at our house now to beware the Portuguese magic that bewitches you and attacks all your senses—you may never be the same again. When you wander down into the local village, sit and have a coffee and relax, as you watch the world go by with the warm sun on your face; or the first time you glimpse the blue shimmering sea from the top of the steps that lead down to the beach—those are the moments that get your heart racing and your mind wandering into the 'what if we lived here?' thoughts that can change forever your perspective on life.

So what makes Portugal so special? Certainly the weather is a big factor, and long summer days of uninterrupted sunshine help enormously, although we know it is not all sun—boy, can it rain here too. And if we are honest, sometimes those long hot summers can even be too hot, as we sit in the shade with the locals and reminisce about the cooler autumn days.

The weather is gorgeous here all year round really, with an average temperature well over thirty degrees in the summer, and over three hundred reported days of sun a year. It is an easy place to market and promote when it comes to the sunshine factor.

But it is so much more than the sun and the weather, as anyone spending any length of time here discovers.

There is a sense that the seasons, the land and traditional farming methods, and the church calendar still give this country its rhythm and pattern. People often say this is what England was like fifty years ago, and there is a feeling of timelessness about this part of the world as soon as you step away from the beach-front tourist areas.

It is not just the place though; it is also the local people. Throughout the region there are gentle, kind, welcoming Portuguese people, whose lives seem to march to a different pace of life; they make time to sit in the sun; greet their friends, and reflect an era long passed away in many other countries. They are polite, reserved, proud of their culture and heritage, and always willing to help you.

There is a different, gentler pace of life here, with the passing of time measured by the local church bells that ring every hour, followed by another church in the distance which chimes away three minutes later. Nobody seems to mind.

And when you are walking along a deserted beach in November watching the sunset, and feeling the sense of calm and peace that only the luxury of free time can give you, with the waves rhythmically and gently curling along the edge of the sand, then you know you have made the right choice and you are exactly where you need to be.

One of the other great things about living here in the Algarve is being able to sit outside in the sunshine and enjoy a leisurely meal in a pretty restaurant, savouring good quality, tasty food.

We really love finding local restaurants, enjoying simple traditional food, surrounded by Portuguese people, where we can still get change from thirty euros for a meal for two.

Prato do dia (which literally translates as 'plate of the day') is very common out here, especially at lunchtime, and if you know where to go, you can have a three-course meal, with a drink and a coffee afterwards for nine euros each. Often there are three or four main dishes to choose from, usually local meat, or fish, and sometimes there is a vegetarian option.

Another food that is very common here is the local favourite of Piri-piri chicken, accompanied by chips and a side salad, and washed down rather nicely with a small beer or two.

❀ೞ✿ಚ❀

We had always joked we were 'too young to retire' and we both had made plans. I had the burning ambition to do two things—to paint and write—and Dave had held a camera in his hands since he was a young boy. We had dreams of transforming our hobbies into something more concrete and professional once we moved out here to live permanently. We did not know if our plans would be successful, but at the very worst, they would keep us busy and out of mischief, and give our days some purpose and opportunity.

We forged our new careers, although neither of us had ever worked for ourselves before, or had any idea what we were doing! We just knew what we loved, and we figured the rest out as we went along. Our first joint exhibition in the Holiday Inn hotel was a scary moment! They gave us a fabulous room to use and loads of support —but said that we couldn't hang anything on the walls! We improvised, Dave created a set of table-top A-frame easels, and we were all set.

I will never forget our first morning opening up, wondering if anyone would come, if they would like our work, or buy anything. Within half-an-hour, we had both sold our first pieces, and we were away. We fashioned our own little 'happy dance' which we jigged around to after each sale. We usually waited until the customer had departed, although I think a few clients might have caught a snatch of our happy little jig!

Almost ten years later, I consider myself an established artist, having sold more than two hundred paintings, and completed over one hundred commissions for clients around the world. Dave is now a well-respected and busy photographer, always happiest getting his feet wet on a deserted beach with his camera and tripod at hand. I am lucky enough to sell paintings almost before they have dried on the easel, which sadly means I do not have the inventory or body of new work needed to host and run our own exhibitions any more. I do miss the excitement of those pop-up events.

It still humbles me to know that people love my work. Dave even photographed a house one day with the rental agent present and spotted one of my paintings on the wall in the lounge. That was a rather surreal moment for him, as the agent said she loved the painting, and Dave was able to tell her that his wife had painted it!

My attempts to learn the language have met with differing

degrees of success. After many years of struggling and suffering, I can now hold a basic conversation with local people and—mostly—understand what is being said to me. I can usually respond with something vaguely articulate, if not always grammatically correct. There are, however, odd words that I just seem to get stuck on, no matter how many times I hear them, or think I know what they mean. Take *doente* for example. Every time I hear this word, I immediately think it means 'dead'. I learnt the hard way...

One of our local elderly neighbours walked past me one day. He always stops to chat, he is a dear old soul and after the usual niceties; he said to me,

"*Minha esposa está doente.*"

My daft brain translated that to mean, "my wife is dead".

"Oh no, I am so sorry, that is terrible," I replied in my best Portuguese. Before I could muster together the phrase for 'I'm sorry for your loss', or offer him my condolences, he spluttered,

"Pah! It is nothing!"

I must have looked as surprised and horrified as I felt, because he looked at me incredulously and said,

"It is nothing, just a cold. She will be fine again in a few days."

Note to self: *doente* means sick—not dead.

✿୨♡୧✿

Our battles with the layers of bureaucracy and processes are legendary. Dave still shudders every time I mention the dreaded SEF office, which we had to visit over and over again to apply for our permanent residency paperwork. And then back again... and again, to sort out the new-style residency cards. 'Mrs Happy' at desk number seven probably still has nightmares about us too. I haven't actually been brave enough yet to let Dave know that, thanks to the delights of Brexit, they are going to be issuing us with new biometric cards. That will undoubtedly require us to visit our local SEF office to go through the whole sorry process all over again. I think I might pop into our local friendly vets beforehand and see if she will give me a tranquilliser dart to take with me. I'm just not sure whether I'll use it on Dave or Mrs Happy—maybe I'll decide when I get there and see how things go.

It's not just the SEF office that gives us headaches, though. Our local bank is also up there in the running for the 'most ludicrous system of the year' award. Dave applied for a visa credit card about two years ago. I did mention nothing happens very fast here, didn't I? We asked at our local branch, in an offhand manner one day, and the lovely bank teller said that of course we could have a credit card. He would set things up and let us know when the paperwork was ready to be signed.

About eight months passed by, we were in the bank again, and suddenly remembered the visa card application. We tentatively asked the same man behind the desk about it, and he looked at us completely blankly. So, we started the whole process again, and we were shunted off to talk to the manager. Progress, we thought. Well, this time, Dave actually signed a form, so we were quite hopeful.

A few more months went by. We weren't really in a hurry for the card, which was a good thing, as they lost the forms and we had to go back and start again. About two years after our first naïve enquiry, Dave finally received a shiny new visa card through the post. You had to ring a special number to authorise it, which Dave duly did. And then he waited for the pin number to arrive in the post. You've probably guessed by now—it never appeared. So Dave had a nice expensive-looking visa card he couldn't use. Well, at least that made my monthly accounting easy.

Out of the blue one day, I received a phone call from our bank's customer service department.

"I'm just ringing to check that you are happy with our service and to find out if there is anything I can do to help you."

"Oh well, actually there is something you can do. Hang on a minute, I'll pass you over to my husband."

I caught Dave unawares (always the best strategy when it comes to anything financial, as he has absolutely no interest in monetary matters and leaves everything to me), and he chatted to the very nice lady on the other end of the phone. I'm sure she regretted making that courtesy call!

The upshot was that she promised that someone would call Dave straight back on his mobile phone number, take him through security, and then try to resolve the issue with the missing pin number for him. I made us both a nice hot cup of tea, asked Dave to put his phone on speakerphone, and settled down to enjoy the ensuing conversation. I wasn't disappointed.

A lovely young man who spoke perfect English rang up. Taking Dave through the security questions was hilarious, it basically involved asking Dave what his name and address was, and the last four digits of the visa card.

Now at this stage, you should remember that we both have a background in policing. Dave, in particular, retired after almost thirty-two years' service, and I clocked up thirteen years before scampering off to work in education. So between us, we've interviewed a fair number of criminal masterminds, who would think nothing of purloining an official-looking letter from a postbox, opening it up, discovering a brand new credit card inside, and going off on a shopping spree. Call us cynical if you like, but they would have a field day over here as all the post boxes for properties are on the outside wall of the house, and you can easily lift up the flap and wriggle your fingers inside. Or maybe it's just me that thinks along those lines...

Anyway, back to the nice young man on the phone who has now scientifically determined that he is indeed talking to the owner of the credit card in question. He checks that yes, the visa card was 'live' and that no, it hadn't been used. That was a relief. I do all the home finances, but as the card is in Dave's name, it doesn't show up when I log on to the home banking site for our account, so I had no way of checking the balance on the card.

The lad helpfully decided that the best thing he could do would be to text Dave the missing pin number directly to Dave's mobile phone. Sure enough, whilst we were still chatting, the phone pinged and in came the magic four-digit number.

That just left us with the small problem of Dave not being able to check his balance. Still chirpy and chatty, the lad then informed

Dave that he did actually have an online account with them, and did he know his password?

It was a good job I had finished my cup of tea by this stage, as I would have sprayed the room with tea as I chortled loudly. Mmm… Dave and passwords. He didn't have a clue.

"Don't worry, Mr Sheldrake, I will text you a temporary password to your phone, then we can get you logged in and set up. Then you will just need to change the password. I can help you do that too."

I wondered if there was a special training course they put their staff through on dealing with 'challenging and financially inept' customers.

Another ping on the phone and we were away. It all went swimmingly well, and Dave updated his password and entered the hallowed pages of the internet banking world. I hoped he didn't get too interested in it all though, as I didn't want him messing up my finely honed and neatly organised system of home finances. Or looking dreamily at the latest camera-gear magazines online, and uttering the immortal words, "I just need another…" (fill in the blanks with any number of expensive camera-related gadgets and gizmos), and then firing up his new credit card.

Up popped a message on the screen, informing Dave that he needed to add his mobile phone number before he could start using the online services.

No problem, we thought. Young, but slightly less keen and chirpy by this stage, our bank lad was still on the line.

"Could you just add my mobile phone number to the account, please?" asked Dave.

"Erm, no, sorry I can't do that."

"Why not?"

"I cannot authorise it now."

"Why not?" repeated Dave, whilst shaking his head at me in exasperation. "It's the same phone number you've sent me the pin code and the password to."

"I cannot do it without going through extra security. Did you receive a 'Cartão Matriz' when you set up your account?"

We set up our joint bank account out here almost twenty years ago. Dave would struggle to find a card he was given last week, let alone at the turn of the last century. I've still got my matriz card, but that's a different story. It's just a credit card with a series of numbers in a table on the back, with columns displaying letters and numbers. The theory is that they ask you what code nestles under the apex of, say, position A2, and you rattle off the answer. I've never used my card.

"I will need to post you a matriz card and then when you receive it you must ring us back so that we can add your mobile phone number to your account. You will need the card before we can authorise that, and we will go through the extra security required."

I'm sure the lad was praying at that point that he would be on a rest day when that call came in.

Dave was suitably unimpressed.

"So, just to recap, you are able to ring me on my mobile phone number—the same one I want to add to my account—and you will happily send me the four-digit pin code for my visa card to that number. Which gives me licence to go mad shopping and spending money. And you can send me the password I need to get into my account online—to the same mobile phone number. But you can't add that phone number to my account until I can tell you some magic numbers?"

"Yes, that is correct, sir."

The matriz card arrived in the post three weeks later. That was about two months ago, and Dave still hasn't rung them back yet. I must remind him… again!

The one good thing about the Portuguese love affair with all things bureaucratic is that you can always find something amusing in there to chuckle over. They usually have a 'system' and there is absolutely no way around it. You just have to learn to live with it. And check your postbox regularly.

It would be fair to say that I have wanted a dog for a long while; I grew up with always having a dog as part of the family and adore the love and companionship they give you. There are so many rescue dogs out here that need a home that it was always going to be a dog in need that would win us both over, but the question was … which one?

Having talked to our friend Ginie from the SOS Algarve Animals (SOSAA) charity about this, we initially toyed with the idea of adopting a young puppy. It was good to talk things through first and we agreed a youngster would be a big commitment when we are both working and would be harder to fit into our lives than we first thought. We happily left it to Ginie, and she promised she would find us the right dog.

Almost a year passed by and it is funny how things turn out to have their own sense of timing. Ginie took a much-needed holiday to see friends in Spain. Her dedication to the charity and the rescue dogs is immense, and all-consuming, so this was a rare chance to leave the kennels behind and travel. She tells the story of how she was driving down a road in a remote village near Seville when a poor scrap of a dog came into view running down the road. Ginie stopped her car, whistled, and the dog promptly jumped into the back of her car and curled up on the seat. More amused than anything that on her weekend away she had rescued another dog, she continued to her friends' house and they fed the dog who was in a pretty poor state.

The next morning, probably as a result of the food, the dog produced milk from her teats, which is when they realised she had recently had pups. A trip back to the exact place they had found her did not produce any reaction at all from her; and a visit to the local vet confirmed she was in such a poor state of health, at best she would have given birth to still-born pups.

The first photos taken of the dog, who they named Olalya after the place she was found, are quite sad to see, although her sweet nature was already evident. It was obvious that Ginie had fallen for her and her gentle ways, as she curled up on the back seat of the car alongside Ginie's own personal pet dog, Cheeky, and happily began her new adventure into a foreign country and new life.

Olalya's coat was in such a bad state that she had to have all her fur shaved off, which made her look even more forlorn, but still lovely, with chocolate-coloured eyes that reflected so much about her life. I saw the photos on Facebook and I was immediately drawn to her. I kept going back to her page and story. It was no surprise then when Ginie called me up and said,

"I have just the dog for you."

I replied,

"I know, I have seen her already."

We both knew we were talking about the same dog.

Dave and I arranged to go over and meet Olalya, and she was the dearest little thing, skinny but happy, quiet but interested in us; and she settled down beside us while we talked things through with Ginie. Dave and I had agreed before we went to see her we would go away and talk about it afterwards and take our time deciding, but I fell for her instantly and Dave later admitted the same thing. It was quite emotional driving away as she trotted quietly up to the gates as we drove out and stood staring up after us as we left.

Two days later we were back to collect her. She recognised us straight away and it was exciting to fill in the papers, pick up her lead and take her home in our car. We were like proud new parents driving her home. She was still quite underweight and a little nervous, but had sweet trusting eyes that took everything in.

Introducing her to her new home was quite something, as she was initially wary and shy of so many things; her own reflection in the shiny oven door made her run; she wouldn't go downstairs or anywhere near our basement stairs as they were going down into the unknown; she walked round drain covers and seagulls overhead made her scarper. But slowly and patiently I worked quietly with her over several days and the transformation was almost instant. If something spooked her, I spent time with her, reassuring her and settling her. Now she stops and looks at herself in a mirror (!) and sits and watches birds and even planes fly overhead.

Her given name by the charity, Olalya, was not an easy name to pronounce; and we thought long and hard about what to call her, toying with several ideas. Dave has a great Monty Python sense of humour though and has always wanted to have 'a dog called cat'. So that's what we ended up calling her … Kat. Initially, it sounded a bit daft, but now it seems to suit her, she's a quirky little girl, and it fits her well. So Kat the dog she is.

The first time we took her to a beach was amusing. I doubt she had ever seen the sea or sand before, and she was a little unsure; however, now she adores the beach, romping around, digging holes in the sand, and playing with us and other dogs along the way. She is mostly a Spanish water dog, with some poodle thrown in there for good measure apparently, but she doesn't seem to like water very much! If there is a puddle on the ground, she will walk around it, although sometimes she goes for a little paddle in the sea. She is not a great fan of swimming unless there is a nice calm river of water with a gentle slope in and out, and it is a hot day and she wants to cool off.

The day she went head-first into our friend's fishpond was hilarious, as she just didn't even recognise that the green stretch of something glistening ahead of her was a pond of water. In she plopped, and came out slightly bemused, dripping wet, but none the worse for her experience.

We took her to the village of Alte one afternoon, which has a lovely river beach with a gentle slope down to the water. And ducks. Did I mention Kat adores birds of all kinds? Off she scampered into the water, had a lovely paddle around, said hello to the ducks (she is very gentle, there is no hint of aggression in her) and then out she climbed, soaking wet and happy. Just in time to greet the contingent from a local coach tour that had just turned up, who were all stood at the side of the river holding their cameras aloft. She made a beeline for them.

Initially there was lots of 'ooh-ing' and 'aah-ing' and someone saying,

"Isn't that a pretty dog?"

And then Kat decided that in front of the whole group was the perfect location to have a shake. She has a nice big fluffy coat in the winter, and it holds a lot of water. And I mean a lot of water. Which landed in giant droplets all over the entire group. They all disappeared rather quickly back into their coach. I have no idea why!

What the SOSAA Charity failed to warn us about was just how much we would fall in love with this little scruffy scrap of a dog. She really is the sweetest, gentlest, most content and well-behaved little girl; happy to be around us, curled up on her bed in my studio while I paint, or out walking on a beach or local village, field or cliff-top with us; or even sat patiently beside Dave while he is out photographing on a beach somewhere. She now sleeps on my bed and I love seeing her little contented face snuggled up on a pillow at night, snuffling gently to herself in her sleep. Her life now must seem a world away from the street-sleeping scavenging existence she knew before in Spain.

It's been lovely watching her personality blossom. She's a very contained and content little thing, and doesn't jump up or lick madly or go wild, but her little stump of a tail and her whole bum wags when she is happy. If I pull out a burr from her fur (which is a daily task as she collects the things for a pastime) then she gently licks my hand as if to say 'thank you'. She charms everyone she meets as she is so gentle and placid; if we meet friends for lunch at a restaurant, she will sit by my feet under the table outside for over two hours with not a murmur.

She is also bright as a button, doesn't miss a thing, loves routine and instinctively seems to know so much, and she adores mashed up sardines on her dinner, and sleeping upside down!

And every time I look at Kat's beautiful face, I am grateful for the day that Ginie stopped and whistled a little scruffy scrap of fur into the back seat of her car.

Our life here in the Algarve has been more than we could have ever imagined. I look back on that day, now ten years ago, when I handed in my notice from work with some trepidation, and started the job of packing to move out here to live. Those first few months of settling into our new home, navigating the bureaucracy and differences, exploring and delighting in every new beach and village we discovered, and the wonderful friends we made, all helped us to feel happy and settled very quickly. We have since moved to live in the western Algarve, in a small town near the ocean, and we are blissfully happy here.

Our creative endeavours, beautiful home, relaxed way of life, and my daily walks beside the river with Kat the dog are all things that bring joy to my soul. I have never regretted our decision to move here, and every year I feel more content and delighted to call the Algarve our home.

I am truly grateful to be 'living our dream'.

(Taken in part and edited from *Living the Dream – in the Algarve, Portugal*.)

✿❀✿❁✿

For more information about Alyson's work as an artist and author, visit her website:
www.alysonsheldrake.com

Top Tips

Many of the contributors to this book also sent in a range of top hints and tips, which have been compiled together below for you.

I have arranged the advice into the following categories:

Moving to Portugal, Settling In, Learning the Language, Navigating the System, Healthcare, and Living the Life.

I hope you find the following information useful. Whether you are planning a move to Portugal or another foreign country, much of what is listed here is generic to a new life abroad.

Moving to Portugal

We all have dreams, and it can take courage to follow them through. Sometimes the timing isn't right, but come and visit the Algarve as often as you can and let your plans evolve.
Cheryl Smith

I would recommend you familiarise yourself with an area and consider living or renting there before making a final move. Things

can be different at different times of day and in different seasons, and not always what you expect.
Johanna Bradley

Just like RVing, moving to another country takes work, determination, and a particular mindset. As a couple making the move, it's not enough for one to humour the other if both aren't fully committed. We've seen it dozens of times before and it never works out in the end. Someone almost always becomes unhappy and eventually resentful. If you dream of moving to Portugal but your partner is thinking more along the lines of France or Spain, that's a yellow light telling you to slow down and re-examine this dream. Even if Portugal is one of the kindest countries, welcoming you with open arms and broad smiles, it's still hard, expensive, and an adjustment.
Evanne Schmarder

Spend time exploring, I have heard some horror stories—make sure the property you are buying or renting is fully legitimate before you sign anything, especially that the boundaries of the property are where they should be. If you have doubts, ask questions, join Facebook groups dedicated to people living in Portugal, they may well have the answers you need, many are very knowledgeable.
Sarah Gadd

Delve deep and reflect on your reason for wanting to move. A change in physical location can provide a fresh outlook, but your problems will follow you wherever you move to.
Alex Englefield

Follow your heart, you only live once. You will spend a long time regretting not doing it. Research, find out as much as possible before arriving. But from the right sources. The internet is great, but there is always an expert, who actually heard it down the bar from 'someone who had been there'.
Debby Burton

My husband, Peter and I visited the western Algarve for just one week to play golf and we fell in love with the region. We bought a holiday home not long after and felt very comfortable. After working for international companies with lots of travelling and being financially secure, we thought of leaving our home country to start a new life here. It took us one year to decide what we wanted to do and then begin the process of creating a Real Estate Agency, which was not easy back in 2004. But if you have a goal and the resources you have to go for it!
Susanna Gross

Choose the location where you live very carefully. Research is important. Make a checklist in selecting a property and the type of area you wish to live in. Go well beyond what the estate agent tells you. Lifestyles are very different in towns compared with rural areas, and luxury resorts. Consider as you get older the amount of work you will need to undertake, as well as costs, in the upkeep of your property.
David Thomas

Before you make the big decision to change your lifestyle and move to the sun, investigate the length and breadth of the Algarve to see what will suit you best 24/7. That quiet beach that enchanted you in early spring might be tourist-packed for months a little later in the year, and that holiday condominium you so enjoyed could be deserted throughout the winter months. If the Algarve is new to you, the best idea is to rent for a few months — perhaps longer, and change locations as you go.
Susi Rogol-Goodkind

When contemplating moving to Portugal, it is important to do as much research as possible and be prepared to integrate into the local community. You can of course live in an *'estrangeiro* bubble' but you will never get the best out of your life here if you do so. I find it a great pity that people living here for so many years know so little about the country, its people, its culture, its government, and simple laws, for example.

Integration is to my mind the crucial step people should be prepared to take. Remember things will be different from your own country and the more understanding you have of how things work, the easier it becomes in enjoying a great life here in this lovely country.

Keeping yourself occupied, I feel, is of key importance. Be it sport or charity work, there is much you can do.

David Thomas

Choosing a location can be the hardest decision. Maybe start by choosing a location based on your interest, if it is surfing then the west coast is best, if you enjoy country walking then settle along the Via Algarviana walking route or any other defined walking route. If you are creative, then perhaps a property near the towns of São Brás de Alportel or Loulé would be ideal to uncover your creative side.

Cheryl Smith

It is a life-changing decision to uproot yourself and your family and move abroad. However many holidays you've had in Portugal, it is altogether different to live here. You'll be leaving lifelong friends and relatives behind. Will you be able to make friends here? Do you really know the area in which you intend to live? Have you experienced it in the winter? Will there be things that keep you awake, even in the dead of night, in the countryside?

So, my three pieces of advice are 1) research 2) research more 3) research even more.

Clive Jewell

You need to find a new home—either a long-term rental which is difficult in the Algarve as most property owners, both foreign and Portuguese, like to rent out in the summer, or purchase a flat or house or do a renovation project.

Trust an experienced real estate agency who speaks your language and is experienced and well trained in this field.

Susanna Gross

If you are looking to build a home, then it would be wise to choose a property with a large enough footprint, otherwise obtaining planning permission to construct a home that does not fit the boundaries of the existing exterior walls may be challenging.
Always ensure that you are correctly advised and that you follow the correct procedures by working together with a reputable English-speaking accountant.
Cheryl Smith

If you are building from scratch, don't deviate from approved plans without checking if you need authorisation. A window in the wrong place, a pool that's edged its way towards the sun—these are the sort of things that can affect getting the habitation licence and the saleability later.
If you are buying an older property, make sure it has the right degree of insulation.
Susi Rogol-Goodkind

Settling In

Be flexible, open-minded, mix with the locals, and learn a bit of the Portuguese language.
To start, you need some financial backing to survive either as a retiree or as a working person. The Algarve does not offer a lot of jobs, those available are mostly in the seasonal tourist sector, and the Portuguese minimum wage is low. The cost of living, although cheaper than most European countries, is rising.
Susanna Gross

Ask questions. That's the first step to discovery.
Have an easily accessible list of phone numbers—from the local hospital and taxis to police and emergency services.
Susi Rogol-Goodkind

Buy a Portuguese car—yes, they may be more expensive than in your 'home' country but don't faff about matriculating or trying to prove your foreign registered car has been here less than six months. It'll save you money in the long run to just bite the bullet.

Research the work opportunities if you intend to work here. It is HARD to make even a basic living here.

Do things properly and above board. Sort out your residency, your taxes, your driving licence, and register with the national health system.

Sue Englefield

When planning to move, do not assume everything in Portugal is cheaper. For instance, electricity and fuel prices are among the highest in Europe. Some imported groceries will be more expensive than from your hypermarket back home. There is usually a tax to pay if you are importing a vehicle. Also bear in mind if you are moving from the UK due to Brexit, it may be more difficult to obtain your favourite products locally and the cost of sending goods from the UK with customs duty will have increased. In other words do the research and budget accordingly.

David Thomas

Really delve into the Portuguese lifestyle by adapting to the culture and customs, since this will transfer you from being a foreigner living in a holiday country to a true citizen.

Karl Heinz Stock

Plan your outdoor space with the climate here in mind. Forget the English country garden … this is a whole different world.

Susi Rogol-Goodkind

Make a concerted effort to establish a trusty group of friends upon moving here. Sharing a new and scary experience with like-minded individuals can drastically improve things for you.

Alex Englefield

Read the *Algarve Resident* and *The Portugal News*, the two weekly Algarve newspapers in English, for news on current affairs and

details of local events including exhibitions, lectures, and entertainment. They are both a good introduction to what's happening locally and the people who live here.
David Trubshaw

Be versatile, don't be afraid to try something new, or make mistakes, we learn from them. Hopefully! It is all part of life's rich tapestry.
Debby Burton

Be open to everyone and everything. Don't go everywhere with your partner, you'll meet more people if you are on your own. Remember Portuguese people are very loving and always keen to help you.
Alisia Alao

There are lots of different types of expats, and you will learn to find your own friends. Just because you both speak the same language doesn't necessarily mean that you will have much in common. But you can also meet new and fascinating people from all nationalities and backgrounds. The Algarve tends to 'flatten out' people socially, and you can find genuine and honest people from all walks of life sat down enjoying a coffee or a beer together.
Alyson Sheldrake

Check out what classes/courses are available. If you have the time and opportunity, take advantage of what is on offer and you could discover new interests that will fascinate you, and new people to share them with.
Susi Rogol-Goodkind

Join AFPOP the Association of Foreign Property Owners in Portugal. Founded in 1987, it specialises in providing a comprehensive range of information services to support foreign residents and visitors to Portugal. They will keep you up to date with new and existing legislation.
Some of the many benefits of membership include regular updated information bulletins, newsletters, and preferential rates on motor,

household, and medical insurance. They also advertise discounts on a wide variety of products and services such as dental treatment, hearing aids, opticians, and language courses.

You can also find discount rates at several hotels—a useful benefit if you are planning to spend time in the Algarve looking to buy a property.

David Trubshaw

Learning the Language

Start learning Portuguese ASAP before moving here, you will need it in order to make the most of integrating into the local community and feel welcomed by your new home country.

Alex Englefield

Learn Portuguese. So many more doors open if you speak the language.

When I first started learning Portuguese, I used Memrise. It is a free app which is really good. The app teaches mainly vocabulary, and as you progress it also adds sentences. It's quite playful and not boring at all. I'm now on module 5 and it just keeps going! My goal is five words a day, five days a week. This usually takes less than ten minutes a day.

I also bought a Portuguese grammar book and I try to do one chapter of theory and exercises a week. But the most important thing is to speak to the locals and practise, practise, practise. I am at a point where I can express myself quite fluently, but I still make lots of mistakes. And that's ok.

My best learning came through teaching yoga in Portuguese—I had to speak it, no matter whether what came out was right or wrong.

Irina Adriaensen

Learn the basics of the language, and how to greet people. Basic manners like please and thank you go a very, very long way with Portuguese people.

Alisia Alao

Learn the language, by this I mean really learning certain expressions of which the Portuguese have many. For example, *"Ter dor de cotovelo"*, which literally translates as having elbow pain, but actually means being jealous.
Karl Heinz Stock

If you have chosen the Algarve as your dream destination, do not worry if you can't speak a word of Portuguese, as English is widely spoken on the Algarve. You won't have a problem communicating with suppliers if you are planning a wedding or conference, or perhaps you are a digital nomad, holidaymaker, or explorer. However, if you plan to live in the Algarve and you can communicate with the locals in their mother tongue, your desire and willingness to understand the language and culture will help you better express yourself, and you will have the opportunity to form deeper friendships.
It is encouraging to know that the subscription-based language learning app, Babbel, did not include Portuguese in their list of 'Six Hardest Languages for English Speakers to Learn'. They based their research on some challenging facts. Some languages require you to memorise thousands of special characters (Mandarin Chinese), or the need to recognise many variations of the language (Arabic). There is also the difficulty in mastering the pronunciation when most vowels are excluded in words (Arabic) or to confuse you the use of the Cyrillic alphabet where the 'b' in the Cyrillic alphabet makes a 'v' sound (Russian). These are just some of the difficult hurdles you could encounter. The six hardest languages that made the list are Mandarin Chinese, Arabic, Polish, Russian, Turkish, and Danish. That makes Portuguese seem quite easy to learn in comparison.
Cheryl Smith

Learning the Language. Well, what can I say, it is a problem. I went to school, I tried to speak it but most of the Portuguese speak English. When they excused themselves to me for not speaking that well, I had to reply in German, as my English is not that good. Over the years I have learnt not to be too shy to speak Portuguese

… it can be fun. The Faust school in Quarteira is very good. You have to try and speak it each day, and keep practising.
Uschi Kuhn

Don't be overwhelmed by the language. If you make an effort, it will be most appreciated.
Maryanne Sea

I believe it is out of respect to a country to learn their language, even if it's just the basics.
June Madilyn Jorgensen

Learning the language will make it much easier for you in terms of understanding and general communication. For some it is easier than others, as I know. In the Algarve, for instance, English is widely spoken, but in many areas it is not. Think carefully about your aptitude in learning a new language. There are many teaching facilities around to help you. Many people find reading it easier than speaking Portuguese.
David Thomas

A popular language app for download onto your phone is Duolingo. The app is free if you don't mind viewing the advertisements in between. This app is used by over two million Portuguese learners and is a fun and easy way to learn but be aware that this app covers Brazilian Portuguese. The main difference is the pronunciation, as the European Portuguese speak without pronouncing the vowels as much as the Brazilian Portuguese, who enunciate vowels longer and wider. In particular, you will notice the difference in pronunciation with the spoken Portuguese words like *bom dia* (good day) and *leite* (milk). However, I found having the app on my phone was convenient to do daily bite size Portuguese lessons and the progress chart feature is very encouraging.

You will not learn a language in a foreign country just by living there. You will need to make time to practise. Make a note of phrases

you are likely to use and write them out several times and say them aloud.
Cheryl Smith

I always recommend taking a Portuguese language course 'in' Portugal and speaking to your neighbours and locals wherever you go in order to practise. The Portuguese language is not easy and needs daily training in the beginning. Portuguese people appreciate any attempt and welcome anyone who tries, which is very helpful when dealing with any authorities. If you try some Portuguese words —most of the time, they will respond and help you with English. They are very genuine and friendly people.
Susanna Gross

My best advice is don't get hung up trying to learn every grammatical tense. It won't happen. Learn the vocabulary relevant to your day-to-day life and get to grips with prepositions and adverbs so that you can link your words in a conversation.
Try to find a copy of the book *Practical Portuguese, Language for Living in Portugal* by Sheila Watts. And watch Portuguese TV, especially news and current affairs programmes, where you are likely to be familiar with the subjects.
Clive Jewell

Navigating the System

Anyone living here knows about the bureaucracy in Portugal. Again, it can be different for each individual. I will only say be prepared for a somewhat backwards and complicated system. A good lawyer helps, as does learning enough Portuguese or having an interpreter to help you with your residency papers or legalities with the government.
June Madilyn Jorgensen

Having spent most of my career running between one meeting and another, while ensuring that I made it to lectures on time too, my northern European clock-watching was supposed to have been left somewhere over the Bay of Biscay when we made the move to the Algarve. I hate to reinforce the myth that the Hispanic attitude to timekeeping persists and that mañana is alive and well in Portugal. For most day-to-day matters the Portuguese are very reliable, however, when it comes to giving a specific time for something to be delivered or completed, a degree of circumspection is needed if you want to avoid disappointment.

Things have improved, in part, thanks to technology and the ability to track deliveries and the like. Unfortunately, deadlines are still a very moveable feast as we learnt with almost every aspect of our different build projects. The Portuguese are polite and non-confrontational, which is compounded and confounded by their ability to be stubbornly mute about when something will or will not be happening. Rather than worrying about causing offence, it would be a lot less stressful if people simply said they do not know or cannot give a guarantee that something will be done when expected. For all of that, the general willingness to help and the relatively calm and somewhat reserved nature of the Portuguese is charming.

John Hough

Everything takes at least twice as long as you would expect it to. It's what makes living here beautiful, but sometimes I'm also pulling my hair out in desperation when I have to deal with bureaucracy.
Have a back-up plan (or three). Starting your own business isn't easy anywhere, so be ready to change some plans and consider it all a wild adventure.

Irina Adriaensen

Do not show your frustration if bureaucratic things move more slowly than the country you are from. They do get done, it just takes a bit longer.

Maryanne Sea

The Portuguese love ticket machines. Expect to take a ticket to

queue up in everywhere from government buildings and the health centre, through to the fresh meat or fish counters at the supermarket. Even if there isn't a ticket machine, or a recognised queue, everyone in front of you will know when it is their turn to be seen. Most official buildings shut for lunch from 12.30 p.m. so even if you were next in line, and the clock strikes, you will have to return after lunch. Most banks are only open until 3 p.m. and it is rare to find a bank that opens on a Saturday morning here.
Alyson Sheldrake

After two years, residents are supposed to exchange their driving licences for a Portuguese model. Thinking this would be an easy process, we were dumbfounded that there is only one place in the Algarve where this can be done. The IMTT office in Faro has to be one of the most frustrating places in the world to visit. The queues form early in the morning and armed with your ticket you can sit for up to three hours waiting to be seen with no guarantee that when you do get to the head of the queue, the official will be helpful. Having visited the office on two separate occasions, when it came to exchanging my licence, I chose to use a document processing service called Doc Lagos, based in the city of Lagos. I still had to visit the IMTT for a face-to-face meeting and to have a photograph taken. The upside of using the service is that all of the required paperwork is sorted in advance of the meeting and you meet with a Doc Lagos employee at the IMTT office. This person sorts out your ticket and who to see, smoothing the process and ensuring that you leave with a letter of entitlement which you can use as a driving licence until such time as your new version arrives. The paper is valid for up to six months. I had to renew this twice through Doc Lagos as it took just over a year for my replacement Portuguese licence to arrive. If you need a licence to drive outside of Portugal, then for a hefty fee, Doc Lagos can issue an international driving licence.
John Hough

Healthcare

Private healthcare can be expensive but good. Trying to see a doctor at the local state-run health centre is often a long and frustrating process, but the costs are minimal. Be prepared to wait for hours; getting an appointment for a specialist can take months.
Many expats go back to their home countries for any serious health issues. I've heard the hospitals are, overall, good, friendly, and helpful.
June Madilyn Jorgensen

I'd like to highlight Portuguese *farmácias*, they have far more 'leeway' than in the UK, so if you can't see a doctor, I would always recommend a chat with your local pharmacist.
Sarah Gadd

Even if you have the best of health insurance, you must register at your local Centro de Saúde so that you can use their services. As a perfect example, the Centro de Saúdes are the only avenue to Covid vaccinations.
Susi Rogol-Goodkind

The local health centre runs an appointment system, but they usually have a 'triage' style system in operation too. If you are ill, turn up first thing in the morning when they open, let the receptionist know what is wrong, and they will determine if you can be seen. It seems to be based solely on how many people have turned up, how many staff they have on duty, and how ill you are. If they cannot see you that morning, they will usually give you an appointment for that afternoon or the next day.
Appointments cost less than five euros, and prescriptions are very reasonable too. You can often buy medicines that would require a prescription in the UK over the counter here at the local pharmacy.
Alyson Sheldrake

Living the Life

Remember things happen more slowly here, *amanhã* (tomorrow) may actually mean *a próxima semana* (next week) or later. Don't worry about it, don't fight it, or you will just stress yourself out.
Sarah Gadd

Another thing you need to know about living in Portugal is the relaxed pace at which everything moves. This is both a good and bad characteristic.
On the one hand, the relaxed and positive atmosphere is what makes the country so special and is one of the reasons why people plan their holiday or even move here. You will rarely get honked at, even driving 20km/h in a 50 zone.
On the other hand, everything takes its time, from construction work to parcels arriving in the mail, but as long as you keep that in mind, the positives definitely outweigh the negatives in my opinion.
Karl Heinz Stock

If you want to offer assistance to some Portuguese people who may be struggling financially, consider the Algarve Network for Families in Need charity. If you want to help animals in need, there are a range of Facebook groups and charities to choose from, including Algarve Dog Re-Homing, whose members work tirelessly on the behalf of many animals.
Maryanne Sea

The Algarve winters, though short by comparison with my former home, are much cooler, especially overnight, than I anticipated. The days are most often bright and blue, but when the sun goes down, you will find yourself shivering.
Houses here are built to withstand heat and I put a warm cardigan or jacket ON when I come indoors. If I had known that, I think we would have paid more attention to the subject of heating our home.
Johanna Bradley

You really will wear shorts and T-shirts every day in the spring, summer, and autumn. You will not need at least eighty percent of the wardrobe of clothes that you brought with you, and you won't need all those posh tops, skirts, or trousers that you packed 'just in case'. Casual means exactly that out here. Even if you go to a posh event, the dress code will still be quite casual. It is too warm here for most of the year to wear anything other than simple attire. Cotton and linen clothes are excellent, polyester and thick man-made fibres are not so great.

You will live in sandals, flip-flops or 'slaps' for around eight months of the year so make sure they are good ones! You will need some warm jumpers, fleeces, and jeans in the winter. And make sure you have a supply of fluffy warm blankets and throws for the sofa and a summer-weight duvet for the winter months.

Alyson Sheldrake

Recalibrate your pace of life ... from coffee shops to government offices, you need to adjust your expectations. Portuguese friends and service people can have what we call a mañana mindset. They're not always on time, but that's their culture, they mean no disrespect. If you want the dinner party to start at 8 p.m. tell your Portuguese friends to arrive at 7 (and consider having enough for the friend or two they may have picked up on the way over).

You might wait in a cash register line for ten minutes while the cashier and the current customer hash out local gossip. Sometimes you'll be surprised; but if you have a government appointment, be prepared to spend at least half the day at the office. While it may be maddening, it's simply how things are done here. And having a coffee? You could sit for hours just chatting, sipping, and watching the world go by. You'll never be asked to leave and when it is time to pay, you must ask for the bill. You'll rarely find an eating establishment with the bad manners to suggest you pay up and leave.

Evanne Schmarder

When we are talking about restaurants, you have to try them for

yourself, everyone's tastes are different. Everybody will tell you with pleasure where they went and where they recommend. Be daring.
Uschi Kuhn

Avoid the alcohol trap if you can. So many people arrive in the Algarve to settle into permanent holiday mode, which is great for a time but really hard on the liver. I've seen people sliding down the slippery slope of beer or wine o'clock getting earlier every day. There is nothing nicer than to sit with your drink, watching the world go by, but don't turn into an old prune if you can help it!
Jessica Dunn

You've probably heard it before, Portugal is a very budget-friendly place to live. Yes, in some ways that's true. Fruit, veg, and fish are dirt-cheap. You can buy an outstanding bottle of Douro red for less than four euros. Handcrafted items can be very reasonable. Property taxes are assessed very differently than in the US. However, while some things are reasonable, others are not. Fuel is pricey. High-end kitchen appliances—when you can find them—are expensive. Nuts and dried fruits are more expensive than we are used to. Then there are items that are seemingly non-existent such as real vanilla extract (they use a powdered *baunilha*) and it required extensive searching before we managed to find 100% all-nut peanut butter (fortunately it is more widely available now).
Evanne Schmarder

Living in a rural area is great for many reasons, but there are things to be aware of and be prepared for such as rural fires, for instance. Good relations with neighbours is vitally important as your neighbour and many others in the village are probably related.
David Thomas

You will miss family and some friends a lot. But you'll miss them at odd times when you least expect it and often right after you have just called them on Skype. But the holidays when you get together will be extra special.

When friends come to stay with you, it will cost you extra. Even if they kindly offer to give you some money to cover their visit. You will stock up the fridge with extra food, eat out more often whilst they are staying with you, and if you are like us, you will of course insist on paying your fair share. And there are only so many times you want to visit a major theme park or attraction, so it is perfectly fine to tell them to have a nice time and see them later when they return.
Alyson Sheldrake

Be patient, Portugal is known for its mañana attitude. Things sometimes take longer to get done here so plan well in advance and enjoy the journey.
Whilst the world is in so much turmoil, making the change to live in the Algarve will continue to offer many lifelong riches like a simpler and healthy lifestyle, countless sunny days, and a slower pace of life, leaving you more time to relax and explore this beautiful country.
Cheryl Smith

I love the close proximity and accessibility Portugal has to other European countries. Overall, it's an easy country for foreigners to live in, even with its minor drawbacks.
June Madilyn Jorgensen

Our expeditions further afield have included Porto and the Douro; Lamego and Viseu, Coimbra, Lisbon, and Evora. One of our favourite repeat visits is to Tomar with a side trip to Batalha and Nazaré. If we are feeling virtuous, we drop in to Fatima to see its amazing Basilica and to light some candles in the grotto.
A great bonus about living in the Algarve is that the transport links are good. Seville and Cordoba are within easy reach and the tour bus operators' ticket specials make for an affordable way of getting to these super cities without the hassle of driving, negotiating city traffic or trying to find parking.
John Hough

Further Reading

If you are interested in finding out more about moving to live in Portugal, I can recommend the following websites.

The British Embassy in Portugal website
www.gov.uk/world/portugal
And the Embassy's Facebook Page: Brits in Portugal
www.facebook.com/BritsInPortugal

Also on Facebook – there is a particularly good and supportive group called British Expats in Portugal. The group has an excellent Files Section with information covering a wide range of 'need to know' hints, tips, and guides for anyone considering a move to Portugal.
www.facebook.com/groups/265570920476558

For Americans considering a move to Portugal, I can recommend the Facebook group Americans and FriendsPT. They have a similar range of files covering everything specific to the American visa scheme and related information pertaining to the US.
www.facebook.com/groups/americansandfriendsPT

If you are not on Facebook, then check out the Expats Portugal Community Forum. They have an active membership with lots of questions and answers about all things Portugal.
www.expatsportugal.com/community/

Dave Sheldrake Photography. He has a selection of high-quality images of Portugal, and especially his favourite beaches, for you to enjoy on his website.
www.davesheldrake.photography/portugal

If this book has whetted your appetite and you are considering buying in the Algarve, then the article *Where to Buy a Property in the Algarve* on our Algarve Blog will be a good starting point for you: www.algarveblog.net/2015/06/10/where-to-buy-a-property-in-the-algarve/

Living the Dream - in the
Algarve, Portugal

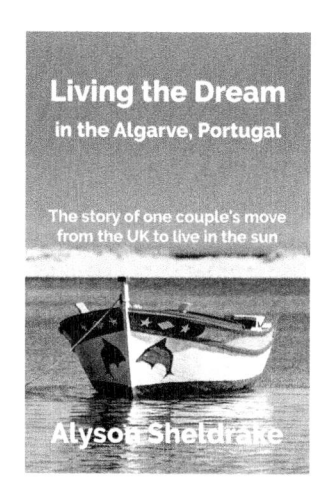

Could you leave everything behind and start a new life in the sun? Have you ever been on holiday abroad and wondered what it would be like to live there?

Alyson and Dave Sheldrake did. They fell in love with a little fishing village in the Algarve, Portugal, and were determined to realise their dream of living abroad. They bought a house there, ended their jobs, packed up everything they owned and moved to the Algarve to start a new life.

Follow them as they battle with Portuguese bureaucracy, set up their own businesses, adopt a rescue dog and learn to adapt to a slower pace of life. Laugh with them as Alyson propositions a builder, they try to master the Portuguese language, and successfully navigate the 'expat' world.

Part guidebook, mostly memoir; this is a refreshingly honest and often hilarious account of life abroad.

Available to purchase now on Amazon worldwide.

For more information visit:
www.alysonsheldrake.com/books

Living the Quieter Algarve Dream

Have you ever longed for a quieter life?
Ever wanted to escape the crowds, walk on deserted beaches, and experience all that a different country has to offer?

Alyson and Dave Sheldrake moved to the western Algarve, far away from the tourists, to live in a rural market town. Surrounded by chickens, rabbits, beautiful beaches, and crazy locals, they settled down to enjoy a more peaceful existence.

Their plans didn't include battling with Portuguese bureaucracy, a life-altering diagnosis, and Kat the dog being rushed to the vets. Brexit, a pandemic, and a house that needed updating ensured that life was anything but tranquil for this creative couple.

In this part guidebook, mostly memoir, find out why the Algarve is a favourite destination for so many, and why this couple have made it their home.

This honest and often hilarious story is the continuation of their Algarve Adventures. It can stand alone as a book for you to enjoy, and is also the follow-up to *Living the Dream – in the Algarve, Portugal*. Available to purchase now on Amazon worldwide.

For more information visit:
www.alysonsheldrake.com/books

Chasing the Dream - A new life abroad

"You're so lucky! I wish I could live abroad."
"I bet you spend all day lying in a hammock on the beach, sipping cocktails in the sun."
20 different stories. One shared dream – the chance to start a new life overseas.
In this anthology of travel stories, twenty established writers share their adventures with you.

Includes work by New York Times bestselling and award-winning authors.
And not a hammock or cocktail in sight.

Chasing the Dream – A new life abroad is the first book in the forthcoming Travel Stories series, curated by Alyson Sheldrake.

For more information visit:
www.alysonsheldrake.com/books

We Love Memoirs

The Facebook group *We Love Memoirs* was founded by Victoria Twead and Alan Parks, two memoir writers who created the opportunity to start a community on social media for both readers and authors to get together. The group now has almost 6,000 members and continues to grow.
The whole genre of memoir was a new thing to me, until I wrote my own first travel memoir. The group has introduced me to so many new themes: from comedy, and travelogues, to other people who

have also upped sticks and started a new life abroad. There are inspirational and moving accounts of people overcoming abuse, illness, and adversity, and tales of animals, adventures, and resilience. There is an enormous selection of books to choose from, and the group's page is full of recommendations, new releases, special offers, quizzes, and prizes. I have also made so many new and supportive friends through the group, both other authors and also avid readers of all things memoir.

Many people describe this as their 'happy place' on Facebook:

www.facebook.com/groups/welovememoirs

Contacts and Links

My artist and author website:
www.alysonsheldrake.com

Email:
author@alysonsheldrake.com

Our Algarve Blog is full of information, photographs, stories, and guides.

Algarve Blog website:
www.algarveblog.net

Algarve Blog on Facebook:
www.facebook.com/AlgarveBlog

Dave's photography website:
www.davesheldrake.photography

Acknowledgements and Dedication

My special thanks go to all those friends who contributed to this book. Thank you for your honesty and willingness to share your lives with me.

My thanks to Mr Chris Sainty, Her Majesty's Ambassador to Portugal, for writing the foreword to this book. I am honoured and most grateful to everyone who has been a part of this exciting project. I hope the result is worthy of your efforts and your stories.

To the beta readers who helped to shape this book, namely Beth Haslam, Lisa Rose Wright, Julie Haigh, Nicole Reed, Simon Michael Prior, Kevin JD Kelly and Kathleen Van Lierop – my sincere and heartfelt thanks.

Thank you to the wonderful members of the Facebook Group *We Love Memoirs*. This really is the best bunch of friendly authors and memoir readers. I have made new friends and read so many wonderful books through this group.

My special thanks must also go to Victoria Twead, of Ant Press publishing company, for her continued support, advice, and encouragement. She has proved that writing books can be fun!

As always, thank you to Dave, my talented, supportive, and hilarious husband. Thank you for being a whizz with a camera. I love you.

Free Photo Album

To view a series of free photographs which accompany this book, please visit my website:

www.alysonsheldrake.com/books/

Keeping in Touch

If you would like to be notified when I publish my next book, please contact me via email and I will add you to my mailing list.

author@alysonsheldrake.com

THE LATEST ART, PHOTOGRAPHY, BOOKS AND NEWS FROM THE ALGARVE

Art by Alyson Sheldrake

www.alysonsheldrake.com
artist@alysonsheldrake.com   author@alysonsheldrake.com

www.davesheldrake.photography
dave@davesheldrake.photography

I also write a monthly newsletter with Dave, which is full of art, photographs, book reviews, and articles about the Algarve. You can sign up to this free via the link here:

www.alysonsheldrake.com/news/

About the Author

Alyson Sheldrake was born in Birmingham in 1968. She has an honours degree in sport and has a PGCE (Secondary) qualification in physical education, English, and drama. She has always loved art and painting, although she found little time for such pleasures, working full time after graduation. She joined the Devon and Cornwall Police in 1992 and served for thirteen years, before leaving and working her way up the education ladder, rapidly reaching the dizzy heights of Director of Education for the Church of England in Devon in 2008.

Managing over 130 schools in the Devon area was a challenging and demanding role, however, after three years her husband Dave retired from the Police, and their long-held dream of living in the sun became a reality.

Alyson handed in her notice, and with her dusty easel and set of acrylic paints packed and ready to move, they started their new adventure living in the beautiful Algarve in Portugal in 2011.

Alyson is the author of the award-winning and popular Algarve Blog, and has also been a keynote speaker for several years at the annual Live and Invest in Portugal international conference. She is also a feature writer for the Tomorrow Magazine in the Algarve.

She is an accomplished and sought-after artist working alongside her husband Dave, a professional photographer. Being able to bring their much-loved hobbies and creative interests to life has been a wonderful bonus to their life in the Algarve. She was also delighted to add the title 'author' to her CV, with the publication of her first book, *Living the Dream – in the Algarve, Portugal*, in April 2020. The subsequent sequel, *Living the Quieter Algarve Dream*, was published in November 2020. When she is not painting or writing, she can be found walking Kat the dog along the river in Aljezur.

Your Review

I do hope you have enjoyed reading this book. If you have a moment, I would love it if you could leave a review online, even if it is just a star rating. I read and learn something from every review that is posted, and I do a happy little dance for every lovely comment that is shared.

Thank you.

Printed in Great Britain
by Amazon